JAILHOUSE STORIES from EARLY PACIFIC COUNTY

JAILHOUSE STORIES from EARLY PACIFIC COUNTY

SYDNEY STEVENS

Foreword by Matt Winters, Editor & Publisher, *Chinook Observer*

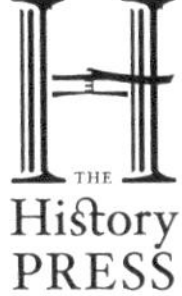

Published by The History Press
Charleston, SC
www.historypress.net

Front cover: "Confiscated Booze." *Courtesy of Pacific County Historical Society*; Joy riding on the Long Beach Peninsula. *Courtesy of the Espy Family Archives*; McKenzie Head, Cape Disappointment, Washington. *Courtesy of Washington State Parks.*

Back cover: Cape Disappointment Lighthouse, Washington. *Bud Cuffel photo*; Roderick Hotel. *Courtesy of the Walter P. Reuther Library.*

First published 2016

Manufactured in the United States

ISBN 978.1.46713.529.0

Library of Congress Control Number: 2016930808

This book is dedicated to my husband, Nyel. Without his support, I could not have spent the hours and days and weeks of research, or the months of writing this book, literally locked up with all these prisoners of long ago. With much appreciation and unfettered love!

CONTENTS

FOREWORD

There's hardly anything more fun than learning secrets we're not supposed to know—even a century late. This book is an exploration of just such secrets, a behind-the-scenes look at the lives of the wretched sufferers who came to the attention of Pacific County sheriffs between 1886 and 1919.

Running a newspaper on the far outer edge of the Pacific Northwest these past twenty-five years, I've come to know there is the news we print, the news we know but will have to leave unprinted until after all the participants are dead and a whole lot of news we don't know and never will. It's a place of secrets, of fresh starts, of people on the run. Folks keep edging farther west until they run out of west and end up here. And so it also was during territorial times and early statehood—maybe even more so back then, when it was easier to go on the lam.

Sheriffs are good at secrets. Some they keep in the pursuit of justice, keeping investigations under wraps until traps can be sprung. Others they keep out of compassion and discretion, keeping mistakes from dogging basically good people. And sometimes I think they just regard facts as a kind of currency that is best saved up.

My friend Sheriff John Didion was a good secret keeper but also someone with a great "sense of story." An NFL center before his law enforcement career, he was a tough guy to move off any spot he chose to defend—or to talk into sharing information he wanted to keep under wraps. But he could be hilarious. I'll always treasure his story of a drunk driver whose pickup was stuck up to its axles in a local mudflat. A deputy tapped on the window, and the drunk tromped down on the accelerator, mud flying everywhere, but the truck didn't move an inch. After a minute, the driver looked to his left, and the deputy was still standing there. Cranking down his window, almost in tears, the drunk screamed, "How are you keeping up with me?"

When I visited Didion in South Bend after he was elected in 1998, he showed me the old Pacific County Jail register—the backstories of crime, punishment and tragedy passed from one sheriff to the next for 112 years. Does it record every juicy detail? Sadly, no, but there are good clues to the kinds of wild stories sheriffs would never have told the newspapermen of their own times.

A dozen years went by before there was a perfect resolution to the mystery of what to do with these jail stories. Historian and author Sydney Stevens became fascinated by the idea of bringing them to life. Sydney knows this puzzling place and its people as well as anyone alive. Her understanding of people on the outer coast—their joys, struggles, dreams and nightmares—is grounded in decades of teaching, writing and empathy. Sydney is uniquely qualified to flesh out these clues to bygone lives, bringing context to the tales of the jail.

So let's join her in remembering these people—with compassion, with humor and with an awakened sense that their lives mattered.

MATT WINTERS
Editor and Publisher, *Chinook Observer*

PREFACE

The first official Pacific County Jail was located in Oysterville, Washington, the town my great-grandfather and his friend I.A. Clark founded back in 1854. The jail was built in 1875, right behind the new courthouse, for in those days—in fact, from 1855 onward—Oysterville was the county seat. By the time I came along, the jail had been long abandoned and the courthouse was no more. The South Bend Raiders from across Willapa Bay had come into town one slushy February Sunday morning in 1893, and while the good people of Oysterville were in church, they stole our county seat.

As Oysterville drifted into quiet old age, the rickety little jail building became Mr. Wachsmuth's chicken coop for a time. Later, when it was no longer in shape enough for chickens or eggs, we kids would go inside it and look for the bullet holes from the long-ago lynching we'd heard the old-timers talk about.

"Watch out for those rotten floorboards!" we'd warn one another. And then we'd stand quietly, enjoying that shivery feeling as we thought about all of the "bad men" who had been locked up there. It never occurred to us that women, too, might have spent time in "the Jailplace," as we'd heard it called.

As it turns out, we weren't far off the mark. For the years that the jail was in Oysterville, there were no women inmates—at least not as far as I can determine. It was not until 1906 that the first female name, Mrs. McMahon, was listed in the prison record. By then, the jail and the

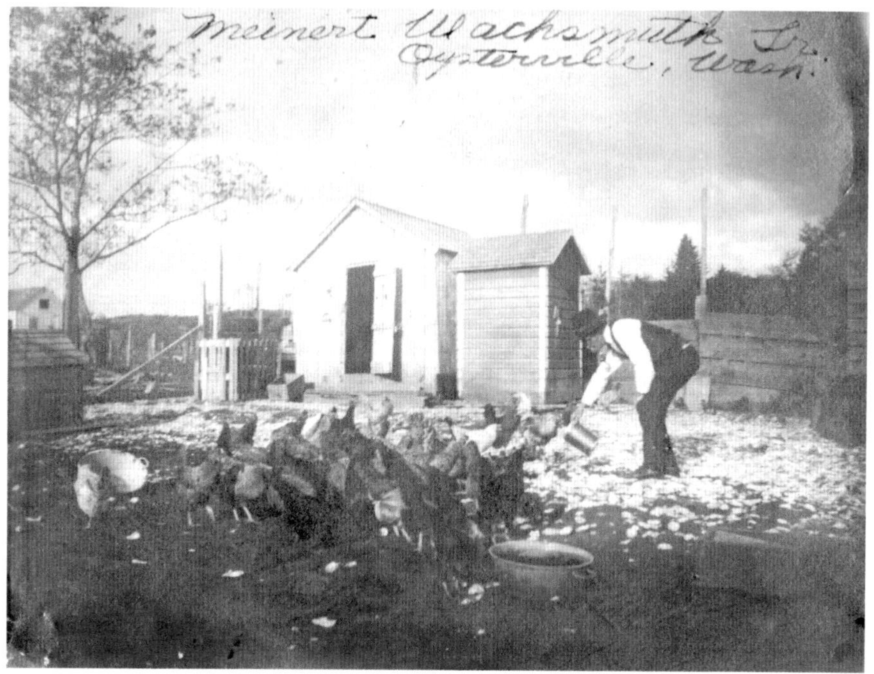

During the early 1900s, the abandoned jailhouse in Oysterville served as Meinert Wachsmuth's chicken coop. It is the larger of the two buildings shown here. *EEA.*

court records had long since been transferred to the new county seat in South Bend.

My information comes almost entirely from a most amazing volume called *Prison Record No. 1 Pacific County*. In it are listed the 591 individuals (give or take the half dozen who might have been repeat offenders) who spent time in the county jail during the years 1886 through 1919. For some, the stay was less than twenty-four hours; for some, it was weeks or months; and for some, it was but a stop on the way to another institution.

The huge, leather-bound book was brought to me by my friend the late John Didion shortly before the end of his tenure as Pacific County sheriff. He had found it in the back of a closet in his office, a long-forgotten relic from the days when clerks used dip pens to laboriously write pertinent information into the record books for posterity.

"With your interest in county history," he said, "I thought you'd like to have a look. You might even manage to find a book in these pages."

And, indeed, I have. It's not quite the book I expected I'd find, though. In a county as generational as ours, and with a total population less than that in average small-town America, I thought I might find the forebears of people I know or maybe even a few of the black sheep in my own family. That was not the case, however.

The "prison demographic" I did find was at once puzzling and intriguing. It caused me to look at statistics and trends far beyond Pacific County and Washington State. I came to few conclusions but found even this cursory look at a bit of Pacific County's hidden history to be an eye-opening encounter. I trust that my readers will find it illuminating as well.

SYDNEY STEVENS
Oysterville, December 2015

ACKNOWLEDGEMENTS

Jailhouse Stories from Early Pacific County would not have happened had not my friend former Pacific County sheriff John Didion (1947–2013) entrusted the *Prison Record Book No. 1 Pacific County* to me some years back. I will always be grateful for his friendship and for his faith that a book would be forthcoming. I wish he could have had the first copy.

Matt Winters, publisher/editor of our local weekly, the *Chinook Observer*, also played a significant role in this story. It was his thought that I do a series for the newspaper—roughly one story every two weeks in 2011 under the title "Behind Bars in Old Pacific County." That was the beginning.

To my neighbor and friend cartographer Paul Staub, my thanks (yet again!) for crafting the perfect map to show Pacific County as "the jumping-off place."

For their assistance in finding and identifying photographs, my thanks to Barbara Minard at the Columbia Pacific Heritage Museum; Andi Day, Cheryl Broom and Drew Foster of the Peninsula Visitors Center; Keleigh Schwartz of BeachDog.com; Steve Rogers and Patricia Neve of the Pacific County Historical Society; Falon Hoven at the Appelo Archives; Nanci Bell Anderson of the Columbia River Quarantine Station at Knappton Cove; Elizabeth Clemens at the Walter P. Reuther Library, Wayne State University; and Stephen Wood, Washington State Parks interpretive specialist. Also, very special thanks to Bryan Pentilla, Bob Swanson, Lisa Farnham, Bud Cuffel and Keith Cox for their assistance and encouragement.

For assistance with microfilmed newspaper articles, I am especially grateful to the Ocean Park Timberland Library staff. For retrieval and help with documents at the Washington State Archives and Records Center, my thanks to Lupita Lopez for the clarifications she made regarding the State Hospital for the Insane; to Tracy Rebstock for explaining the way in which the prison book was most likely used; and, especially, to Jewell Dunn, who alerted me to the bullet that was contained in the very thick file of Lum You's trial record.

As always, I am grateful to Jean Hazeltine Shaudys and her late husband, Vince, for their safekeeping of the old issues of the *South Bend Journal* and for, time and again, finding important nuggets of information for me.

A very special shout-out, too, to Michael Lemeshko, whose generosity in explaining the convoluted paths of governmental research helped me immeasurably. And last but never least, to my "cuzzin" Ralph Jeffords, whose mastery of all things genealogical has been inordinately helpful once again.

The images in this volume appear courtesy of the Columbia Pacific Heritage Museum (CPHM), the Espy Family Archive (EFA), the Pacific County Historical Society (PCHS), the Knappton Cove Archive (KCA), the Dobby Wiegardt Collection (DWC), Washington State Parks (WSP) and others as noted.

INTRODUCTION

Jumping-off place: 1) a remote or isolated place; 2) a place or point from which an enterprise, investigation, or discussion is launched.
—Merriam-Webster's Collegiate Dictionary, *Deluxe ed. (Springfield, MA: Merriam-Webster Inc., 1998)*

Pacific County, once a part of Oregon Territory, then a part of Washington Territory and now the most southwesterly corner of Washington State, has always been referred to as "the jumping-off place." Back in the 1840s and '50s, when the first white settlers began arriving here, they understood that description to mean they were so far from civilization that they could travel no farther. They had reached the end of the road, and there were only three choices to be made: to return from whence they had come, to take root where they were or to jump off the continent entirely. I've always wondered why they didn't simply call it the "jumping-in place" since to go any farther west would have put them into the Pacific Ocean.

Those who came to the Pacific shore, whether from the sea or by land, were adventurers and explorers. At first, they were mostly men—some young, some older, but all seeking that elusive something called "their fortune." Some were running to something, perhaps to a dream of respectability or to the establishment of an empire or a dynasty. Others were running from something—from an unhappy past or from trouble with an employer or with the law. Whatever the reason, they came for a new start.

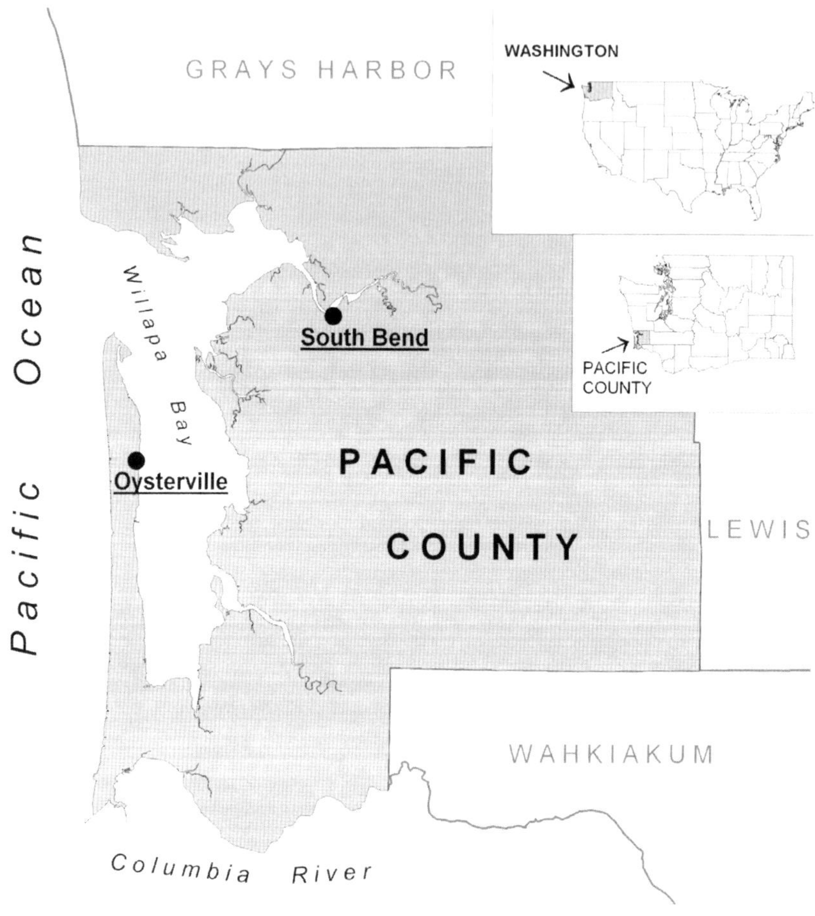

Pacific County, Washington, with its 576 miles of ocean, bay and river shorelines, was often called "the jumping-off place" by early settlers. *Paul Staub map.*

Many are the tales of the independent, free-spirited folks who came to the jumping-off place looking for a new life without the constraints and confining rules of polite society. These days, in fact, residents take pride in the many characters who have left their mark on Pacific County and whose live-and-let-live sentiments set a tone of rugged individualism.

In the mid-nineteenth century, there was space enough to give even the most offensive characters a wide berth. There was little need for the formality of a jail. In fact, early Pacific County sheriffs had so few demands on their time with respect to administering law and order that they often served in the capacity of assessor as well.

One such hapless servant-of-the-people was Charles Green, who was appointed sheriff in 1869. The position of assessor was added to his duties the following year, and shortly thereafter, while on his tax-collecting rounds, he disappeared. His remains were never recovered, and it is assumed that he was waylaid and murdered for the tax money he carried, at the time estimated to be about $2,000 in gold coin.

It was a few years later that the first county jail was built in Oysterville. At first, it was seldom occupied, but as settlements flourished and the population increased, so did the incidence of crime. Tolerance for lawbreakers decreased and, inexorably, as the years passed, the incidence of prisoners in "the Jailplace" increased accordingly.

The old jail book recently discovered in the back of an unused closet in the county sheriff's office gives a glimpse of many of the unfortunates who spent time in the Pacific County Jail from 1886 to 1919. Those were the years that Pacific County was still finding its way out of the Wild West and into a more civilized way of life. It's not the whole story, of course. No book ever is.

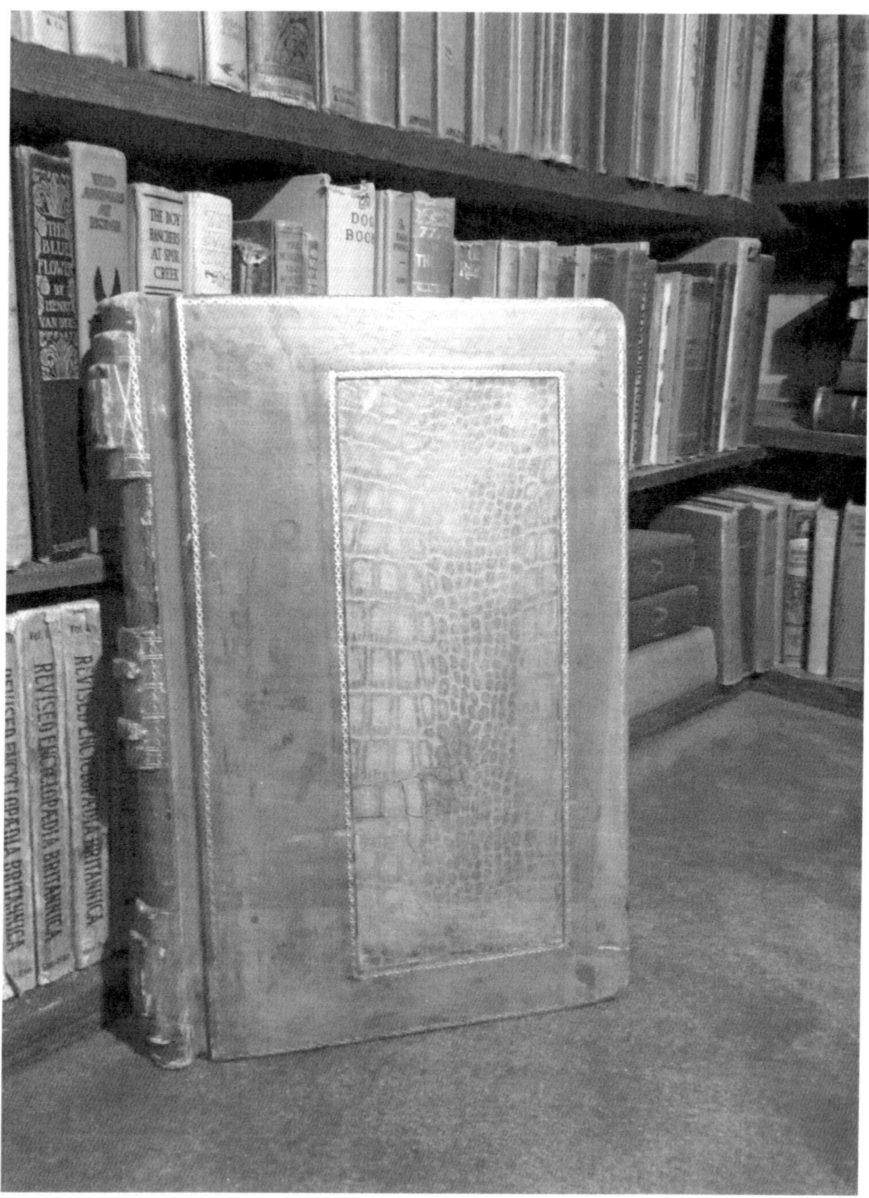

The jailhouse book, *Prison Record No. 1 Pacific County*, measures sixteen inches high, eleven inches wide and one and a half inches thick and weighs eight pounds. *Sydney Stevens photo.*

1

JUSTICE IN A TIMELY MANNER

...the facts in the case fully justify this action.

On Thursday, April 15, 1886, Norwegian native Markus Schuldrup was booked into the county jail at Oysterville, Washington Territory, on the authority of M.S. Griswold, justice of the peace.* Schuldrup was thirty-two years old and six feet, two inches tall, with light hair, blue eyes and a fair complexion. His arrest involved an assault with a deadly weapon.

Mr. Schuldrup had the distinction of being the first person listed in the fine new logbook called *Prison Record No. 1 Pacific County*. By today's standards, the oversized leather-bound volume is impressive, indeed. So are the many handwritten notations, entered in the appropriate boxes and spaces in nineteenth-century inked perfection. As official as the book appears, however, it tells only part of the story. Justice Griswold also kept a ledger (docket), and in it he recorded a bit more of Schuldrup's unfortunate circumstances.

* It was the justice of the peace's sworn duty to "administer summary justice in minor cases, to commit for trial and to administer oaths, and perform marriages." It is said that early Washington citizens, suspicious of federal judges appointed and assigned to the territory from far-off Washington, D.C., created the office of the justice of the peace as a way of maintaining local control over the business of justice. The system was called the "fee justice system" and was in place from territorial times until 1967, when the office was replaced by the district court plan.

Filling in the Blanks

The fine new volume with the decisive-sounding words, *Prison Record No. 1 Pacific County*, embossed in gold on its spine, was purchased (at the direction of the Pacific County commissioners) by mail order from George D. Barnhard and Company in St. Louis, Missouri. It is formidable looking, indeed, even after all these years.

The book is leather bound, measures sixteen inches high, eleven inches wide and one and a half inches thick and weighs eight pounds. Its endpapers are marbled, and its 160 pages appear to be of a linen-based paper stock, preprinted. The volume's first twelve-page section is an alphabetically tabbed index (two or three letters per tab) in which prisoners' names were evidently added periodically, in the order they were jailed. After each name is the page number (or sometimes numbers) on which the details of the prisoner's stay in the county jail can be found.

The bulk of the volume contains preprinted pages with the heading "Register of Prisoners Confined in the County Jail" across each double-page spread. Each page is further divided into lined boxes with additional headings at the top of each column. On the left page are the categories: "Number," "Name of Prisoner," "Age," "Height (Ft. In.)," "Hair," "Eyes," "Complexion," "County or State in which Born" and "Special Marks or Peculiarities as to Prisoner or History." Categories continued on the facing page include: "When Committed (Month, Day, Year)," "By What Authority Committed," "For What Offence and for What Term," "Date of Leaving Prison (Month, Day, Year)" "Escaped or Discharged; If Discharged by What Authority" and "Remarks; Action Taken if Prisoner Escaped."

In all, 591 prisoners are listed in the book, and the blanks, when filled in, provide fascinating reading. As I made my way through page after page, it became apparent that entries in the book reflected the changing concerns and attitudes of the Pacific County citizens as the years progressed. Arrests mirrored the social anxieties of the times—problems with immigrants at the turn of century, alcohol-related misadventures during Prohibition and deserters and draft-evaders during the Great War.

Unfortunately, not every blank was filled in for every prisoner—especially those crucial blanks on the right-hand page that give at least a cursory look at "the rest of the story." Too often there is no answer to the question "What ever happened to him or her?" and, unless the case merited the attention of the press or resulted in a trial with the attendant court records, the jail book provides the contemporary reader with as much frustration as fascination.

I suspect that some of the incomplete information occurred because of the circumstances under which a prisoner was logged in and logged out of jail. Perhaps more time was available at the beginning of the process for dotting the *i*'s and crossing the *t*'s. And once justice had been served, were jailers, like their prisoners, eager to put the experience behind them, forgoing the opportunity to complete the record-keeping?

One more important aspect of the book needs to be kept in mind: not every county prisoner was necessarily logged onto the pages of *Prison Record No. 1 Pacific County*. At various times, prisoners were housed in private homes—perhaps that of the sheriff or his deputy. Later, when the county seat was moved to South Bend, that city's jail was sometimes rented by the county to relieve the crowded conditions at the county lockup. This was especially useful in separating prisoners who might have been in collusion regarding a crime or to separate women from men during the years when the single iron cell was still in use.

When all is said and done, of course, even a thorough examination of the prison book gives but a cursory view of life behind bars a century and a half ago—comparable, perhaps, to understanding the nuances of a nineteenth-century fox hunt by looking at the names and remarks in the *Manor House Guest Book*. Even so, it is a compelling window through which to view our forebears on both sides of the law here in Pacific County.

According to Griswold,* Mr. Schuldrup first appeared before the court on Sunday, April 11, charging one Don Ross with breach of the peace. He told the justice that Ross had threatened himself and his wife by shooting a gun, causing the Schuldrups to fear for their lives. Griswold immediately

* Though his ledger was nothing more than a hard-cover lined notebook with pre-numbered pages, Griswold carefully headed each entry: "Territory of Washington, County of Pacific, In Justice's Court for Oysterville Precinct," thereby denoting its official status as the docket of the court proceedings.

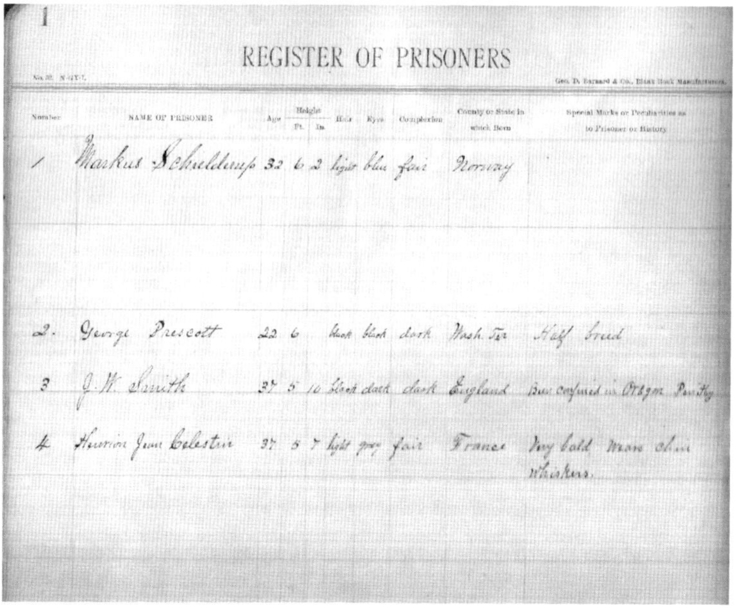

On the left half of each double page in the jailhouse book is recorded the personal information for each prisoner. *Sydney Stevens photo.*

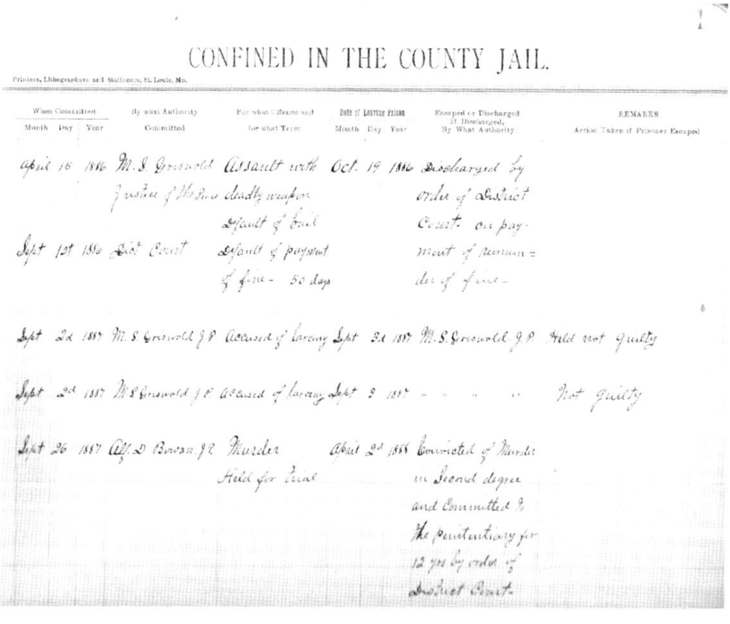

The circumstances of each prisoner's incarceration are written in the appropriate spaces on the right-hand pages of the jailhouse book. *Sydney Stevens photo.*

issued a warrant for Ross, as well as subpoenas for witnesses William and Peter Johnson.

Exactly what the justice meant by "appeared before the court" is uncertain. Most likely, Griswold (who took his office and its attendant duties very seriously) was referring to himself in his capacity as justice of the peace. He may well have spent his Sunday afternoons at his office in the courthouse, and Schuldrup may have approached him there. Or perhaps Schuldrup was upset enough that he marched right up Main Street to Griswold's home and knocked on the door. It is possible that Griswold conducted his court business then and there.

Fifty years later, when my own grandfather Harry A. Espy served as justice of the peace in Oysterville, the courthouse was no more, having been stolen by the South Bend Raiders in 1893. "Papa" (as his children and children's children called him) performed all marriages out of his home, feeling, perhaps, that since he was not an ordained minister it would be unseemly for him to officiate at the church across the street. However, when he was asked to arbitrate a legal dispute, Papa always met the contesting parties at the schoolhouse so that any "blue language" would not reach the ears of his family. It wasn't a very formal arrangement like it had been in the days when Oysterville was the county seat and legal business could be conducted at the courthouse.

In any event, back in 1886, the next steps in the Schuldrup case were taken on weekdays, presumably during regular office hours at the courthouse on School Street. In his ledger, Justice Griswold noted each ensuing incident: "Return of the warrant was made April 12, 1886 and Defendant brought into court and court opened Marcus [*sic*] Schuldrup, Peter Johnson and Wm. Johnson were sworn and examined and evidence taken down."

Meanwhile, Don Ross had not taken kindly to the accusations made against him. On April 14, he initiated a counter suit against Schuldrup, telling the court that Markus Schuldrup had "assaulted *him* with a deadly weapon, deprived him of his liberty, et cetera. Warrant was issued same date as the law denotes, also subpoena for Peter Johnson."

Two Trials in One Day

Justice Griswold lost no time in scheduling trials for both Schuldrup and Ross. They proceeded in a timely manner, both on Thursday, April 15. About the *Territory of Washington, Pacific County v. Don Ross*, Justice Griswold wrote:

The court then proceeded to examine the witnesses and found that if positive threats had been made to which none but the complaining witness testified, they were entirely conditional and the judgment of the court is that the evidence does not show any present disposition to put any threats whatever into execution...It is therefore ordered and adjudged by the court that the defendant be discharged and the case dismissed.

At this point, things began going badly for Mr. Schuldrup:

And it is further ordered and adjudged by the court that the charge is unfounded and that Markus Schuldrup the complaining witness pay the costs in the case as the statute directs amounting to forty-one and 50/100 dollars, as ascertained and adjudicate...Dated April 15, 1886.

Legal costs in the case:

Justice cost 4.50 for papers 12.00	$16.50
Sheriff	$14.60
Peter Johnson, witness	$4.00
Wm. Johnson, witness	$6.40
Total cost	$41.50

Justice Griswold then proceeded immediately to consideration of the matter of "*Territory of Washington, Plaintiff v. Marcus* [*sic*] *Schuldrup, Defendant*":

April 15th at five o'clock Sheriff brought defendant into court and the case was opened…

Upon due consideration of the evidence it is found by the court that it is sufficient upon which to hold the Defendant to appear at the District Court for trial and it is therefore ordered and adjudged by the Court that Defendant enter into a bond with sureties to the amount of $150.00 for his appearance at the District Court for trial…

The Defendant could not procure bail and was committed to Jail as the law directs.

THE PRICE OF JUSTICE

Griswold carefully enumerated the costs for this trial as well, which were added to Mr. Schuldrup's ever-growing obligation to Pacific County, Washington Territory.

Legal costs in the case:

Justice's costs complaint and aff. [affidavit?]	$0.50
Warrant	$1.00
Commit to Jail	$0.50
One Subpoena	$0.25
Serving three witnesses	$0.45
Executing judgment	$0.50
Filing six papers .90	$5.40
Sheriff's cost	$5.00
Witness Peter Johnson	$2.20
Total	$15.80

Whereupon Mr. Schuldrup was locked up in the County Jail while awaiting trial at the District Court.

However, that was not the last of Justice Griswold's dealings with Mr. Schuldrup. Four days later, on Monday, April 19, Griswold noted in his journal:

> *Whereas it is reported to the Court that the defendant is suffering in his health by confinement in the Jail, and that his mind and reason are liable to be affected by such confinement, and;*
>
> *Whereas the Court believes that his wife's care and management are necessary factors in the man's physical and mental-wellbeing;*
>
> *Whereas his wife, Christine, has and does promise for his good behavior and appearance at court;*
>
> *Wherefore it is ordered and adjudged by the court that the defendant be released on his own and his wife's recognizance for good behavior and for his appearance at court.*
>
> *This Bond is filed and approved and Defendant released from custody.*
>
> *M.S. Griswold, Justice of the Peace*

It is further believed by the court from personal examination that the facts in the case fully justify this action, and that it is one of those cases that call for exercise of that discretion with which the law clothes courts in the interest of humane and public justice.

M.S.G.

Back in Jail

Schuldrup's name does not appear again in Justice Griswold's carefully written notes. But he does show up once more in the jail book. Seemingly, Griswold's trust in Schuldrup and his wife, Christine, was not warranted. On Wednesday, September 1, Schuldrup was locked up once again. According to the jail book, Schuldrup was "in default of bail and default of payment of fine." This time, he was sentenced to fifty days or "until payment of all monies owed the county." On Tuesday, October 19, one day short of the maximum required confinement, he was discharged by order of the district court upon payment of the remainder of his fine.

That is the last mention of Markus Schuldrup among the pages of the "Register of Prisoners Confined in the County Jail." Perhaps his experience

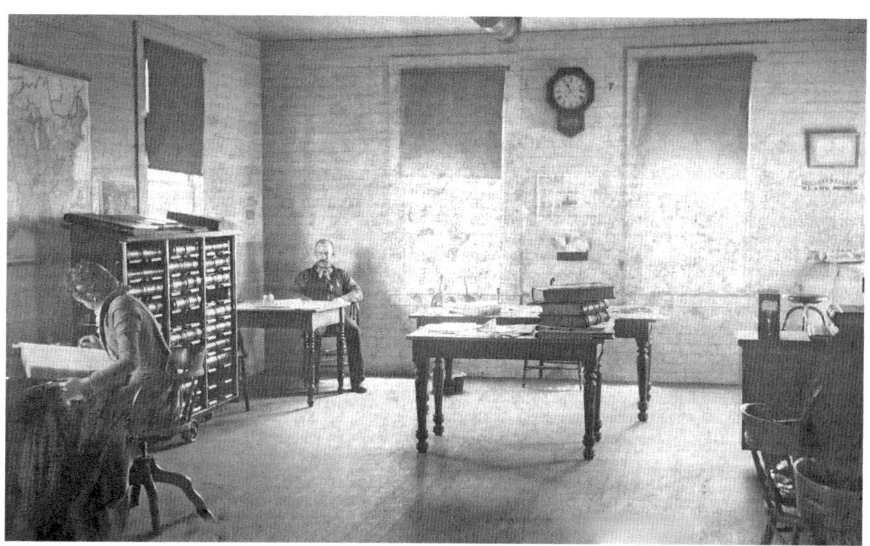

Large volumes of Pacific County records, such as the jailhouse book, were kept in the auditor's office at the Oysterville County Courthouse. *CPHM.*

with justice in Pacific County served as a deterrent to further complaints and/or crimes. On the other hand, Schuldrup's name does not show up in any other Pacific County records—not in the cemetery records and not in the territorial census of 1887 or in the census of 1880, for that matter. Perhaps he and Christine were just "traveling through." Or perhaps they found life here less congenial than they had hoped.

Not too many years later, Griswold's name also disappears from local records. The last mention of Justice Griswold was in 1895. Fifteen-year-old

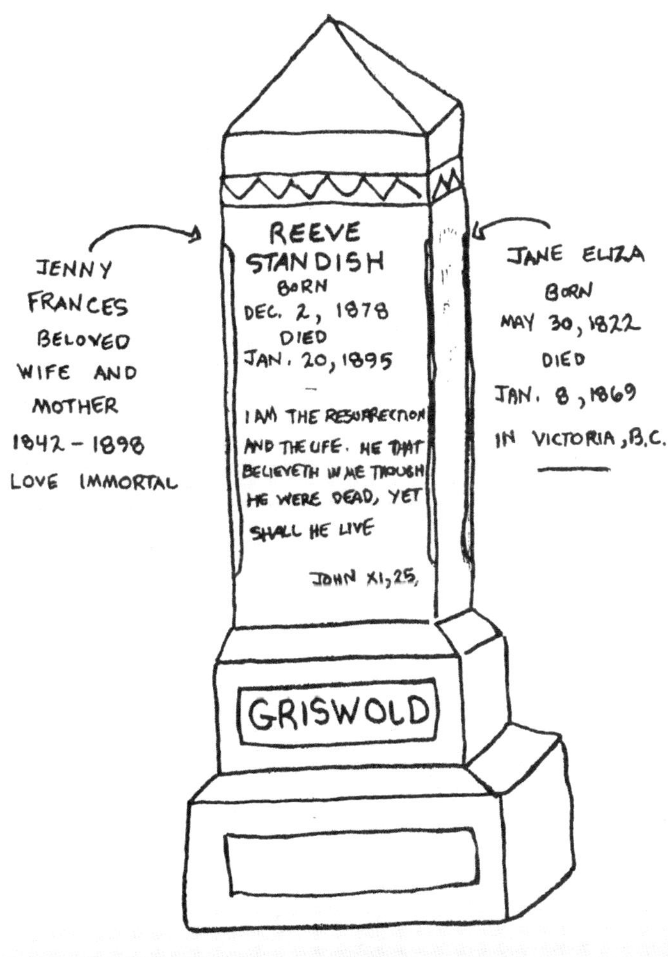

This imposing tombstone at the Oysterville Cemetery lists only M.S. Griswold's wife, Jenny; son, Reeve; and sister Jane. *Drawing by Larry Weathers, ©1977.*

Reeve Griswold had been buried in January of that year at the Oysterville Cemetery, and on April 13, 1895, it was noted in the *Oysterville Baptist Church Record*: "During his talk, Brother M.S. Griswold referred very pathetically to his son Reeve, our deceased brother of the church." Beyond that, there is no information concerning M.S. Griswold.

M.S. Griswold: A Man of Parts

Miles Standish Griswold arrived in Oysterville in the 1850s, shortly after its founding. He was a Harvard graduate who had turned down a professorship there in favor of going to sea. Landing in San Francisco, Griswold took a job as cook aboard an oyster schooner headed for Shoalwater Bay. In the 1860 census, he was thirty-three years old and listed himself as a "farmer," but by the next census, in 1870, he was calling himself an "oysterman."

He was called several other things by the local populace. During his tenure as the first county school superintendent in 1875 and 1876, the students of the district nicknamed him "Old Baldy." The adults of the community, however, referred to him (probably behind his back) as "the Wrath of God" and spoke of his wife, Jenny, as "the Love of God," hers being a gentler disposition.

Perhaps his nickname came from the rigorous standards he set for teachers, including not only their teaching methods but also "their ability to discipline, neatness of the school room and assessment of the teachers' appearance, habits and manners."

Ten years later, using those same standards, Superintendent Mrs. Adda Brown Hicklin recorded the following evaluation of a teacher: "Salary, $35.00; Enrollment 28; Attendance 14; Methods, poor; Discipline, very poor; Government, poor; School, 50%; Rank of teacher, 60%; Remarks: This lady ought to marry. She will never make a teacher."

Like many of the Pacific County pioneers, M.S. Griswold was talented in a number of areas, and in spite of his reputation for sternness, he was considered by his Oysterville neighbors to be "a man of parts." He had served as a representative in the First Territorial Legislature

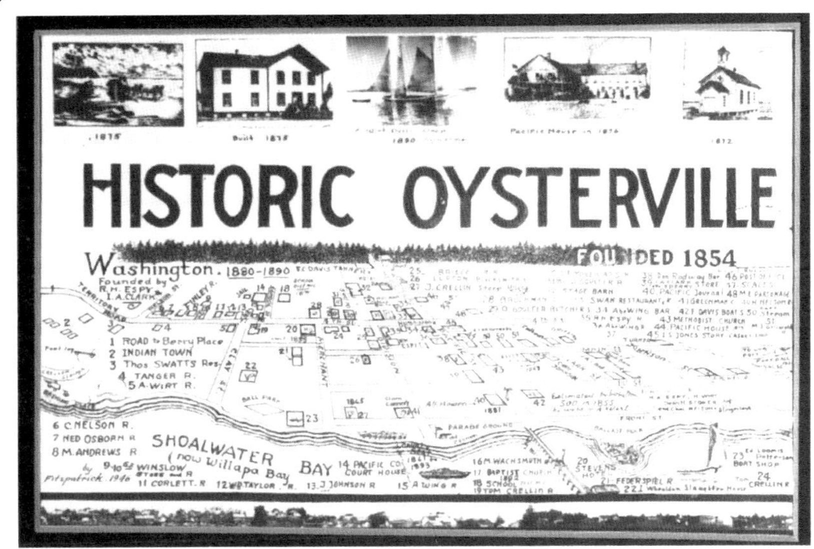

On this composite map of Historic Oysterville, the courthouse is shown as No. 14, and Justice Griswold's house is shown as No. 51. *EFA.*

and was the fifth Oysterville resident to be elected justice of the peace. Perhaps voters felt that such service would allow him an official forum for his assertive tendencies.

More may be known, however, about Schuldrup's nemesis, Don Ross. In an 1876 reminiscence called "New Year's Day in Old Oysterville," published in the winter 1967 *Sou'wester*, Isaac H. Whealdon of Ilwaco wrote:

> *Don Ross at one time drew a very good likeness of I.A. Clark with the old Methodist Church, its pastor and a small congregation riding on Mr. Clark's back and this was certainly true, for "Nosey" as we used to call him did literally carry the old M.E.* [Methodist Episcopal] *Church through all the days of its infancy in Pacific County.*

So perhaps Mr. Ross was an artist, and perhaps he lived in Oysterville in the early days. A Don H. Ross (b. December 19, 1819–d. December 20, 1900) is buried in the Ilwaco Cemetery. His age seems to fit. Are all these Don Rosses one and the same?

The pages of the "Register of Prisoners Confined in the County Jail" for the years 1886 to 1919 provide a good deal of insight into law and order in the early days of our county. But like most historical records, there are more questions raised than answered.

2
"PECULIARITIES AS TO PRISONER HISTORY"

...appears to be slightly deranged.

During the twenty-seven-month period from September 1887 through November 1889, thirteen prisoners were booked into the county jail at Oysterville. They were prisoners #2 through #14 in the jail book, and their particulars were duly noted in the appropriate spaces. All were men of working age, the youngest being twenty-two and the eldest forty-seven. If they were in any way similar, it was that most were from faraway places.

They came from Norway, Sweden (two), England, France, China, Finland, New Brunswick, Illinois, Ohio and one "unknown." Only two came from Washington Territory. The information was neatly filled in under the "County or State in Which Born" column in the "Register of Prisoners Confined in the County Jail." Of the twenty printed headings that march along the top of each double-page spread in the hefty old ledger, it is the column headed "Special Marks or Peculiarities as to Prisoner History" that catches the eye.

The Wild West

In spidery Spenserian script, the notations leap across the century and a quarter since they were written. No politically correct statements, these. In

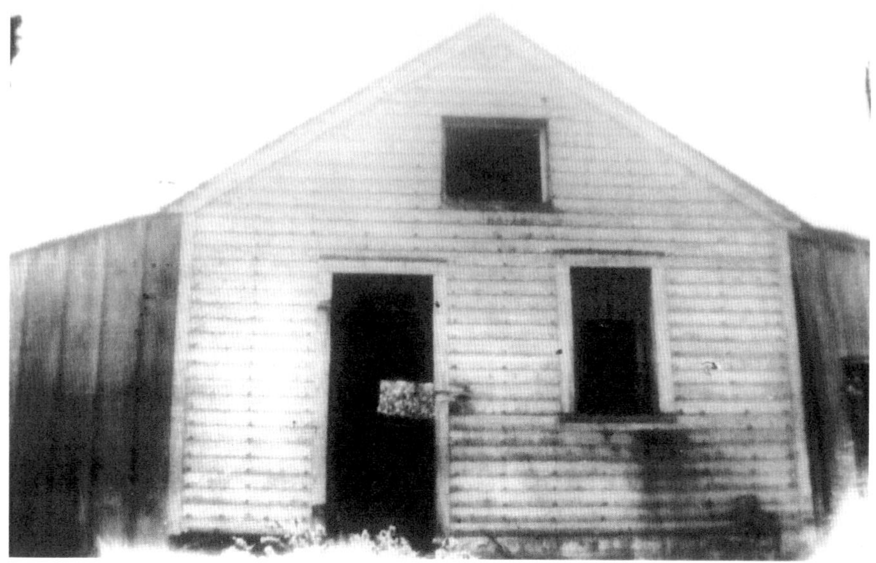

Built behind the courthouse at Oysterville in 1875, the jail building was abandoned in 1893, when the Pacific County seat was relocated. *EFA.*

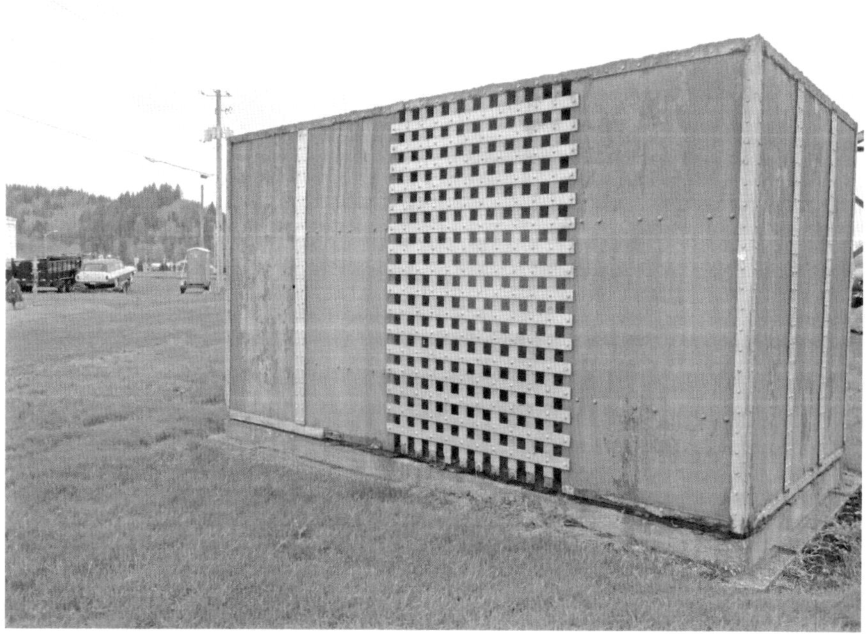

In 1880, this two-bunk cell weighing four tons was shipped around the Horn and was placed in the Oysterville jail for added security. *Sydney Stevens photo.*

the 1880s, they definitely called 'em as they saw 'em. This was, after all, still considered the Wild West. The infamous gunfight at the O.K. Corral in Tombstone, Arizona, had taken place only six years previously, and gunslingers and lawmen such as Wyatt Earp, Bat Masterson, Pat Garrett and Butch Cassidy were still hard at work becoming legends.

At the county seat in Oysterville during the last years of the 1880s, there were no legendary figures booked into jail. The thirteen prisoners of 1887 through '89 came down in history as names in the jail book only. Except for a few notes in Justice Griswold's own ledger, the Pacific County records are silent on the men and their eventual fates.

In the "Peculiarities" column, "half-breed" is the notation for twenty-two-year-old George Prescott and also for twenty-five-year-old Joe Gouchy, though his actually says, "Indian half-breed." They are the two young men who were born in Washington Territory. Prescott was booked on September 2, 1887, and Gouchy on November 10, 1888. In each case, the charge was larceny, and each was dismissed by order of the court for insufficient evidence.

"Larceny" is often listed in the jail book as a reason for arrest. I wasn't totally certain how larceny differs from theft, so I looked it up. I'm still not sure. Apparently, larceny has meant different things at different times and in different places, but in general, it involves personal property that can be possessed and carried away in one form or another. Theft is a more comprehensive term that, in recent years, has been expanded to include identity theft, intellectual property theft and so forth.

Opium Fiend

"Addicted to Drunkenness," "Opium Fiend" and "Hard Drinker" are noted, respectively, for William Senior (39), Chu Chu Lee (28) and John Doe (28). In all three cases, their offenses, as well as time served, appear to relate more or less to their noted "Peculiarities."

Senior was booked on January 27, 1888, for provoking a quarrel and was discharged after five days. One month later, on February 27, "Opium Fiend" Lee was charged with selling liquor to the Indians and served ten days in the jail at Oysterville. John Doe was arrested on June 13, 1889, for being drunk and disorderly and was released a week later.

And what about the name John Doe? Traditionally, "John Doe" is used as a placeholder name for a male party whose true identity is unknown or must be withheld in a legal action, but if this was the case, it is not mentioned. There are no indicators that this was not the man's actual name—no quotation marks around the name, no aka notations.

Oysterville in the 1880s was still a rough-and-ready place. Not as rowdy, perhaps, as in the years immediately after its founding in 1854 but still a town with a frontier atmosphere. Although the oyster business was beginning to suffer from overharvesting and weather-related environmental problems, business was still brisk in the saloons and restaurants along the banks of Shoalwater Bay—especially during the weeks when court was in session and the town was crowded with attorneys and their clients.

Greater Downtown Oysterville

When the fine new courthouse was constructed on School Street in 1875 (the first Pacific County courthouse to be built with taxpayers' money), Oysterville's population was at its zenith. Just the year before, a two-story schoolhouse had been built to accommodate the burgeoning student population of the town. It replaced the twelve-year-old "little red schoolhouse"–a prefabricated eighteen-by-thirty-foot building made of redwood lumber, sawed in California. It, like almost every commodity in Oysterville, had been shipped north as ballast aboard one of the oyster schooners of the Shoalwater Bay trade.[+]

Both the school and the courthouse were on School Street toward the south end of town. Both were built by master carpenter John Peter Paul, who was paid "$1,526 in gold coin" for the courthouse, according to the minutes of the November 2, 1874 commissioners' meeting.

With the two imposing new buildings across the street from each other, the south end of town took on a distinct air of importance

+During the mid-nineteenth century, following the discovery of gold in California, many easterners poured into the state. Their hunger for oysters, a familiar "taste of home," resulted in a flourishing oyster industry. The fact that Shoalwater (now Willapa) Bay was the principal source of fresh oysters for California in the 1850s and the 1860s caused the business to be known as the Shoalwater Bay trade. Oysters were shipped from Washington in sailing vessels that took about six days to reach San Francisco. The trade was so large that several ships were engaged exclusively in carrying oysters.

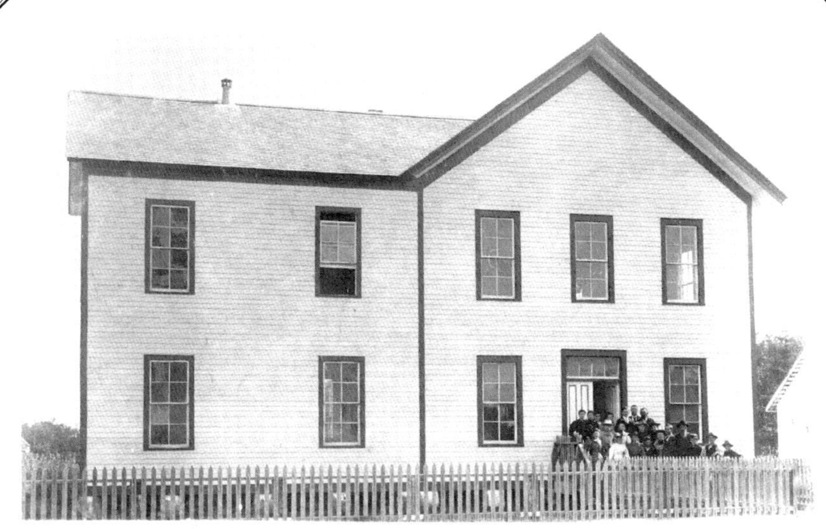

By 1895, the abandoned courthouse in Oysterville had been opened as Peninsula College, an endeavor that lasted only two short years. *EFA.*

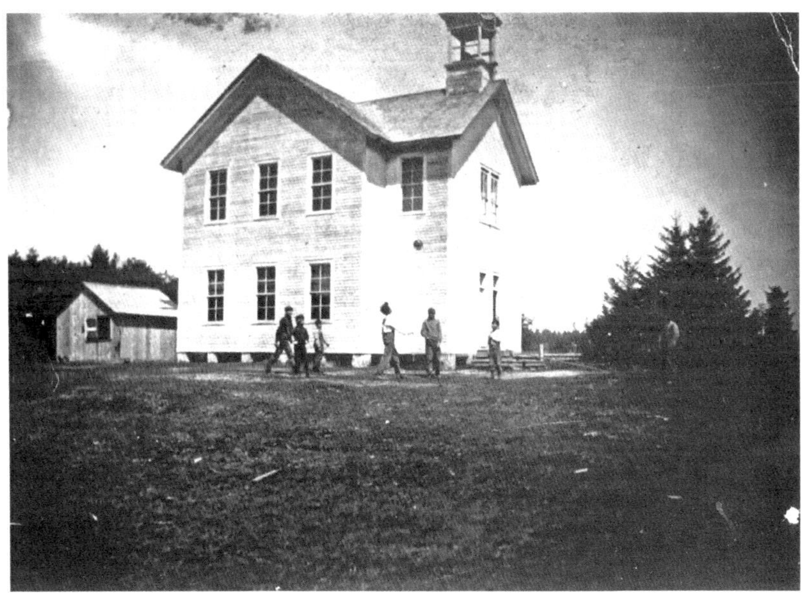

If schoolchildren noticed prisoners being taken to and from jail just across the street, they neglected to leave any pertinent commentary in their copybooks. *EFA.*

and respectability. Up until this time, and with the exception of the Winslow Store on Territory Road and the Stevens Hotel two blocks to the north, the southern half of town was a neighborhood of single-family residences. Most commercial enterprises—the boardinghouses and saloons, the restaurants and stage barns, the newspaper and even the casket maker's shop—were to the north beyond Division Street.

These were the peak years of Oysterville's prosperity. The oyster industry dominated village life, and Oysterville, itself, dominated the Shoalwater Bay region. But by the mid-'90s, Oysterville's fortunes would turn. Three cataclysmic events, one right after the other, would cause a decline in the town's fortunes.

In the 1880s, a series of environmental events caused the native oysters to "fail." In 1889, the long-awaited railroad terminated, not in Oysterville as promised, but in Nahcotta, four long miles to the south. And finally, in 1892, Oysterville lost its status as county seat. Although a tenacious few hung on through one setback after another, the town never recovered.

Oysterville was isolated, more so then than now. The only access was by water and stagecoach. For some, it was a good place to hide out or at least lay low for a time. My Great Aunt Dora Espy, born in 1872, used to tell the following story about the Oysterville of her childhood.

Outlaws in Town

I remember the stage coming lickety-cut. In those days, there was a lot of shanghaiing done because Astoria was a big shipping place. But shanghaiing was against the law. Pete Grant and Larry Sullivan, later a well-known politician, were competitors in the shanghai business. Whenever anybody was in a jam, they'd come to Oysterville. There was a Methodist church on one corner and a saloon on the other. There were seven saloons. When these outlaws would come to stay awhile, they would bring a bunch of girls with them and hire the hall and dance.

The post office was in back of the saloon. Mother never let me go to the post office when that crowd was in town. She didn't want me to talk to the pretty

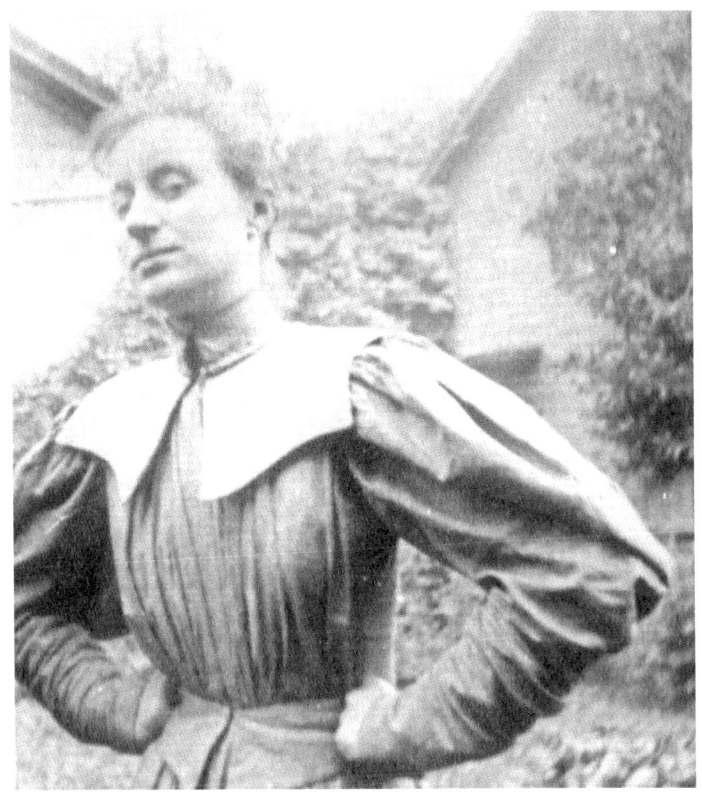

Right: Dora Espy Wilson (1872–1955), pictured here in 1892, loved to tell about the rip-roaring days of her childhood during Oysterville's boom years. *EFA*.

Below: Driver John Morehead described the Oysterville-to-Ilwaco stage as "a primitive affair, resembling a prairie schooner with both ends closed and an entrance on either side." *EFA*.

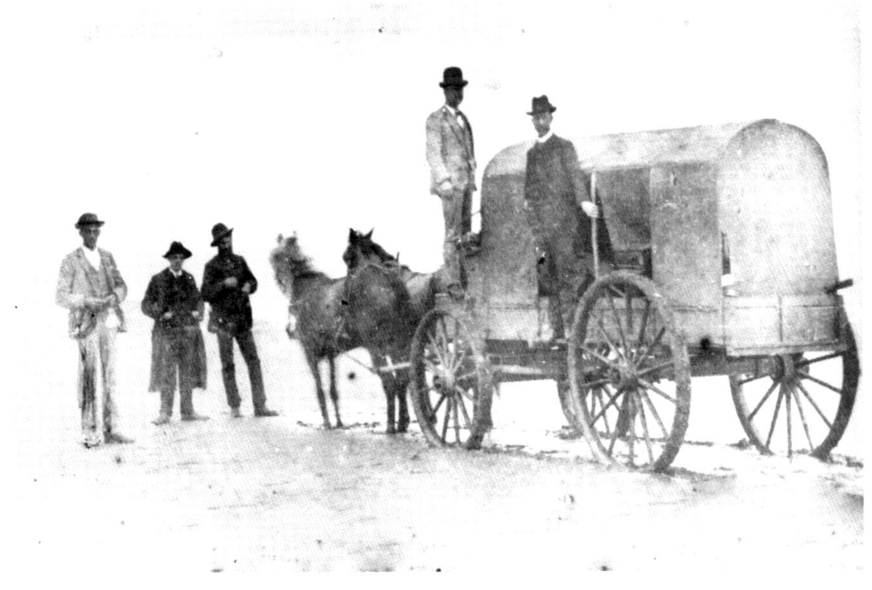

girls. Father owned the hall. I would help him sweep it out and stay for two or three dances. A one-legged Indian would saw out the tunes on an old fiddle. I thought those girls were the most beautiful creatures with ribbons in their hair.

Mother bought some turkey-red calico for something. I tore strips off the side and made bows and tied them on my hair. I would walk down the street, and people would say, "Hello, little girl. Where did you get your bows?" Mama wouldn't let me take money from people, but I would take peppermint candy. Well, in a few months, the outlaws would return to Astoria and the excitement would be over.

Hiding out in Oysterville may have been fairly popular. Two of the thirteen jailed during the 1887–89 period had previously served time in the Oregon Penitentiary at Salem, a fact that was duly noted in the "Peculiarities" column of the jail book.

J.W. Smith (37), who had been confined in the Oregon Penitentiary, was arrested on September 2, 1887, for larceny but was released the next day. "Not guilty," according to Justice Griswold. He apparently was in cahoots with young Prescott—same alleged crime, same arrest date, same outcome.

The other "alumnus" of the Oregon Penitentiary prior to his sojourn in Pacific County must have given his Oysterville jailers quite a headache. He was A.C. Carlson (24), from Finland. His complexion was listed as "florid," and under "Special Marks or Peculiarities," it was noted that he had a "scar over both temples; Had Served 3 years' term in Oregon penitentiary for burglary."

Escape!

Carlson was booked into the jail at Oysterville, again for burglary, on August 19, 1889, on the authority of Justice D.A. Rodway (known around town as "Dapper Dan"). The justice knew a bit about the seamier side of Oysterville life, for in addition to serving as justice of the peace, he was the proprietor of Rodway's Saloon on the corner of Pacific and Main Streets. It was a popular watering hole in the bustling community, and presumably, Rodway was well accustomed to customers of Carlson's ilk.

Carlson was held to appear before the grand jury. He was convicted of the crime of burglary and sentenced by Judge Allyn to three years in the penitentiary. On August 31, Carlson escaped from jail.

Perhaps escape was the norm in the 1800s.* Next to the printed heading "Date of Leaving Prison" is the heading "Escaped or Discharged; If Discharged, by What Authority," leading one to assume that escape was a viable outcome of confinement in prison. The final column on the right-hand page calls for "Remarks," and opposite Carlson's name is written: "Descriptive Circulars sent to all Police Officers in Territory, Reward of $50 offered by Sheriff."

Mr. Carlson wasn't apprehended, at least as far as is noted in the jail book. However, the authorities in Pacific County must have kept his file open, so to speak, for more than nine years later, someone neatly clipped and pasted a small news item concerning Mr. Carlson next to the remarks about him, providing a sort of closure to the case:

> *"Back Among Old Friends"*
> *Andrew Carlson was received at the penitentiary Friday, for the third time. In each case, being convicted of larceny and his last case is the lightest of the three. August 20, 1884, Carlson was received from Clatsop County, for a term of three years for larceny. He was discharged April 14, 1887. January 25, 1895, he was received from Multnomah County under two convictions for larceny, and sentenced to terms of two and three years, which were served concurrently, and he was discharged September 15, 1897. January 28, 1898, he was received from Lincoln County, sentenced for one year for larceny.*

Penitentiary Bound

In unrelated cases, Heurion Jean Celestin (37) and John Thompson (47) were both accused of murder; booked into the county jail on April 2, 1888, and

* Lulu Brown Bunnell grew up in South Bend in the 1890s, just after the county seat had been moved there from Oysterville. In later years, she recalled several jailbreaks that she had witnessed. She described seeing one prisoner fleeing for the woods while another was "squeezing through the gap where one of the bars had been cut away from a window…It must have been between 1895 and [the] 1900s," she remembered. On another occasion, her father, Zack Brown, who served as deputy under Sheriff Tom Roney, told of sending out a posse to hunt for an escaped prisoner. Since he had to drop back due to a lame leg, he gave his gun to an unarmed posse member, and as the others followed the trail into the woods, he rested for a moment under a tree. According to his grandson, "He looked up and saw the prisoner standing on a branch above his head. Grandpa knew the man had heard the conversation about the gun, but he said, "Hadn't you better come down and go back to jail?"" The escapee agreed and went back without incident.

August 19, 1889, respectively; held for trial; and, ultimately, sentenced to twelve years in the penitentiary. Their "Special Marks or Peculiarities" were duly noted. Celestin was "very Bald; Wears Chin Whiskers." Thompson "has wound on top of head; Appears to be slightly deranged; Tattoo on right arm the name of J. Adolph, head of woman and shield of liberty."

J.M. Kelly (30), the man of unknown origin, had no "Special Marks or Peculiarities." He spent November 10 through 12 in jail on suspicion of larceny but was then released.

D.R. Whitace (32), described as a "dead beat" who went by the alias of George Evans, was also held for two days in 1889 for obtaining money under false pretenses. He went to trial and was discharged for failure to convict. M.S. Griswold served as justice of the peace.

The last man booked into jail that year was Eugene Russ, described as "ruptured and subject to fits of insanity." He was booked on November 16, 1889, on the authority of C.C. Dalton, justice of Ilwaco, for assault with intent to kill. It is noted that he was to be held until the next term of the Superior Court. That's the end of the entry. No other information is forthcoming in the jail book concerning Mr. Russ.

It would be nearly four months before the little jail would be occupied once more, and then, four men would be booked simultaneously. Their imprisonment and subsequent fates would become one of the most famous of all Pacific County's cases: the Frederiksen murders.

Doing Hard Time in the *1880*s

Notations in the old *Pacific County Jail Book* often indicate that an inmate was tried, found guilty and committed to the penitentiary. But the record is sometimes silent about *which* penitentiary he or she was sent to, even though, by 1887, there were several in Washington Territory.

In the very early days, there were no prison facilities other than county jails such as the one at Oysterville. Local sheriffs were paid one dollar per day to keep territorial prisoners, and the lawmen were allowed to use convict labor as they wished. This led to abuses, both of the prisoners and of the legislative funding.

Presumably, it was to McNeil Island that the two Pacific County Jail inmates—Heurion Jean Celestin and John Thompson—convicted of murder were sent in 1887. The notations say only "sent to penitentiary." It was not until 1892 that Walla Walla was specified as the penitentiary where Alfred E. Wendall was sent to serve one year for his conviction for burglary. Whether any of the prisoners noted in the jail book were taken to the Territorial Penitentiary at Seatco is unknown, though it's probably unlikely. Seatco closed in 1887, just one year after the *Pacific County No. 1 Prison Record* was begun.

McNeil Island

In 1867, Congress authorized the establishment of a prison in Washington Territory, and three years later, the United States government bought land on McNeil Island near Steilacoom in Pierce County. There, the first federal prison facility in the Northwest would be constructed. The contract to build the first cell house,

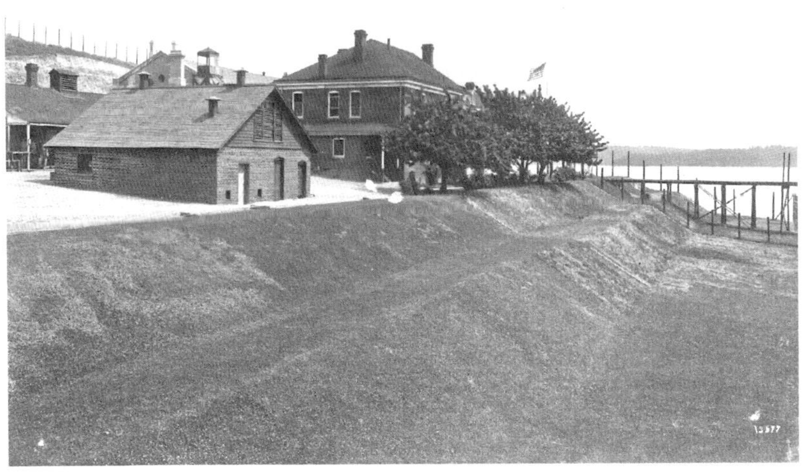

This 1890 photograph shows the federal penitentiary at McNeil Island (1875–2011), the oldest prison facility in the Northwest. *Department of Corrections, Washington State.*

according to plans submitted by the attorney general, was given to Isaac C. Ellis of Olympia.

Construction began in 1871 and was scheduled for completion by November 1873. The building was a large brick and stone shell with back-to-back cells, none against an outer wall, to prevent escapes. The interior cellblock held forty-eight double cells, three tiers high. Each cell measured six by eight feet, with a seven-and-a-half-foot ceiling. However, there was one astonishing omission. The prison had no auxiliary facilities—no kitchen, bathrooms, offices or accommodations for the guards—and there was no provision for water or heat.

The Washington Territorial Penitentiary officially began operations on May 28, 1875, when Marshal Kearney arrived with three prisoners. After being logged in the daily journal by the guard on duty (the only admission procedure), the prisoners were issued black-and-white-striped prison garb and promptly put to work cleaning up and grading the prison yard.

Marshal Kearney required prisoners to work all day every day except Sunday. They were provided with only the basics: necessary work clothes and food. In order to make money for extras such as tobacco, soap or matches, prisoners were allowed to make cedar shingles. The shingles were sold in the nearby mainland town of Steilacoom, and the net profits went into a prisoner's fund, which could be used to buy those extras for the inmates.

By the end of the year, the inmate population had increased to nine.

Seatco

Because the Washington Territorial Legislature was unwilling to spend public funds on a penitentiary, during its first quarter century the territory had no place other than county jails in which to hold felons. The frugal territorial legislators finally decided that it would be more viable financially to house all prisoners in one place, and the Seatco (pronounced See-at-co) facility was established at Bucoda in 1878, not far from Olympia, the territorial capital. A half dozen years earlier, the Northern Pacific Railroad had located a station there, which made transporting prisoners relatively easy, assuming they were coming from or going to a point near a rail line. However, that would not be the case for Pacific County for some years to come.

The prison was built in 1878 by a group of private businessmen who were then paid seventy cents a day per prisoner by the territorial legislature. Thirty-six cells, each with a single six- by twelve-inch iron-barred window, were designed to hold a maximum of three prisoners each. The cellblock was unheated, and there were no sanitary facilities other than a bucket for each cell. The second floor held the kitchen and dining area and quarters for the guards and for an occasional female inmate.

Seatco prisoners were put to work cutting wood for the railroad, mining coal and working on farms. A little later, they were also employed making bricks or working in a sash and door plant and in a cooper shop.

There were many charges of brutal treatment and harsh working conditions, but in those days, when punishment rather than rehabilitation was the expectation, the public took little notice. There were no visiting days, and only rarely was a clergyman allowed to hold religious services at Seatco.

Most of the complaints by prisoners concerned the heavy leg irons they wore twenty-four hours a day. These irons, called "Ringquist cuffs," were the invention of a Steilacoom blacksmith. Depending on an inmate's reputation, iron balls of up to twenty pounds were attached to the irons. Despite leather cuffs around them, the irons caused severe skin abrasions and subsequent infections. They also made almost any kind of work difficult at best and often hazardous.

Walla Walla

In 1886, the legislature decided to take the incarceration of felons out of the hands of private contractors and to build a territorial penitentiary at Walla Walla. In May 1887, the last of the Seatco prisoners were loaded on a train and transported to the new facility. Early cells were made of iron, with strap-iron grill doors. Lighting was by candle until 1902, when electric lights were installed for cell illumination. To provide needed jobs for the prisoners, a one-story jute mill for the manufacture of sacks was built in 1892.

Prisoners were required to observe absolute silence during meals; staring at visitors or gazing about the dining room was strictly forbidden.

Officers, too, were under stringent regulations and were to refrain from whistling, scuffing, immoderate laughter and other ungentlemanly conduct while on the penitentiary grounds. The first escape was made by two inmates who jumped over the walls on Independence Day 1887. Following the escape, it was announced that the prison walls would henceforth be guarded.

3

HELD TO ANSWER ON THE CHARGE OF MURDER

Has anyone seen Mr. and Mrs. Jens Frederiksen?

The small, two-bunk iron cell suddenly became crowded beyond its capacity when, on Sunday, March 30, 1890, four men were booked into the Pacific County Jail at Oysterville. According to the jail book, they were to be held for examination on charges of murder.

The four were confined by the authority of the justice of the peace, Bay Center Precinct, and the following information was listed about each:

> *John Edwards: Age, 38; Height, 5 ft. 9½ in.; Hair, dark; Eyes, grey; Complexion, dark; County or State in which Born, Indiana; Special Marks or Peculiarities as to Prisoner or History, hard of hearing, is a hotel cook.*
>
> *George Rose: Age, 18; Complexion, fair; County or State in which Born, Washington.*
>
> *John B. Rose; Age 65: Height 5 ft. 8½ in.; Hair, grey; Eyes, grey; Complexion, Medium Lt; County or State in which Born, Belgium.*
>
> *Ed Gibbons: Age 32; Height 5 ft. 10 in.; Hair, brown; Eyes, blue; Complexion, fair; County or State in which Born, Nova Scotia.*

As is the case with many entries in the old jail book, information is sparse and leaves a great deal to the imagination. With regard to these particular four men, however, much has been written in subsequent years, and large parts of their tragic story—one of the most dramatic in Pacific County history—can be pieced together.

According to data in the opinions of the Washington Supreme Court and Court of Appeals of 1891:

> *John B. Rose was a man 70* [sic] *years old who had resided in and near South Bend many years. He kept a hotel at which some 40 people were regular boarders, and was well known to everybody about there.*
>
> *Edwards...was a young man, employed by Rose to attend to the cattle and other property at the ranch, and lived there alone; but it had been for some time arranged that he should quit his employment.*
>
> *Gibbons was a young man who had, within three weeks only, come to the neighborhood a stranger, boarded at the Rose house, and was engaged with several others in slashing timber near the town.*

The following statement was given by young Rose at the initial trial in Pacific County and was quoted in the Supreme Court record: "My name is George Rose. My age is 19 years. My father's name is John B. Rose."

The four men were accused of murdering Danish immigrants Jens Frederiksen and his wife, Neilsine ("Sine"), who were the uncle and aunt of Sahra Frederiksen Layzell. Sahra was just a little girl when the murders took place, and it wasn't until 1955, a full sixty-five years later, that she wrote her story. Even then, it would be another twenty-three years before the account was published and the long-silenced murder story was brought to light again. In all, eighty-eight years had gone by since Edwards, Gibbons and the two Rose men (father and son) had been booked into jail and "held for examination on charge of murder."

The Fortune Teller's Prediction

Jens and Neilsine "Sine" Frederiksen were married on August 3, 1887, in Astoria. For a while, they gillnetted salmon on the Columbia, Sine acting as boat puller for her husband. She had arrived recently from Denmark, having been sent for by Jens, and according to family stories, she had visited a fortune teller in New York City before coming west.

"Your next-door neighbor is going to kill you and your husband!" the fortune teller warned.

But Jens was older (thirty-five to her twenty-one), and he was a man of some experience. He had served in the Danish army and then had spent time at sea before joining his parents and siblings in Astoria, where they all strove to make a new life for themselves in this fine, pristine country. As long as young Sine was close by her husband, working on the wide river, she gave little thought to the fortune teller's prediction.

Soon, however, Jens was "bitten by the oyster bug," family members later recalled, and the couple moved to Bruceport on Willapa Bay. Jens spent long hours away from home that summer, learning the oyster business, and Neilsine, with time on her hands, began to grow fearful. Eventually, the stories go, she would become hysterical and wouldn't enter her house alone.

Before long, the Frederiksens moved once again, this time to a 160-acre claim across the bay to an area now known as Frederiksen Slough. They worked hard there to establish a farm, but in a letter she wrote to Denmark, Neilsine spoke of pressures put on them to sell their property. "Our home is <u>not</u> for sale," she said. And she confided that she was pregnant. A farm was a good place for raising children.

Many years later, Mrs. Lillian Ehsanullah had this to say: "If the neighbors of Jens and Sine Frederiksen were really their murderers, then the prophecy of the gypsy in New York City indeed came to pass. Whether or not the true facts of who murdered my relative and his wife ever will be known, the real murderers must be dead now, and all will have received their just desserts in the Hereafter."

"Recollections of Sahra Frederiksen Layzell" was published in the spring 1978 issue of the Pacific County Historical Society's quarterly magazine, *The Sou'wester*. Editor Ruth Dixon prefaced the story with this explanation:

> *The narrative is presented because it is part of our history, a reflection of the times of the great land boom era on the Willapa River and Bay. It is also presented in an effort to accurately and dispassionately tell a story which needs sympathetic understanding of the persons and situations involved.*

It is a story that rocked the county in the 1890s.

Missing Couple

Contemporary documentation of the murder story had begun in early February 1890 with a somewhat ominous-sounding article in the first issue of South Bend's newspaper, the *Enterprise*.* The paper carried a small item asking if anyone had seen Mr. and Mrs. Jens Frederiksen, who had left Bruceport for South Bend, where they intended to make some purchases for their farm across the bay. Their animals had gone untended, and some uneasiness was felt for their safety. It is at that point that Mrs. Layzell picked up the story:

> *When this first notice appeared, George Rose, the son of John Rose, who owned a nearby farm, reported that he had seen the Frederiksen skiff capsize in the storm and the couple drown. Since George was so positive in his description of the capsizing, the evidence that this was not true was withheld for a time, and suspicion was focused on him.*
>
> *When George Rose was accused of the murder, Sheriff Turner heard John B. Rose tell his son to stick to the truth and say that the people went out in their boat and were drowned. This cast suspicion on him, too. The Rose ranch adjoined the Frederiksen place.*

In a later issue of the same paper, dated February 21, 1890, a second news item appeared:

> *A young couple named Frederiksen left Bruceport in a small, flat-bottomed skiff to buy household goods at South Bend about the first of this month, but not hearing from them, their friends naturally concluded that they were visiting somewhere during the stormy weather which occurred about that time, but a few days ago their boat was found swamped on the beach near Toke's Point, a bailer and an old ax shows that the boat was not upset. It is supposed that they perished from cold and exposure incidental to a trip in such a boat and in such weather, as no information can be obtained of their whereabouts. They have been married but a short time.*

Again from the Supreme Court record:

> *The Frederiksen couple only a month before their death, had taken up their residence upon certain government land adjoining the land of John B. Rose, and were living in a boat-house floated up on some logs at high-water mark.*

* Later that year, the *Enterprise* would be renamed the *South Bend Journal*.

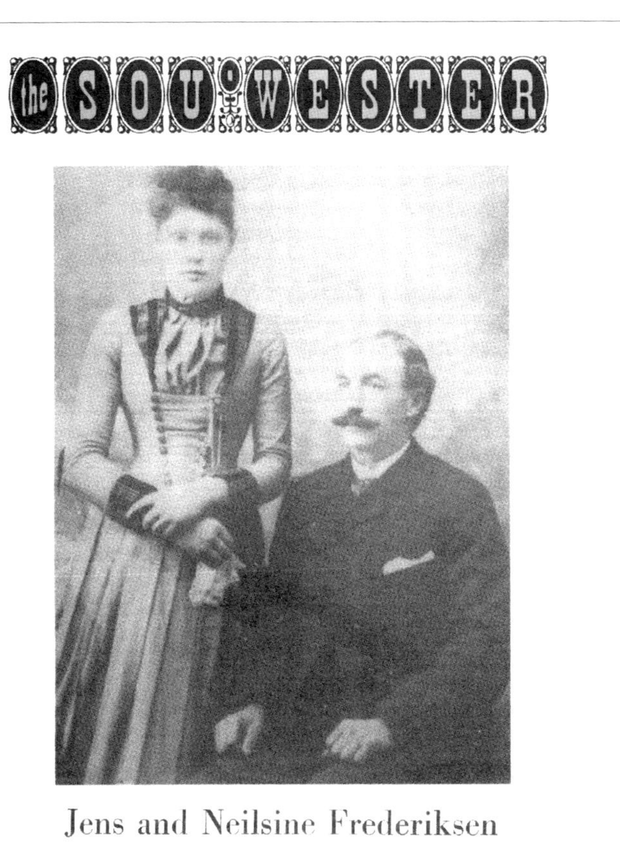

the SOU'WESTER

Jens and Neilsine Frederiksen

Wedding Photo
August 3, 1887, at Astoria, Oregon

SPRING 1978

$1.00

Volume XIII
Number 1

More than three-quarters of a century after the tragedy, the Pacific County Historical Society's *Sou'wester* article about the Frederiksen murders set tongues wagging once again. *PCHS.*

> *The land had been previously several times occupied by different claimants, who had abandoned it, and Frederiksen intended to prosecute a contest in the land-office to clear the record of former filings.*

The property was described by Mrs. Layzell as

> *a 160 acre claim across the bay* [from Bay Center], *a jewel-like setting which is now known as Frederiksen Slough. Nearing milepost 7 on the*

Raymond–Tokeland Road, look toward the Bay and you will see a dike which still encloses a tideland prairie. Beside the deep highway fill, the outlines of a small farm complex are still visible, with fruit trees and the ruins of what was once a comfortable home, a barn and outbuildings.

The Rose Place

The adjacent property was owned by the John B. Rose family, early homesteaders in the area. In 1888, they had moved from there to the new community of South Bend, to a large piece of property that ran from Memorial Avenue almost to Nob Hill. Though they kept their homestead on the banks of the Willapa, their primary residence was now located behind the present-day Pacific County Historical Society Museum, near the telephone building at First and Alder.

Soon, the Roses built the three-story Crescent Hotel and Bar at the corner of Alder and Water Streets. According to Pacific County historian Senator Robert C. Bailey (1918–2005), "John Rose...was one of the new town's leading investors and citizens. He was active in the Land Company promotions and building activities."

Referring to the Rose property, the Supreme Court record continued:

The Rose place consisted of something over a hundred acres, and had upon it a farm-house and outbuildings, an orchard, etc. It had been settled for many years, and was used by Rose as a place to keep cattle and poultry, and for the raising of supplies for his hotel in South Bend, where he lived. No other person lived in the vicinity of this land, and the country around was wild, rough, and uncultivated. The only means of travel upon it seems to have been the waters of the bay and river.

A Search for the Bodies

Continuing the story of her missing relatives, Mrs. Layzell wrote:

Sheriff Turner and others searched for the bodies. Then, following the cattle to the barn over a narrow, muddy trail, F.O. Frederiksen [the missing

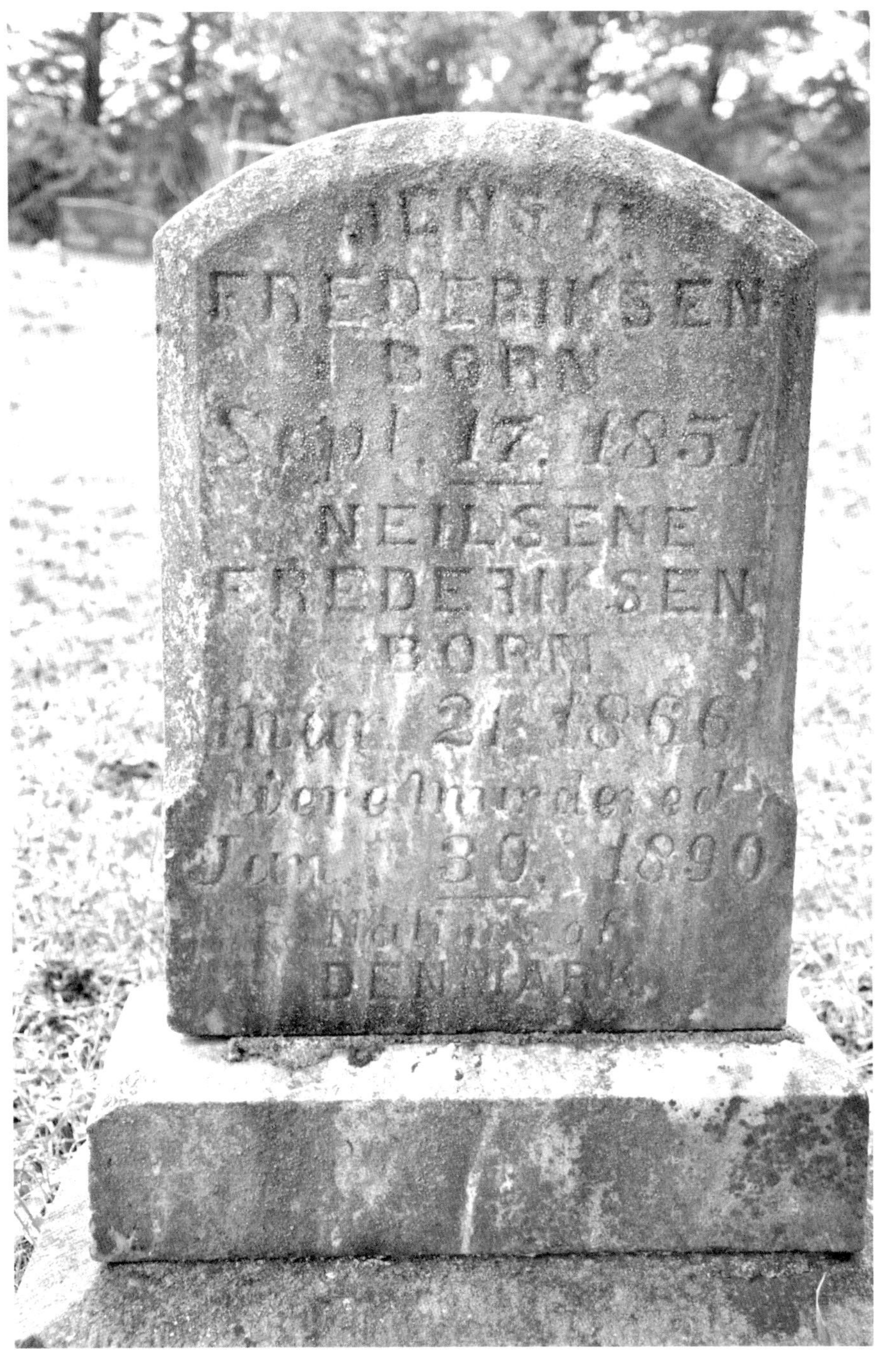

These tombstone words read, "Jens F. Frederiksen, born September 17, 1851; Neilsine Frederiksen, born March 21, 1866. Were murdered January 30, 1890. Natives of Denmark." *Sydney Stevens photo.*

man's brother] *was shocked to see emerge, from under their hoofs, a human arm. The authorities were called and dug up the body of Jens. Then a search began for the body of Neilsine. It was noticed that a manure pile had been disturbed as if something had been removed from it and a search of the Rose ranch divulged that she had been reburied in the pig pen.*

F.O. Frederiksen noted in his Danish family Bible: "Found and buried Jens the 29th of March. Sine buried the 1st of April, 1890. God be with you both. Amen."

The bodies were brought to the local boat shop in Bay Center, where the autopsies were held. They were then buried in the Bay Center Cemetery, and on their tombstone is written: "Jens F. Frederiksen, born September 17, 1851. Neilsine Frederiksen born March 21, 1866. Were murdered January 30, 1890. Natives of Denmark."

H.H. Brown, "Administrator of the estate of Sena [*sic*] and Jens Frederiksen, deceased," carefully detailed the costs associated with the settlement of their estate and their burials:

William Mills	6.75
I.S. Jones, coffin Trimmings	20.00
E.O. Reed	30.00
Pacific Journal	7.50
Eagle Canning Co.	7.15
Board and Stakes	2.25
A.S. Bush, fees	33.40
Geo. A. Hill, head stone	30.00
Wm. B. Copas, fencing grave	25.00
H.H. Brown, lumber for grave	15.00
Joseph McBride, W.B. Clarke, Joseph DeRoos, Appraisers	12.00
Joseph DeRoos, Witness fee for Frederiksen	7.00
E.B. Stone, Posting Notices	5.00
E.B. Stone, Attorney Fee	60.00
F.O. Frederiksen	25.00
Bounties for recovery of bodies	200.00
H.H. Brown, for services	25.00
H.H. Brown 1, Trip to Portland	25.00
H.H. Brown 1, Trip to Vancouver	25.00
Ilwaco Advance	7.50

The Trial

On Thursday, April 3, 1890, just two days after the Frederiksens were laid to rest, the following notation was made in the jail book after the names of each of the imprisoned men, Edwards, Rose, Gibbons and Rose Sr.: "Held to answer on charge of murder." Their trial did not begin for another three and a half months.

On Friday, July 18, 1890, the following article appeared in the *South Bend Journal*:

> *The Superior Court convened at Oysterville on Monday last (July 14), Judge Bloomfield on the bench. The work of impaneling the grand jury being over, the charge against John and George Rose, John Edwards and Ed Gibbons, with the murder of Jens Frederiksen and his wife in February last was brought up for hearing on Tuesday, with the result that a true bill was found against each of the prisoners on Wednesday morning.*
>
> *There were two bills of indictment: one charged Edwards with having killed Frederiksen with a shotgun in the presence of the other three; the other that the woman had been killed by one of the prisoners (which one the jury were unable to determine), aided and abetted by the others.*
>
> *The counsel for the defense entered pleas yesterday for a change of venue. At present it is doubtful whether this will be granted. It is the desire of the prisoners that the trial be proceeded with at once.*

The following account of the trial was copied from the records in the office of the Pacific County clerk, at the courthouse in South Bend:

> *No. 121*
>
> *July 16, 1890 Murder of Sine Frederiksen State vs. John B. Rose, James E.* [Ed] *Gibbons, John Edwards and Rose.*
>
> *Grand Jury: True Bill: J.H. Turner, Sheriff, George H. Bloomfield, Judge.*
>
> *July 17, 1890: all made the plea of "NOT GUILTY"*
>
> *July 30, 1890: JOHN EDWARDS, On trial Separately.*
>
> *Jury: Andrew Wirt, Phillip Moore, M. Feldburg, Curt Masser, E.J. Ford, John Adamson, Thomas Roney, J.C. Deuton, F.A. Mauldin, Freeman Albright, F.H. Cannaris, James Cady.*
>
> *Verdict: August 2, 1890: "We, the jury in the case of the State of Washington, plaintiff, against John B. Rose, John Edwards, (on trial*

separately), J.E. [Ed] *Gibbons and George F. Rose find the defendant, John Edwards, guilty in the first degree as charged in the indictment."*

August 5, 1890: JOHN B. ROSE, On Trial Separately.

Jury: Edgar Brookes, C.H. Shubbe, Ansmus Brix, Frank Salsbury, Benjamin Hutton, James R. Hall, Phillip Patton, Wilson Graham, W.W. Campbell, Chas. Patton, Amos Wirt, Jerome Gable.

Verdict: [same wording as for John Edwards]...*find the defendant, John B. Rose, guilty in the first degree as charged in the indictment.*

According to Ruth Dixon:

> *Both men* [Rose Sr. and Edwards] *were committed to the custody of the Sheriff, each to be "kept in confinement in the County Jail until the time hereafter to be set for his execution, and at the same time, not less than 30 days and not more than 90 days from this date at the County Seat, to-wit: "At the town of Oysterville in said county, that by the Sheriff of this county he be taken to the place of execution prepared for that purpose, and that he be then and there hanged by the neck until he is dead, and that he pay the costs and disbursements of that action."*
>
> *George F. Rose had been the principal witness, and he told substantially the same story as when he made his first confession—namely, that his father, Gibbons and Edwards first lured Jens Frederiksen away from his house, and Gibbons deliberately shot him. After that, they enticed Sine Frederiksen out and shot her in cold blood. Together, the men rifled Jens' pockets and divided his money. All helped to bury the bodies to cover all traces of the murder.*
>
> *Change of Venue*
>
> *There was a great feeling of anger against the defendants, and threats were made against them and their witnesses. On August 6, 1890, the state requested that the trials of Gibbons and George F. Rose be moved to the November term of the court at Montesano. These men were then committed to the custody of Sheriff Bush (of Chehalis County) to be confined in the Chehalis County (now Grays Harbor County) jail. Gibbons is reported to have become mentally unbalanced and committed to an institution, where he died.*
>
> *George Rose disappeared from the Montesano jail in December 1890, and a $100 reward was offered for his return. There were many rumors as to his whereabouts, none proven. Many years ago,*

> *an old gentleman who said he was there confessed to "Ye Editor" that George was handed over to a group from Pacific County, of whom he was a member, and that he was marched out to where a new railroad was being built to Ocosta. He was shot and buried in the soft earth at the end of the fill, and the next morning the body was covered deeply and new tracks laid over it. The old man said that if railroad records showed the day-by-day progress of the work, the remains could be easily found.*

Bailey had different information. In an article written in the autumn 1994 *Sou'wester*, he noted:

> *Shortly after George was sent to Montesano, an Indian is said to have walked down the street in broad daylight and attempted to rob a passerby of a watch. He was arrested and placed in the jail with George. Soon after, a morning checkup showed that the would-be robber and George Rose, the chief witness against his father and Edwards, had disappeared. George Rose was never heard of again, but it was the subject of almost annual speculation for many years as to where he was buried, or someone said "he had been seen at some place or other.**

Of the four accused men, now only John Rose and John Edwards remained. Both were still confined in the jail at Oysterville awaiting the result of an appeal to the Washington State Supreme Court. Their judgment came on March 16, 1891. The decision of the lower court, which had convicted Edwards and Rose Sr. of the murder of Jens and Sine Frederiksen, was reversed. A new trial was ordered, largely due to the weak testimony of young George Rose (now mysteriously missing) against his father and Edwards.

* The subtext underlying all of the stories surrounding the fate of young George is that his father, Rose Sr., from his jail cell in Oysterville, had arranged for his son's disappearance, ensuring that there would be no witness left to testify against himself and Edwards.

All Their Worldly Possessions

Recently, the estate accounting of murder victims Neilsine Lauritzen and Jens Frederiksen came to light after being tucked away for more than one hundred years in an Ocean Park attic. The house, now the Wiegardt Gallery, once belonged to Laurine Lauritzen Wiegardt, sister of murder victim Neilsine Frederiksen and great-grandmother of watercolor artist Eric Wiegardt.

According to Eric, the papers concerning the Frederiksen estate were among a number of letters and documents—many in Danish—that he had found and set aside some years ago when he was renovating the old house for use as a gallery. When Eric and his father, Dobby,

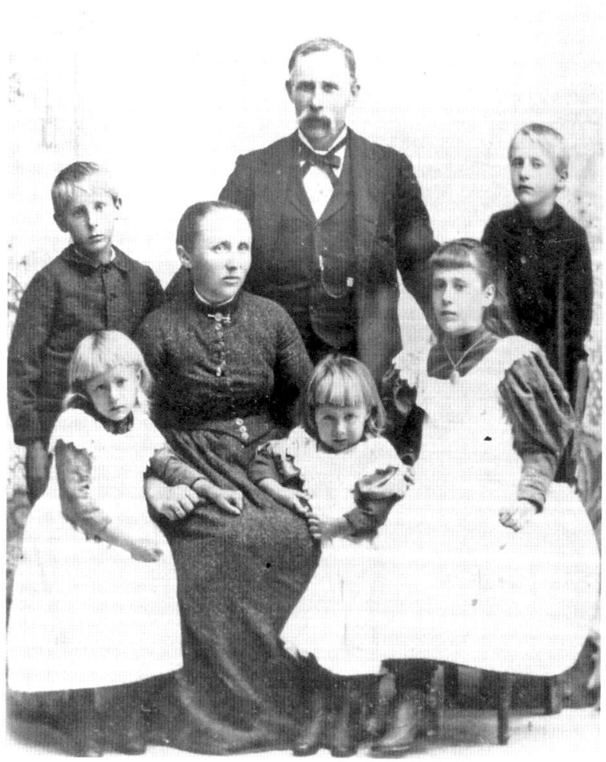

Neilsine Frederiksen's sister, Laurine Wiegardt, shown here surrounded by her family, was the heir to all of the Frederiksens' worldly possessions. *DWC.*

finally began going through the documents, long since forgotten information about the Frederiksens came to light.

One of the documents, the "Decree of Distribution," had been filed in the Superior Court of Pacific County on November 28, 1892. It explains the reason that Laurine Lauritzen Wiegardt was the primary heir to the Frederiksens' estate:

> *It also appearing to the satisfaction of the Court that said Jens Frederiksen was assassinated and died prior to the Assassination and death of his wife the said Sena [sic] Frederiksen; and it further appearing to the satisfaction of the Court that said deceased died without issue and that the whole of said residue descends to heirs of said Sena Frederiksen deceased.*
>
> *It is therefore ordered, adjudged and decreed that said residue be and is hereby distributed as follows, to wit:*

To H.H. Brown Administrator	$45.99
To Andrew Olsen [Notary Public]	$30.00
To Laurine Wiegardt	$74.46

> *It is further ordered that said Laurine Wiegardt be and she is hereby held responsible to any and all co-heirs she may have for the payment of a co-equal share or share-out of said last mentioned sum.*

Dobby Wiegardt pointed out that the "co-heirs" were siblings still living in Denmark.

Also among the papers was an accounting of the Frederiksen estate listing each of the possessions, the date it was sold and the amount obtained for it.

SEPTEMBER 26, 1890	
1 Clock	$5.00
1 Trunk	$4.00
1 Shotgun	$10.00
1 Fruit Jar and Wash Tub	$2.50
1 Table	$2.50

1 Bedspread	$1.50
1 Bedroom Set furniture	$30.00
1 Wash board & Pitcher	$1.00
Teaspoons	$1.50

NOVEMBER 7, 1890	
Bedstead & Mattress	$30.00
DECEMBER 1, 1890	
1 Fishing Boat	$120.00
1 Watch	$15.00
DECEMBER 27, 1890	
1 Fish Net	$20.00
JULY 1, 1891	
Cash from A.S. Bush	$300.00
JULY 8, 1891	
Oyster bed	$30.00
1 Skiff	$2.00
1 Trunk	$1.00
AUGUST 15, 1851	
3 Volumes History	$5.00
1 Gun	$4.00
1 Fishnet and fixtures	$25.00
Bedding	$8.00
Valise	$1.00
Fixtures	$12.00
Chairs	$3.00
Lamps	$3.00
TOTAL	$657.00

A letter from Andrew Olsen accompanied the decree and the list. Interestingly (from our perspective of more than a century later), the letter was sent to Laurine's husband, Heinrich Wiegardt, and instructed *him* concerning the next step his wife would need to take: "Friend Weigardt [*sic*], I have at last after untold trouble got the Frericksen [*sic*] estate settled. I inclose [*sic*] you a copy of the Decree so that you will see how matters stand. I also inclose receipt for Mrs. Weigardt to sign and when you go to Bay Center Brown will pay you the $74.46."

4

THIRTY MASKED MEN

The sentence was death...

By the middle of March 1891, when the Washington State Supreme Court delivered its verdict in the Frederiksen murder case, the courthouse and jail were the focus of attention throughout Pacific County, and the feelings of South Bend citizens had reached fever pitch. The big events of 1889—the completion of the little narrow-gauge railroad from Ilwaco to Nahcotta in May and the admission of Washington Territory to the Union as the forty-second state in November—now paled in comparison to the drama being played out in the county seat.

Only two of the four men initially jailed at Oysterville on March 30, 1890, on the charge of murder were still behind bars. John B. Rose, by now in his late sixties or early seventies (there are conflicting reports in the records), and John Edwards, now thirty-nine, still occupied the two-bunk cell.

On Friday, April 10, 1891, Rose Sr. and Edwards were anticipating a trip to Chehalis on the following day. The change of venue had been ordered for their re-trials by the Washington State Supreme Court, which found the circumstances of their first trials troubling.

Supreme Court Decision

In an Oysterville courtroom the summer before, with Judge Bloomfield presiding, Rose and Edwards had each been found guilty, in separate trials, of the murder of Jens and Neilsine Frederiksen. Each was sentenced to death by hanging. On appeal, however, three of the four presiding state justices expressed the belief that

> *the principal witness* [George Rose] *was an accomplice, who had told a number of conflicting stories, sometimes taking the murder entirely upon himself, and at other times charging it upon others. He admitted numerous falsehoods, and testified that defendant* [John Edwards] *committed the murder, and that he himself had no previous knowledge that murder was intended.*

The justices on the high court also took exception to the jury's verdict in that first trial:

> *The verdict was guilty, and the sentence death. For the verdict we see no way to account, except upon the theory that the jury totally misconstrued the value of the testimony…which they might well do, in view of the court's refusal to direct an acquittal; or there was such prejudice and passion created in their minds that they were incapable of rendering a verdict according to the evidence. There were many assignments of error which we have not touched upon, but we are so thoroughly satisfied that the appellant should have a new trial, on the ground referred to, that it is not necessary to consider them. The judgment is reversed, and a new trial granted.*

In Pacific County, emotions were climbing to dangerous levels. The attorneys for Rose and Edwards had asked for and were granted a change of venue for the safekeeping of their clients. It may have been about the same time that Sheriff J.H. Turner took the Rose women into his home in Oysterville as a way of providing them with protective custody. The late Martha Turner Murfin (1918–2011), Sheriff Turner's granddaughter, said that the murders and what followed were an unspoken subject in their family when she was growing up:

> *I do know that my grandparents were friends with the Rose family and that my grandfather was concerned for the safety of the women during*

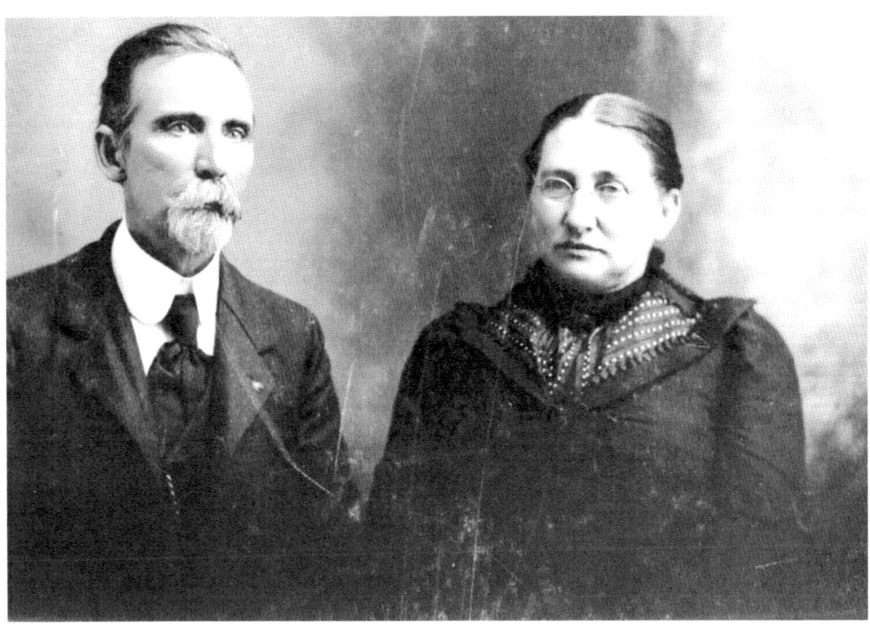

Sheriff Turner and his wife gave sanctuary to the women of the Rose family, who feared for their lives in early 1891. *Murfin family collection.*

> *the time the men were in jail. He must have been very upset at the final outcome because once he had served out his term of office,* he did not run again for sheriff, and not long afterward he and my grandmother and their children moved back to South Bend. I think my dad was about ten when the lynching took place.*

The Fourth Estate

A.C.A. Perkes, editor of the *South Bend Journal*, was also alarmed at the rising public sentiment against Rose and Edwards. In a passionate editorial written on April 10, 1891, shortly after the Supreme Court decision, he declared:

* Turner had been elected sheriff in 1884 and thus was the last sheriff to serve in Pacific County while Washington was still a territory. He ran again and was reelected in 1889, this term being the first during Washington's statehood. During his terms of office, he and his family lived in Oysterville, presumably to be closer to the courthouse and jail. At the completion of his second term, they returned to South Bend, where Turner served as postmaster until his untimely death in 1905.

Men of Pacific County, the highest Court of Justice created by the glorious Constitution has told you THAT YOU WERE WRONG in condemning John B. Rose upon the evidence you found against him; and that nothing but blind prejudice made you do it!...Do you think you can right it by committing another wrong, and by defying the highest tribunal you have placed over yourselves. Perish the thought! For the fair name and fame of our county, desist, or your own children will learn to revile you.

Many years later, the victims' niece, Sahra Frederiksen Layzell, recounted the next part of the story in *The Sou'wester*:

The prisoners were to be removed to Chehalis on Saturday, April 11, but the night before, at about 1:15 a.m., about thirty masked men landed at Oysterville from two plungers and went quietly to the jail. William Brown, the jailer, was lying on his bunk in the jail hall when he suddenly heard blows on the outside door and several voices speaking in unison demanding that the door be opened. Brown, after receiving threats of dynamite, pulled the bar and attempted to get through to spread the alarm.

Instead, his rifle was taken from him, and he was tied hand and foot. Five shots were fired through the barred windows into the cell; the bullets ricocheted around the walls, killing the two prisoners, who were crouching out of range in a corner.

The mob slunk away into the night, and the incident has gone down in history as the only lynching ever to take place in Pacific County. My great-uncle Cecil Espy, born on November 28, 1887, was not yet four years old, but later that morning, his father walked him the three and a half blocks from their home to view the bodies still lying in their blood. "My boy," R.H. Espy told his young son, "this is what you get for breaking the law." Cecil never forgot the incident, though he lived well into his nineties.

Several items in the April 17, 1891 issue of the *South Bend Journal* related to the tragedy:

The Remains Buried
Last Tuesday, a large concourse of friends boarded the steamer EDGAR and escorted the bodies to Rose's ranch, where they were laid to rest, the last funeral rites being performed by the Reverend Sprague Davis.

John B. Rose's Will
The last testament of John B. Rose bequeaths his earthly possessions to the widow. The estate is variously estimated to be worth from $30,000 to $100,000. Judge Holcomb is appointed administrator without bonds. The Will will be offered for probate in the coming week.

"Pacific County's Shame"
(Editorial comment by A.C.A. Perkes)
The wheels of the Journal press had hardly cooled last Friday night (April 10, 1891) after their efforts in putting before the people of Pacific County a last solemn warning in the interests of right and justice and an earnest protest against the unlawful shedding of more blood, when a mob of inflamed, misguided men forced an entrance into the county jail and shot down in cold blood the defenseless men who were charged with murder of the Frederiksens. Too much cannot be said condemnatory of the unlawful and brutal act.

While we do not defend the character of John B. Rose and John Edwards, nor proclaim their innocence, we contend that they never were proven guilty of the crime charged, and that a great, big doubt exists in the minds of all who have carefully studied the testimony produced during the trial, as to their guilt. The prejudice existing AGAINST THE MURDERERS OF THE Frederiksens was naturally intense, as the crime was most horrible. Why this prejudice should have become all the more intense when directed against Rose, until tangible, and corroborated testimony had been adduced, proving clearly his guilt, we are unable to understand. The crime of killing defenseless prisoners who, in the eyes of the law, are innocent until proven guilty, was equally as great as the monstrous butchery which the unnatural son of John B. Rose charged against his father. In case the true facts regarding the murder of the Frederiksens are ever made known, and clearly demonstrates the innocence of Rose, the consciences of those who took part in the bloody work last Friday night will fasten upon them retribution severe indeed.

Not everyone agreed with Editor Perkes's sentiments. A headline in the *Seattle Post-Intelligencer*, for instance, read, "Pacific County Men Overrule the Supreme Court," and the story went on to say, "While the taking off of these men was awful in the extreme, yet nearly all feel that it was justice. They have paid the penalty for their butchering of a defenseless woman and an honest man with their lives."

A Social Phenomenon?

Much more recently, in 1999, Professor Michael J. Pfeifer examined the Oysterville lynching in a scholarly paper called "Lynching and Criminal Justice: The Midwest and West as American Regions, 1878–1920."

"The 1891 Lynching in Oysterville, Washington," he said, "was part of a significant social movement, the collective killing of persons accused of homicide, that flared in the late nineteenth-century Midwest and West."

Pfeifer went on to say that

> *mid-western, western, and southern lynchers shared a commitment to what I call "rough justice," the harsh, informal and often communal punishment of serious criminal behavior...Lynchers and their defenders argued that their actions, while outside the purview of law, were actually socially and morally beneficial because they afforded a degree of justice that the criminal justice system could not or would not provide.*

A Conspiracy of Silence

On what followed, Senator Bailey had this to say:

> *Feelings ran so high that when the boat bearing the body of John Rose was brought to South Bend, the citizens refused to let it be unloaded and it was necessary to take it to the Rose homestead for burial.*
>
> *While this was a black mark on the reputation of the town, old-timers interviewed in the 1930s all asserted it went with the boom philosophy: develop and make money. They contended, almost to the man, that it was John Rose's hope to plat and market his homestead as part of the land boom but that the Frederiksens had acquired property between that of Rose and the platted areas upriver, making the Frederiksen properties highly necessary for the proposed new plat.*
>
> *It was much later, in 1910, that the Rose ranch and surrounding area was platted into "Willapacific," a short-lived, nonexistent town site which hoped to be the terminus of the Milwaukee road. It never materialized beyond platting.*
>
> *For years, the South Bend newspapers refused to carry stories about the case in deference to the large Rose family living in the community. Mrs. Rose and her daughter continued to run the Crescent Hotel and every member of*

the big family became active and a good citizen in the South Bend of that time and the future.

Although the Rose name remains prominent in Pacific County to this day, there are apparently no direct descendants or relatives of the John B. Rose family in the area. Nor do the transcripts of that long-ago trial remain in Pacific County records. Years ago, Senator Bailey combed the files at the courthouse and found all references missing or, as he quietly speculated, "expunged."

Like Martha Turner Murfin, Jean Hazeltine Shaudys remembers that the murders were not a subject for discussion during her childhood. Her grandfather F.A. Hazeltine bought the *Enterprise* turned *South Bend Journal* from A.C.A. Perkes just as the Frederiksen/Rose drama was drawing to a conclusion. He was one of the Pacific County newspaper editors who agreed to the moratorium on news articles about the tragedy.

Dobby Wiegardt, too, says he heard very little about the story when he was growing up in Nahcotta. His grandmother Laurine Lauritzen Wiegardt was the sister of Neilsine Lauritzen Frederiksen, and as the murdered woman's only relative in America, she was the primary heir to the meager Frederiksen estate. But even though Dobby lived only a few blocks from his grandmother's Bay Avenue home in Ocean Park and was close to her throughout his childhood, he does not remember her ever discussing the horrific Frederiksen murders.

However, Dobby does have a vague recollection of a family story about something that happened some years before his grandparents moved to Ocean Park from Bruceport. It was before Dobby—or, for that matter, before even his father, Dobby Sr.—was born.

"For some reason, Mrs. Rose went to see Grandma," Dobby relates. "And during their visit, Grandma noticed that Mrs. Rose was wearing a ring that had belonged to Neilsine. I can't remember who told me that story," says Dobby, "but I know it wasn't Grandma."

After all the long years of silence about the case, and after all of the verbiage that finally was written about the tragedy and that fateful Saturday morning, April 11, 1891, at the Oysterville jail, nothing is more final or more definite than the few words written in the *Pacific County Jail Book* nearly 120 years ago:

John Edwards—Killed by Mob April 11, 1891
George Rose—Broke Jail at Montesano Nov. 30, 1890
John B. Rose—Killed by Mob April 11, 1891
Ed Gibbons—Discharged by Order of the Court

5

A YEAR OF PEACE AND QUIET

Sent to friends in Portland, Oregon…

By July 1891, life had pretty much settled back to normal in the Pacific County seat of Oysterville. There had been plenty of time to scrub the bloodstains from the walls and floors of the jail cell—blood from the lynching of John Rose and John Edwards in the early morning hours of April 11.

The newspapers and tongue-waggers of the county had stopped speculating about the whereabouts of George Rose. How he had disappeared from his cell in Montesano and whether he was alive or dead were no longer important. His testimony would not be needed now that his father and Edwards were dead. As horrendous as the Frederiksen murders and their aftermath had been, it was time to move on. As the summer gained momentum, visitors flocked to the North Beach Peninsula.* They came from the hot inland valleys of Oregon, arriving on paddle-wheelers from Portland and taking the Peninsula's little narrow-gauge railroad train to their final destinations near the cooling breezes of the Pacific.

More and more beach cottages were springing up in Long Beach (still known as Tinkerville until the official name change in 1922) and Seaview.

* Although the finger of land jutting north from the mouth of the Columbia River is still officially called "North Beach Peninsula," a concerted effort by the city of Long Beach in the 1920s succeeded in making "Long Beach Peninsula" the common reference, even on state and local maps.

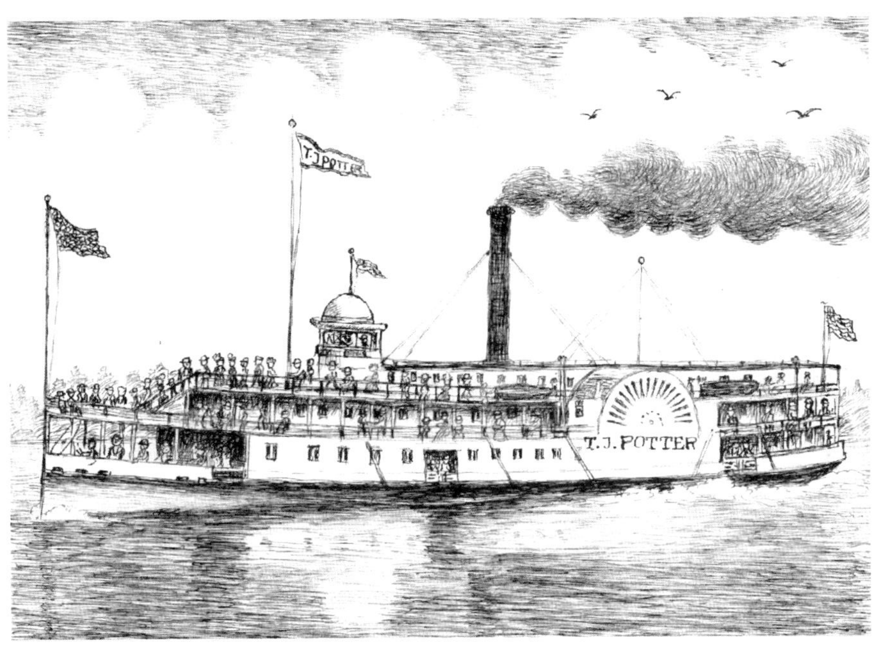

The elegant side-wheeler *T.J. Potter* made the tourist run between Portland, Oregon, and Ilwaco, Washington, from 1888 to 1921. *EEA*.

Members of the Methodist Episcopal Camp Meeting Association were buying up property in newly platted Ocean Park. The land boom in South Bend was on in force. There was a feeling of progress and prosperity in Pacific County.

Few Prisoners

Following the Rose lynching, the jail remained empty until A.S. Kirk was booked on Thursday, July 2, 1891. He was forty years old, originally from Indiana, and was imprisoned on the authority of the justice of the peace of Ilwaco. On page four of the five-year-old jail book, he was listed as the nineteenth prisoner and under "Prisoner History"; it was also noted that he was insane. Kirk was held in Oysterville for five days, whereupon he was sent to friends in Portland, Oregon.

Three other men were jailed that summer. Benjamin Gricks (24), an Australian native, was booked on July 14 for larceny and held for twelve days. On August 4, John W. Gardner (31), a timber cruiser from Montana, was booked for failure to pay a fine. He was discharged by county attorney Marion Egbert on August 13.

The last inmate of the summer was Erikson Makelin (26), originally from Finland. He was committed by the authority of C.C. Dalton, justice of the peace, on August 26. Under the heading "For What Offence and for What Term" is noted, "Insanity; for examination." Makelin was discharged the following day by court commissioner Phil D. Barney.

Again, the jail was quiet for a few months. It was not until October 28 that Martzel Baer, a thirty-six-year-old native of Germany, was jailed on the authority of W.F. Wallace, JP, of South Bend. The charge was once again "Insanity," and he was held for examination. It was noted that his hair was light, his eyes were blue and his complexion was fair:

> *Mr. Baer was held for thirteen days at which time he was committed to Hospital for Insane by the Judge of the Superior Court. The final notation in the Jail Book concerning Baer under "Remarks" states: Had on person cash $47.50, one silver watch—Taken to Asylum at Steilacoom Wash. by Dept. Sheriff Carruthers.*

A Matter of Majorities

Well before Pacific County's first jail was built, the insane asylum at Steilacoom was up and running. The facility had originally been founded as Fort Steilacoom by the United States Army in 1849. It was one of the first U.S. military fortifications built north of the Columbia River in what was to become Washington. It was constructed due to civilian agitation about the 1847 massacre at the Whitman Mission+ and, a few years later, became the headquarters for the U.S. Ninth Infantry Regiment during the Indian War of 1855–56. In 1868, the fort was decommissioned as a military post, and Washington Territory

+The massacre at the Whitman Mission occurred on November 20, 1847. Oregon missionaries Marcus and Narcissa Whitman and eleven others were killed by a party of Cayuse Indians in a dispute that erupted over Dr. Whitman's inability to cure Cayuse tribal members who were suffering from an outbreak of measles.

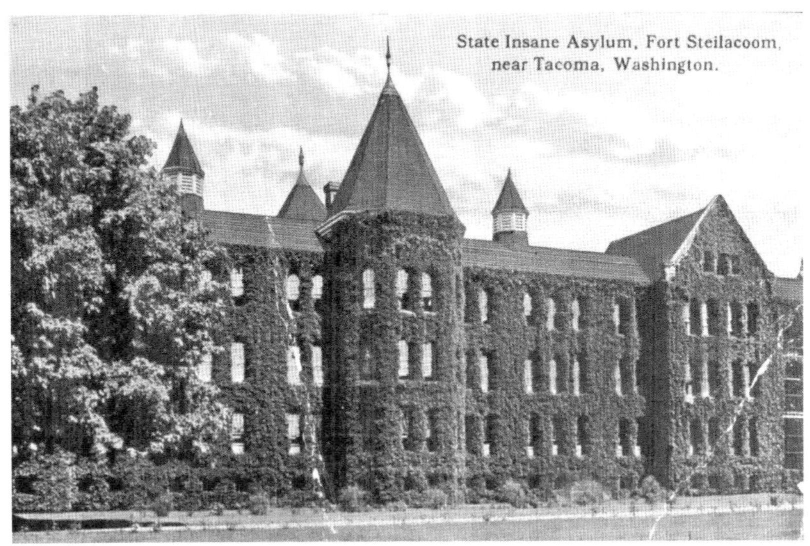

Founded by the U.S. Army in 1849, Fort Steilacoom was decommissioned in 1868 and repurposed as an insane asylum in 1871. *EFA.*

repurposed the fort as an insane asylum, with the barracks serving as patient and staff housing.

Throughout the pages of the jail book, there are notations concerning prisoners who were judged "insane" and were sent to the asylum at Steilacoom. Although it is usually apparent from the few words inscribed in the appropriate box just who sentenced the offender to the asylum, it is not at all clear who diagnosed his or her infirmity. The following short article from the March 10, 1888 *Weekly Astorian* put the problem in perspective, at least according to one Pacific County resident:

> *Before a commission in lunacy yesterday appeared Jacob Adams, a resident of Oysterville, who, being adjudged insane, will be sent to Steilacoom. He appears to be a little off on religion, and being asked how it was that the Oysterville folks believed him crazy, said it was purely a matter of opinion; that he believed that they were crazy, and, of course, they being in the majority, he had to give in. So this insanity question resolves itself into a matter of majorities.*

From the time of Baer's release on November 10, 1891, until February 5, 1892, the iron cell in Oysterville remained empty. Then, twenty-seven-year-old Charles S. Johnson, a native of Illinois, was held to answer on charge of robbery. He was five feet, seven and a half inches tall, with brown hair, gray eyes and a fair complexion.

Written under "Special Marks or Peculiarities as to Prisoner History" were these notations: "Lame in both legs caused by rheumatism. Walks with cane. Sandy mustache. Heavy set. Johnson was arrested for Robbery and held to answer. He was convicted of petit larceny*—10 days in jail. The final note on February 20, 1892, says Discharged—Expiration of Term."

County Seat Talk

During the first months of 1892, there began to be talk of moving the county seat. South Bend, especially, was eager to become the center of the county's political and business activities. After all, it would not be long before the final bit of track would be laid, making South Bend the western terminus of the Northern Pacific Railroad.

Furthermore, plans were underway to encourage maritime traffic into Shoalwater Bay and up the Willapa River. Realtors spoke in glowing terms of making South Bend the "Baltimore of the Pacific." Key to this plan was petitioning the United States Board on Geographic Names to change the name of the bay from Shoalwater to Willapa. "Shoalwater," the South Bend developers thought, discouraged ship's captains from entering the bay, "shoal" being the nautical term for shallow. Seemingly, no one gave thought to the expertise with which mariners read their nautical charts, where depths were carefully noted.

* Petit larceny, according to Webster's New World Law Dictionary, 2010: "Originally distinguished from grand larceny as a matter of degree. A theft of something valued at 12 pence or less was considered petty larceny, and the death penalty was not invoked. Today, the amount differentiating between petty and grand larceny is in dollars and varies from state to state."

A Whale of an Idea!

During the summer of 1892, talk of the impending "county seat election" was overshadowed for a time by the arrival of two Pacific humpback whales. The first arrived near the Loomis Mansion, south of Ocean Park. South Bend tailor and taxidermist John Hudson lost no time in traveling to the beach to claim the leviathan on behalf of Washington's World Fair Commission. He posted notices that all persons mutilating the whale would be prosecuted.

Hudson had obtained an appointment from the Fair Commission to collect specimens of Pacific County's birds, fish and animals. His contract specified that he was to collect and mount families of elk, deer, mountain sheep and mountain goats and single specimens of other animals and birds of Washington. They would be exhibited in Chicago the following year at the state's building at the Columbian Exposition, popularly known as the World's Fair. The prospect of a whale skeleton as the exhibit's focal point was a bonus he could not pass up, despite the difficulties he needed to surmount.

Before he had even set eyes on the beast, the Portland *Oregonian* reported that the mammal had been so long dead that "people over on the edge of the next county began using disinfectants and burning rags to offset the heavily-freighted air that came from the vicinity of the animal." Though Hudson himself seemed undaunted, saying only, "It surely is a very disagreeable job," he was hard pressed to hire necessary workers and ended up with only one helper. To compound his problems, before he could even get started in removing the whale's organs and separating its flesh from the bones, the *Oregonian* was reporting that "relic hunters had removed the last vestiges of its jaw as well as the whalebone [baleen]."+

+Baleen is a filter-feeder system inside the mouths of baleen whales such as the humpback. The baleen system works when a whale opens its mouth while submerged and takes in water. The whale then pushes the water out, and animals such as krill are filtered by the baleen and remain as food for the whale. People formerly used baleen (usually referred to as "whalebone") for making numerous items for which flexibility and strength were required, including backscratchers, collar stiffeners, buggy whips, parasol ribs and corset stays. Nowadays, synthetic materials such as plastic and fiberglass have replaced baleen and, of course, items such as buggy whips and corset stays are no longer de rigueur.

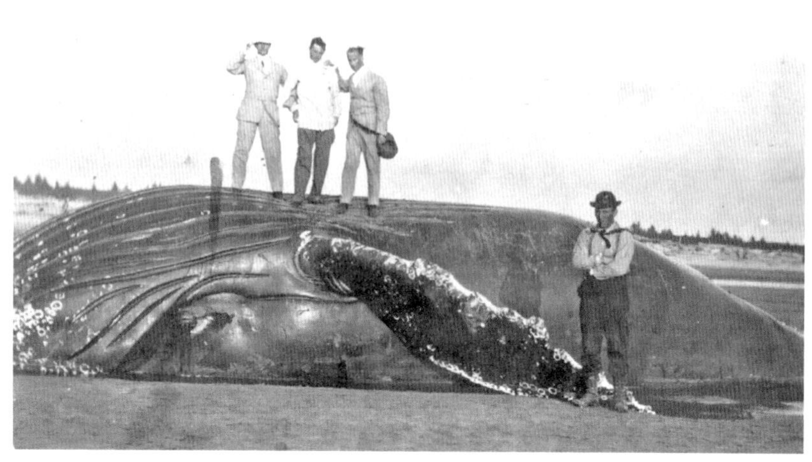

Whales periodically wash ashore onto the Long Beach Peninsula and, invariably, draw the curious and the souvenir hunters, as seen above in 1923. *Verna Oller collection.*

Hudson pooh-poohed this latest report, responding that the monster was still intact and that *Oregonian* readers visiting the World's Fair would be able to pass through the jaws "as Jonah did of old." Whether or not he was simply putting a good face on things is not known, for just about that time a second whale washed ashore not far from the Oysterville approach road, and Mrs. Julia Briscoe, Oysterville's postmistress and wife of Judge John Briscoe, claimed the monster in Hudson's name.

As luck would have it, this, too, was a whale of "the same sex and species measuring 44 feet long, 3½ feet shorter than the first whale," according to Hudson. He made arrangements with Mrs. Briscoe to keep an eye on the beast so that he could eventually take from it the parts that were missing from the first whale. However, the baleen and part of the jaws of this whale also "disappeared," and despite threats of prosecution, Hudson had to be content with retrieving only the jawbones.

Eventually, the whale skeleton was exhibited in an exposition in Tacoma, as well as at the Chicago World's Fair, and it finally went to Chicago's Field Museum. In response to a rather disparaging headline in the *South Bend Journal* about the items in the exhibit, Hudson retorted, "They drew more attention to the county and its location than all the printed matter distributed in the state of Washington by South Bend in the past year."

As for Hudson's threats of "prosecution," the record is silent. Certainly there is no mention made in the jail book nor in Griswold's log concerning those who made off with parts of either of the whales. On the other hand, my own grandmother reported that, on her first trip to Oysterville in the summer of 1897, she was amazed to find that her future mother-in-law, Mrs. R.H. Espy, was "using whale ribs for chicken perches!"

Sealand, just four miles to the south of Oysterville, was also thinking about the advantages of becoming the county seat. It had been less than three years since the rival town of Nahcotta, just across the new railroad tracks, had become the northern terminus of the Ilwaco Railway and Navigation Company's little Peninsula railroad. In the face of Nahcotta's increasing name recognition, residents of Sealand hoped to avoid total oblivion by becoming the county seat in November's election.

The citizens of Oysterville were also gearing up for the election. The decision in 1889 by their very own neighbor, transportation magnate Lewis Loomis, to end his new narrow-gauge rail line at Nahcotta had been a great blow to the community. A number of businesses had left town and moved the four miles south, correctly anticipating that both the ease of transporting goods and the influx of passengers would be a great boon to business. Only when court was in session was there anything "doing" in Oysterville now, and residents feared that losing the county seat would put the finishing touches on the town's ghostly atmosphere.

Meanwhile, as much as possible, it was business as usual over at the courthouse and the nearby county jail. On April 22, Alfred E. Wendall was booked into jail on the charge of burglary. Like all of the recent prisoners, and no doubt like a majority of the county's population, Wendall was from afar. A New Yorker, he was five feet, one and a half inches tall, with black hair, gray eyes and a fair complexion. The jail book notes: "Upper left tooth out. Thick lips. Uses morphine. Clean shaven."

Under "For What Term," it is noted that Wendall would be "held to answer at next term of Superior Court, July 1892. Convicted of burglary and Sentenced to one year in the penitentiary on July 14, 1892. Taken to penitentiary at Walla Walla by James Binder, D.S."

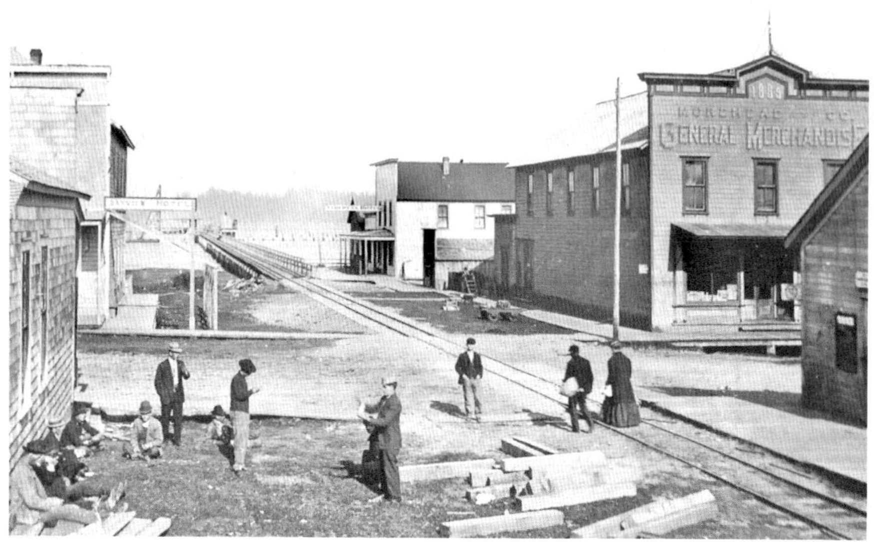

In 1889, the tracks for the new IR&N Railroad bisected Sealand (left) and Nahcotta (right) and made Oysterville all but superfluous as an economic force. *CPHM.*

As of July 15, 1892, the county jail was empty once more. For the next five months and thirteen days, there would be no inmates in the small iron cell. The citizens of Oysterville could devote their full-time attention to the upcoming election and their efforts to retain the Pacific County seat. It wouldn't be until well after that fateful election that blacksmith Andrew Gordon would be booked into the jail on a manslaughter charge and would gain the distinction of being the "Last Prisoner in Oysterville."

6

THE LAST PRISONER IN OYSTERVILLE

"I'll shoot you, too!"

Even after the November 1892 election, when the good citizens of Pacific County voted to move the county seat to South Bend, life continued at much the normal pace at the courthouse in Oysterville. No serious effort to pack up the offices was being made. In fact, there were grumblings about irregularities in the election procedures. "Transients, a-workin' on the railroad had been allowed to cast their votes in South Bend" went the rumor.

Ever hopeful of continuing as the center for county business, Oysterville residents appealed the election results, and plans for a move across the bay were temporarily halted. County commissioners continued to meet in Oysterville, court continued to be held in Oysterville and the county jail, empty since July 15, stood ready to welcome those who broke the law.

It wasn't until the day after Christmas that Andrew Gordon was booked into jail. He was destined to be the final prisoner to serve time in the jail at Oysterville. In fact, there would not be another man booked into the Pacific County Jail until July 14, 1893. By that time, the iron cell had been moved to the new county seat in South Bend, and there it had stood vacant for four months.

Mr. Gordon, a blacksmith, was sixty-four years old and five feet, eleven and a half inches tall, with gray eyes, brown hair and a full sandy beard. He was from Kentucky and had family in Kansas.

One notation in the jail book said, "Small scar on right leg caused by cut." Under "Remarks" was written, "Had on person $31.75 which was placed in Sheriff's office to his credit. Mr. Gordon was committed to jail on December 26 by the authority of Superior Court on the charge of Manslaughter."

"A Vile Name"

Gordon's trial took place on February 21, 1893, with Judge W.W. Langhorne presiding. According to the February 24 issue of the *South Bend Journal*, witnesses testified that Gordon was one of six or seven men who had gathered on Christmas Eve at the shanty of the Northern Pacific Railroad's gravel pit boss, William Kelly. The men were playing cards, drinking and talking, but by midnight, only Kelly, Gordon and two other men, witnesses Mr. Murphy and Mr. Collins, remained.

The witnesses said Kelly called Gordon "a vile name," whereupon Gordon took out his revolver, purchased only the day before, and shot Kelly, who fell over dead on his bunk. Gordon then said, "I'll shoot you, too," but the witnesses, who by then had sought cover underneath the bed, were unsure whom Gordon meant—perhaps even himself. They heard several more shots, and Gordon then walked across the street to the home of the Lilly family, where he visited for a while. Gordon testified that he had but a "glimmering recollection" of being at the Lilly home.

According to the *Journal*, Kelly was known to be a quarrelsome character, whereas Gordon had a "good name," was reputed to be "even tempered," had been a member of the Methodist Church and had served for three and a half years with the Ohio Cavalry during the Civil War.

Apparently weighing the reputations of both men and taking into consideration the name-calling that precipitated the shooting, the jury voted ten for acquittal, one to convict for manslaughter and one to convict for murder in the first degree.

A compromise was worked out, and Gordon was convicted of involuntary manslaughter and sentenced to two years hard labor at the state penitentiary in Walla Walla. He was escorted there by Sheriff Thomas Roney, who reported on his return, according to the March 3 edition of the *South Bend Journal*, that the trip had been "uneventful."

Apocryphal Story

Over the years, the story has come down that Andrew Gordon was not only the final prisoner in Oysterville but also that he actually traveled with the jail when it was barged over to South Bend. In that rendition of history, the only question was whether Gordon made the trip still locked in the iron cell or if he was allowed outside to ride on the deck in style.

A long-forgotten article in the March 2, 1893 issue of the *South Bend Journal* provided some clarification. Concerning recent actions by the county commissioners, it was reported that payment of $47.00 was made to Sheriff J.H. Turner of Oysterville for boarding Gordon for forty-seven days. Additionally, A.E. Caierns of South Bend was paid $10.50 for boarding the prisoner for six days.

It would appear, then, that Gordon did not await his trial in the jail cell for all the days between his December 26 arrest and his sentencing on February 22. For whatever reason—perhaps because the transfer of the courthouse records and jail seemed imminent—Gordon was kept in the Oysterville jail only until January 1, after which time other arrangements were made.

Furthermore, according to the March 3 *Journal*, W.R. Gray, who was contracted by the county to remove the safes and the jail from Oysterville, "ran into difficulty" and had to tear out the side of the jail building to remove the cell. J.M. McIntire was subcontracted to load the jail onto the barge, and the March 10 paper noted that he had been paid for that job.

Although information is sketchy concerning the exact day that the jail arrived in South Bend, it seems likely that Mr. Gordon was already ensconced in the penitentiary at Walla Walla well in advance of the jail's journey across the bay.

On Court Street and Diaper Alley

Considerably more is known about the jail itself than about the last prisoner it held. The jail's history began on May 4, 1875, according to the minutes of the county commissioners' meeting: "A great portion of the afternoon session having been occupied in discussing of a jail suitable for the wants of the county." Again, on May 5: "Plans for jail discussed." And on May 6: "Jail 14x18 with 9 foot walls ordered."

The builder was master carpenter John Peter Paul, who had built the two-story schoolhouse the previous year and had just finished the courthouse.

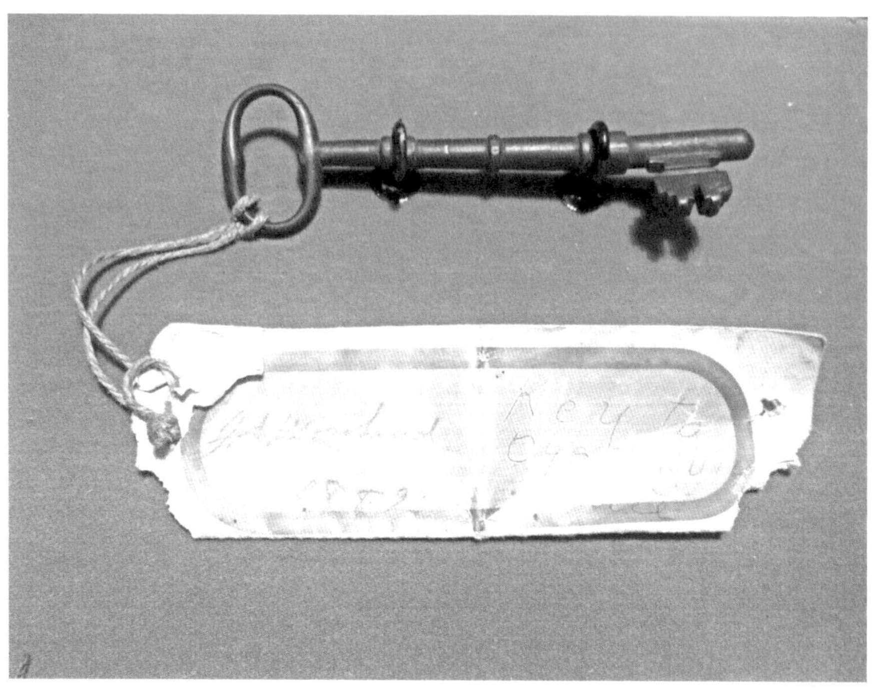

The label attached to the old iron key says, "J.A. Morehead Key to Oysterville Jail 1882." (Morehead served as county commissioner for fourteen years.) *EE4.*

The *Commissioners' Minutes* for February 7, 1876, ordered that "J.P. Paul be allowed for building County Jail according to contract out of current expense fund $450."

The building was constructed of two-by-sixes laid flat and spiked together. It stood two feet off the ground on wood posts and had shiplap cedar siding and a tarpaper roof. The entrance door had a sturdy lock and also could be secured from the inside by a wooden bar and latch arrangement. Heavy iron bars had been installed in the large window by the door, and there was an additional smaller window in the attic.

Accoutrements in the little structure included a woodstove for heating and cooking; a shelf on which sat the frying pan, coffee pot, linens and a few dishes for the convenience of the prisoners; and a cot for the jailer and one or two cots for the prisoners. Lest it be thought that this arrangement was an especially "cozy" one, it should be noted that the county was apparently well supplied with both shackles and handcuffs. On July 2, 1860, the *Commissioners' Minutes* indicate that the sheriff was directed to purchase "Pr. Feet Shackles 8.00, pr. Hand Cuffs 5.00," and again, on May 4, 1868, "3 pr. Shackles $7.50" are listed.

The building was located behind the courthouse on the corner of Court Street and "Diaper Alley" (which was the name affectionately assigned to the path that ran behind some of the houses on Territory Road giving access to back doors and to the back gardens where housewives hung their laundry in fine weather).

Although Pacific County had just celebrated the twenty-fourth year of its founding, public funding thus far had been authorized by the commissioners for only one other building: the two-story schoolhouse built just the year before. Previously, those who conducted county business had met in private homes or in buildings rented for the purpose. Lawbreakers, however, had not necessarily been given such mindful consideration.

Pioneer Jail Facilities

During the early years in the rowdy pioneer settlements of the county, transgressions were generally overlooked. Those who clearly needed to be locked up were held in whatever room, house or public building could be secured by a sheriff or local constable. Perpetrators of serious crimes were occasionally sent to Astoria, which had the nearest true jail facility.

In 1853, when the county seat was still located in Chinookville (east of present-day Chinook, beyond the Fort Columbia Tunnel), a zinc cabin belonging to Bill McCarty was used as a meeting place, a courtroom, a jail and for any other county purpose. When not in use by the county, the building served as a storage facility for fishing gear.

Typical, also, of early law and order were the arrangements made in 1854 at Bruceport, as described in a firsthand account by James G. Swan in his book *The Northwest Coast, or Three Years Residence in Washington Territory*:

> *A miserable loafer that had found his way into the Bay, and who was known by the name of Joe, was caught in the act of stealing a pair of boots from the grocery store; and he was also accused by Captain Hillyer of setting his boat adrift…After the charges were made, Joe acknowledged stealing the boots, but said he knew nothing about the boat…*
>
> *Dick Hillyer then proposed that Joe be tied up, and his back warmed with a rope's end to freshen up his memory, and we were each requested to give our views on the case.*
>
> *Now it so happened that the very night previous, old Toke had started off from his lodge in a fit of rage, and Suis* [Toke's wife] *supposed he*

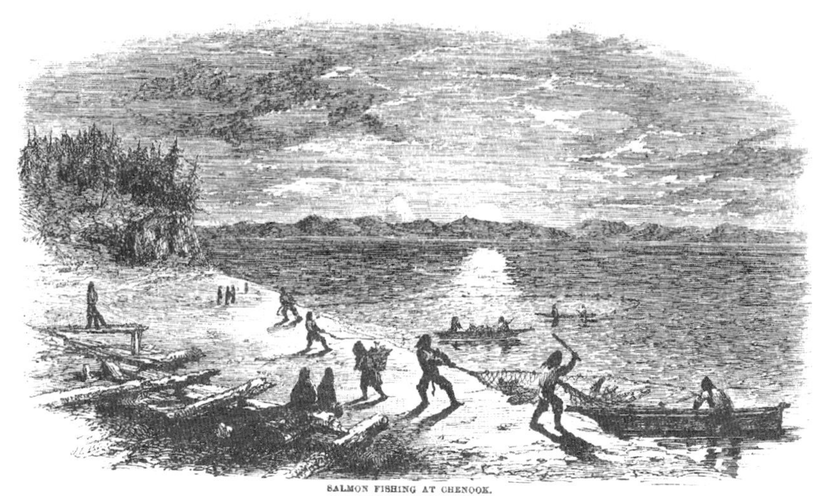

SALMON FISHING AT CHENOOK.

This etching of Chenook (or Chinookville) by James G. Swan appeared in his 1857 book, *The Northwest Coast, or Three Years Residence in Washington Territory*. EFA.

had crossed the Bay to another lodge he had at Toke's Point...I therefore suggested that we put Joe into Champ's hen-house, and secure him till someone should cross the Bay and see whether Toke had the boat or not.

Now Champ's hen-house was not a slim affair built of slats, as its name might import, but was a solid log house, as strong as a fort.

Joe begged that he might be put there till he could prove himself innocent of the boat charge. He was accordingly incarcerated among the poultry, and left to his own reflections.

That afternoon Toke returned, bringing back the boat...

Dick then went to liberate Joe, and found him very quietly engaged in sucking eggs. This new felony enraged Squire Champ, who was for having Joe immediately flogged; but the people, thinking he had been punished enough, put him on board a boat bound to the portage, and started him out of the Bay...

Around the Horn

For five years, the little wooden jail building at Oysterville was used "as is." Then, in 1880, the county purchased a two-bunk iron cell from the Pauly Jail

Building and Manufacturing Company of St. Louis, Missouri, and had it transported by ship down the Mississippi and around the Horn to Oysterville.

It was constructed of riveted steel plates and half-inch-thick bars and weighed four tons. The cell bears an inscription stating that it was patented on September 15, 1874. According to all reports, its massive lock, patented on June 6, 1878, requires a hefty foot-long, two-inch-high key.

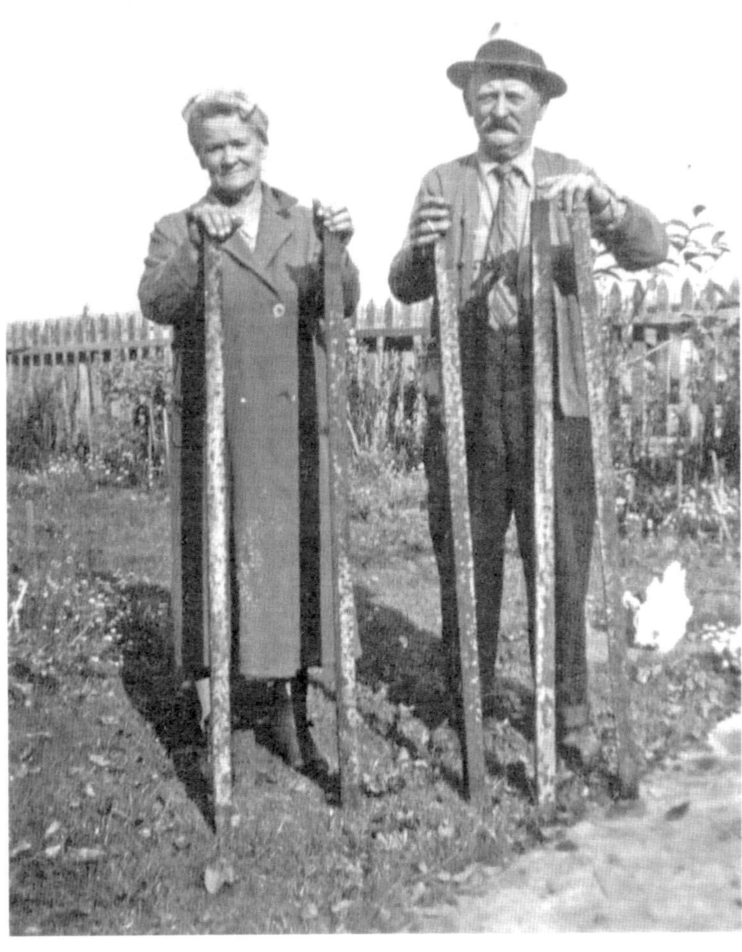

Louise and Harry Wachsmuth of Oysterville donated the bars from the old jail building to the World War II scrap metal drive. *Tucker Wachsmuth collection.*

On February 7, 1880, the *Commissioners' Minutes* stated:

> *Ordered that the cage put in the County Jail by the Pauly Jail Company be accepted and that an order be drawn on the Treasury of the County for the balance due on said contract ($1,690.90), which sum includes the cost of preparing the jail for the reception of the cage and installation costs.*

The installation of the cell into the sturdy little jail building was intended to provide an added measure of security. But security for whom? As it would turn out, not for the prisoners themselves.

Usually, prisoners were booked into the jail singly; once in a while, two men occupied the jail. But in 1890, it was into this small iron cell—close quarters even for the two prisoners for which it was intended—that the four men accused of the Frederiksen murders were placed. There is no record concerning how the crowded jail conditions in Oysterville might or might not have contributed to the unfortunate circumstances that followed. The iron cell itself bears witness—albeit silent—to the unlawful ending of the case; the bullet scars can still be seen on the walls.

Although the jail cell was barged over to South Bend, the wooden jail building remained in Oysterville. Eventually, when the county sold its Oysterville property and the remaining buildings, the little wooden jailhouse became Meinert Wachsmuth's chicken coop. Still in place were the five thirty-pound bars that had been put into the front window of the building upon its completion in 1875.

During World War II, Meinert's son and daughter-in-law, Harry and Louise Wachsmuth, donated those bars to the local scrap iron drive. The donation was made on Sunday, October 18, 1942, and with the bars went the last visible sign that prisoners, not chickens, had once been housed in the old shed.

A Long History of Quiet Service

The Pacific County seat moved "in stages" from Oysterville to South Bend in 1893, as there were "difficulties in removal of the jail," according to the news from the *South Bend Journal*. The next week's paper reported that a bid of $330 had been accepted by the county for the removal of "safes (from the courthouse) and jail (cell from the jail building)."

The side of the jail building had to be taken out so that the four-ton iron cell could be removed and placed on a barge for the voyage to South Bend. No description was given of how the cell got from its location near Diaper Alley onto the deck of the barge.

After its arrival in South Bend, the little cell's initial placement is unknown. By that time, the courthouse offices had been temporarily located on the first floor of the Bristol-Leonard Building—now the approximate location of Powell Seiler & Co. on Robert Bush Drive. It is known that the Knights of Pythias occupied the second floor of the building and that their hall was used as an interim courtroom. If the protocol of courtroom-jail proximity established in Oysterville was followed, the iron cell was undoubtedly nearby.

On January 1, 1894, upon completion of the first South Bend Courthouse on Quincy Street, between Montana and Oregon, the jail cell was placed in the basement of the new building. It was used by the county for the next seventeen years, when the present-day courthouse was built in 1910–11.

Before construction began on the new (and final) courthouse, a debate raged in local newspapers over where the jail should be located. Some felt it should be placed in the basement of the new building. Such placement, it was argued, would be cheaper than constructing a separate facility—$20,000 cheaper, according to some estimates. Besides, the courthouse campus and landscaping would be more attractive if there were only one building went the argument.

Ultimately, though, the county commissioners decided to build a separate jail. Perhaps this was the decision that tipped the scale financially and caused the new courthouse complex to be dubbed "The Gilded Palace of Reckless Extravagance" by local newspaper pundits—more a jibe at the spending policies of county officials than at the new courthouse itself.

With the building of the new jail facility, the old iron cell became superfluous for county purposes, so it was presented to the City of South Bend. It was installed in the city hall, which was then located near the corner of Willapa Avenue and First Street. There it stayed until the building was gutted by a fire ignited by an inmate. The iron cell, of course, survived the fire just fine and was subsequently installed by crane into the jail section of the "new city hall" while it was under construction.

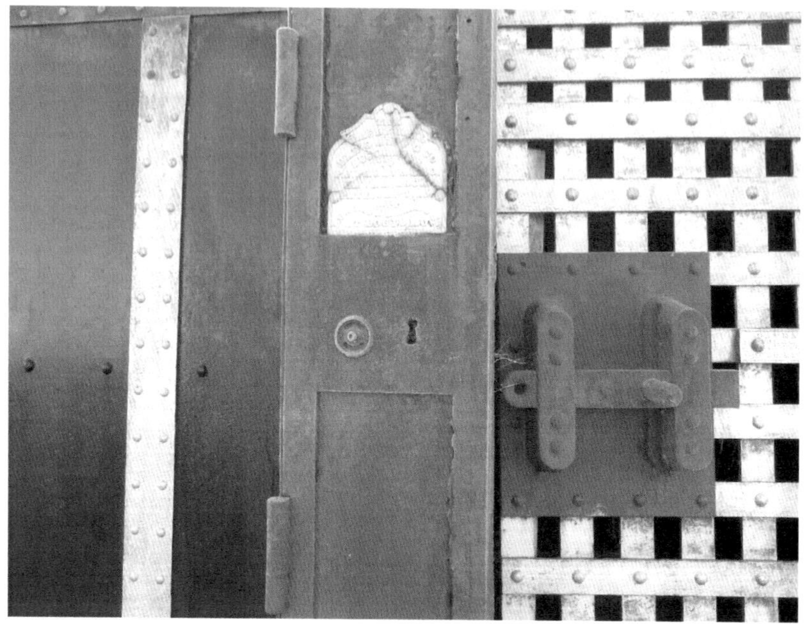

Unhappily, the sturdy locking mechanism for Pacific County's jail cell door was not an absolute guarantee of security or safety. *Sydney Stevens photo.*

The old Oysterville jail cell—"the steel-plated cage" or "the County Bastille," as some termed it—sat in the South Bend City Hall until the 1970s, when it was removed and placed in Robert Bush Drive Park near the city dock and the present-day Boondocks Restaurant. In the early 1990s, it was moved once again to the newly dedicated Margaret Olson Park on Highway 101, several streets below Hangman's Park (so named for another infamous county prisoner) on Montana Street. It is there today.

All in all, the little iron jail cell was used for almost a century. It served both the county and the City of South Bend well, surviving bullet-fire as well as arson. If only those walls could talk...

7

COUNTY GROWING PAINS

Taken to the asylum.

The Pacific County seat had been officially changed to South Bend by election in 1892, and it had been unofficially removed from Oysterville in February 1893. Plans quickly got underway to build a new courthouse, but until it was ready, the temporary quarters on Bristol-Leonard Street sufficed.

Construction took nine months. During that time, only one prisoner was booked into the jail. He was Peter Hoakinson of Sweden, arrested for assault and battery on July 14, 1893. He was described as thirty-nine years old and five feet, nine and a half inches tall, with light hair, gray eyes, a fair complexion and a cut over his left eye. It was also noted that he had on his person a watch and seventy-five cents.

Mr. Hoakinson was tried in Superior Court and sentenced to thirty days in the county jail. A further notation, however, says, "Let out by order of court July 17, 1893." The discrepancy in the length of his sentence and the time he served, like many notations in the old jail book, is left unexplained.

For most of the next year, there were no arrests recorded in the jail book. It was not until June 4, 1894, that John C. Swanson, also from Sweden, was booked into the jail for reasons of insanity. Mr. Swanson was forty years old and five feet, eleven inches tall, with light hair, blue eyes, a fair complexion and a heavy beard. He was released the following day and taken to the asylum (at Steilacoom).

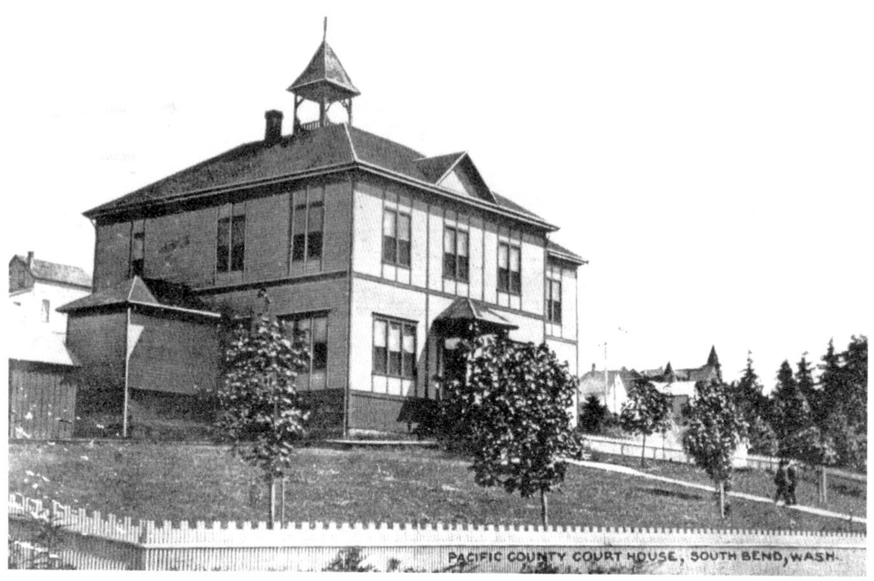

Located on Quincy Street, this second Pacific County Courthouse to be constructed at public expense would not be the last one built in South Bend. *PCHS*.

Mr. Swanson had the distinction of being the first occupant of the jail in its newest location—the basement of the newly completed Pacific County Courthouse on Quincy Street, between Montana and Oregon. This was the second courthouse built by the county at public expense, and as far as anyone could foresee, it would be the last. As it would turn out, however, the citizens of the fast-growing city of South Bend would find the Quincy Street location of the courthouse exceedingly inconvenient. But it was not until 1910 that construction began on a new, more substantial courthouse building on Quality Hill, nearer to the center of the town's business district—the courthouse still in use today.

Boom and Bust

Meanwhile, the town continued to boom. It had been just five years since three real estate promoters, George U. Holcomb, Louis N. Eklund and Captain Philander Wheeler Swett, had arrived in the area with big plans in mind. After looking the harbor over, they had made a proposal to the South Bend Mill Company to boom their town site and build a city where there was then only a mill, a mill store and a few houses for mill employees.

Finding the idea unacceptable to the mill owners, the three enterprising men soon moved up the river a short way, formed the South Bend Land Company and purchased property, which they immediately platted into lots and blocks. They quickly proceeded to get options on all the settlers' lands that bordered the river on both sides for several miles. By mid-1893, the motley collection of homestead properties had boomed into a bustling town.

Taking the Shallow out of Shoalwater

It was Lieutenant John Meares of London's East India Company who charted and named "Shoal-water Bay" on July 5, 1788. In the log of his ship, *Felice Adventurer*, he wrote:

> *At noon our latitude was 47°01' north, and the lofty mountains seen the preceding day bore east-northeast distant seven leagues. Our distance might be four leagues from the shore, which appeared to run in the direction of east-southeast and west-northwest, and there appeared to be a large sound or opening in that direction. By two o'clock we were within two miles of the shore, along which we sailed, which appeared to be a perfect forest, without the vestige of a habitation. The land was low and flat, and our soundings were from fifteen to twenty fathoms, over a hard sand. As we were steering for the low point which formed part of the entrance into the bay or sound, we shoaled our water gradually to six fathoms, when breakers were seen to extend across it, so that it appeared to be quite inaccessible to ships. We immediately hauled off the shore till we deepened our water to sixteen fathoms.*
>
> *This point obtained the name of Low Point (now Leadbetter Point), and the bay that of Shoal-water Bay, and a headland that was high and bluff which formed the other entrance, was also named Cape Shoal-water (later, Toke's Point)...*
>
> *We had concluded this wild and desolate shore was uninhabited; but this opinion proved to be erroneous, for a canoe now came off to us from the point with a man and a boy.*

Little did Meares realize that, some one hundred years later, the name Shoalwater would be blamed for discouraging ship's captains from entering the bay. South Bend promoters, in an effort to increase maritime traffic coming up the Willapa River to their newly platted town, began a concerted public relations campaign extolling the benefits of the Willapa Harbor and aimed at changing the name of Shoalwater Bay to Willapa Bay.

As part of the campaign, the 1891 issue of *Northwest* magazine ran an article by E.V. Smalley titled "Willapa Bay, an Excellent Harbor." According to Mr. Smalley:

> *The depth of water upon the bar at the entrance to Willapa Bay is not a matter of conjecture or a theme for argument. The question was officially settled long ago by the United States Coast Survey and the following letter shows the official record taken from the charts of 1868:*
>
> *U. S. COAST & GEODETIC SURVEY OFFICE,*
> *WASHINGTON, D.C. November 7, 1889.*
> *Mr. Henry Wood, Union League Club, Philadelphia*
> *DEAR SIR:*
>
> *In response to your letter received at this office November 5th, I have to say twenty-one feet can be carried over the bar into Shoalwater Bay, Washington Territory, at low water, and that the tide rises eight feet, thus giving a depth of twenty-nine feet over the bar at high water.*
>
> *Yours respectfully,*
>
> [Signed] *T.C. MENDENHALL,*
> *Superintendent*

Even the local newspapers got into the act. The *Pacific Journal* moved from Oysterville to Sealand and changed its name to the *Willapa Republican.* When the paper later sold to C.A. Heath, he renamed it *Willapa Pilot.* A few years later, he moved it to South Bend and renamed it once again: *Willapa Harbor Pilot.* Yes! The name change game was on in earnest.

As things turned out, while the South Bend "Harborites" were successful in changing the name of the bay to "Willapa," local wags and newspaper pundits were quick to point out that they couldn't change the nature of the bay itself, and the lofty dreams of maritime greatness did not materialize. The grand scheme of creating "The Baltimore of the Pacific" was not to be.

Wharves were built, commercial buildings and residences went up in short order and it was predicted that Portland, Seattle and Tacoma would soon be playing second fiddle to the fast-developing "San Francisco of the Northwest." In 1890, an agreement was reached with the Northern Pacific Railroad to build its Pacific terminus in South Bend. The following year, the three-story Albee Hotel was built on Water Street in a convenient location for train travelers.

Getting There, Circa 1900

The Northern Pacific Railroad "came in" to South Bend in 1893. Its arrival had been long anticipated, especially by members of the South Bend Land Company who, in 1889, had secured large tracts of the most desirable land along the Willapa River in order to establish a commercial city there.

They had immediately entered into contracts with parties representing the Northern Pacific Railroad, which agreed to build a line to this promised metropolis on the Willapa River, and the work of construction began the same summer. The proposed route would cover the fifty-eight miles from Chehalis in Lewis County to South Bend on the banks of the Willapa.

Press releases that promised completion of the line within six months had the entire Willapa Bay region agog. People flocked to South Bend in great numbers, and land speculators converted the forest into town lots in short order. In actuality, however, track-laying took nearly three years to complete. Inclement weather and labor problems, exacerbated by poor working conditions, long hours and delays in providing paychecks, caused the work to drag. When finally finished and open for business, details like signage and water barrels were yet to be installed.

Nevertheless, from the onset, the line was hugely successful. Now, people could travel between South Bend and Chehalis in every kind of weather. For a time, two passenger trains and two freight trains ran each way daily. The short run was so successful, in fact, that it became one of the most profitable in the state of Washington.

Chehalis, the seat of Lewis County, had long been the commercial center for farmers and loggers of the area. With the completion of the Northern Pacific line to South Bend, connections to Puget Sound and the Columbia River further expanded the markets for Chehalis farmers and businesses. According to "Lewis County to Willapa Bay by Rail" in the 2006 summer/fall issue of *The Sou'wester*, for the first quarter of the twentieth century, it was common for downtown Chehalis stores to put on extra clerks in the mornings. They were needed to take care of the customers from more than two dozen mill towns up and down the line who would come by train to do their business and shopping.

The old depot in Chehalis, once a hub of Northern Pacific activity, is now the site of the Lewis County Historical Museum. The South Bend station—built at the end of the line and once the western terminus for the Northern Pacific System—is no more.

In response to the rapid development, civic groups and a chamber of commerce were organized, and a city government with a mayor and council was established. Soon, there was a fire department and a cemetery. By the time the ribbon was cut inaugurating the new courthouse on January 1, 1894, the town boasted two thousand inhabitants. Whether this included the large immigrant population imported to work on the railroad was a matter of conjecture, particularly by the residents of Oysterville, who claimed these "transients" had been allowed to vote in the matter of moving the county seat.

But even before county officials had moved into their new offices, the great financial Panic of 1893 had made itself felt in South Bend. Called the greatest of all the financial panics of the nineteenth century, it was triggered by railroad overbuilding and shaky railroad financing, which set off a series of bank failures. It was worst in mill towns. In South Bend, it wiped out personal fortunes,

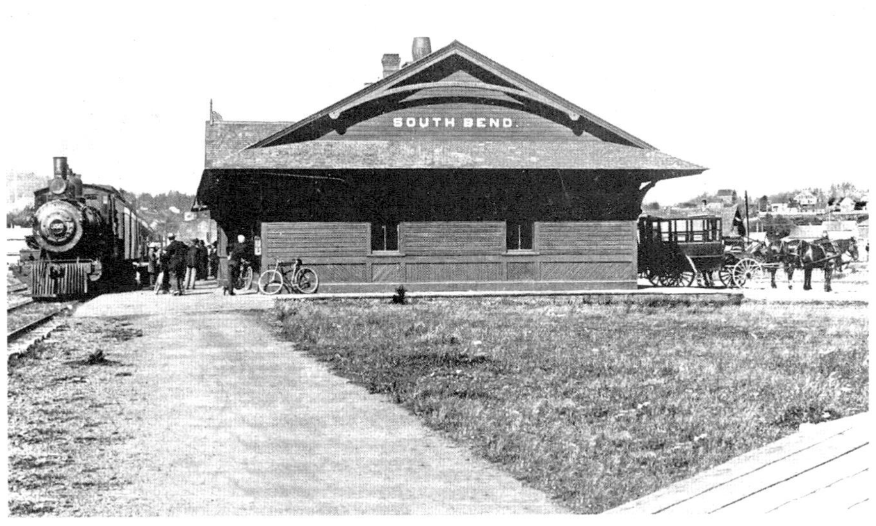

On December 18, 1892, at 9:15 a.m., when the last rail was laid, South Bend became the western terminus for the Northern Pacific Railroad. *PCHS.*

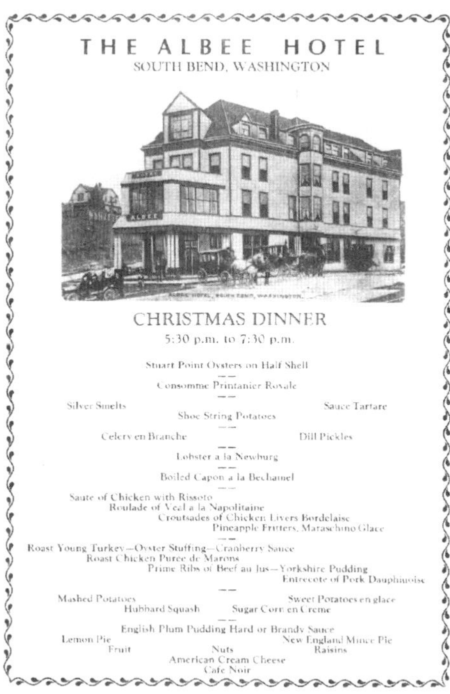

This 1907 newspaper advertisement for South Bend's Albee Hotel depicts the horse-drawn carriage that delivered guests to and from the Northern Pacific Railroad Station. *PCHS.*

industries, factories, institutions, businesses and railroads, among the latter the Northern Pacific Railroad, which was forced into receivership for three years.

South Bend's boom had suddenly become a bust. No great seaport materialized despite all the dreams and tremendous labor and expense. Financial setbacks continued in the last half of the 1890s, many of the "boomers" moved away and South Bend's heyday became but a hazy memory.

But even as the remaining residents of South Bend struggled to maintain their town's foothold on the banks of the Willapa, not many changes were manifest at the county jail. A slow but steady stream of prisoners were locked into the old iron cell during the last years of the decade. Including Mr. Swanson, there were five occupants in 1894, twelve in 1895, three in 1896, two in 1897 and five in 1898. No one at all occupied the jail in 1899.

Foreign Born

As had been the case since the jail book records were begun back in 1886, all of the prisoners were men, and the prisoner information continued to show a high percentage of "foreign born." Between 1893 and 1899, exactly half of those arrested had been born in foreign countries: fourteen of twenty-eight. They came from Sweden and Germany, China and Norway, Denmark and Australia and Bohemia.

Perhaps these figures were a reflection of the increasing numbers of immigrants coming into the United States through both East and West Coast portals. Another manifestation of this influx of immigrants in the Northwest was the establishment in May 1899 of the Columbia River Quarantine Station at Knappton Cove,* soon to be called the "Ellis

* In 1889, Congress enacted a national quarantine law stipulating the exclusion of "all idiots, insane persons, paupers, or persons likely to become public charges, persons suffering from a loathsome or dangerous contagious disease and criminals." For immigrants bound for the United States via the Columbia River, the voyage took them upriver to naturalization in Portland. Incoming vessels moored on the Columbia River for health inspections. If they passed, they were permitted to proceed, but if they failed, the vessels were ordered to the quarantine station. Passengers disembarked and went inside for showers, while their belongings were taken to be deloused. Meanwhile, the ships were sealed and fumigated. Forty-eight hours later, the ships and their passengers were permitted to continue on unless they needed to be confined to the "pest house" for a time to recover from an illness. Passengers deemed too ill or likely to become public wards were sent back to their homelands.

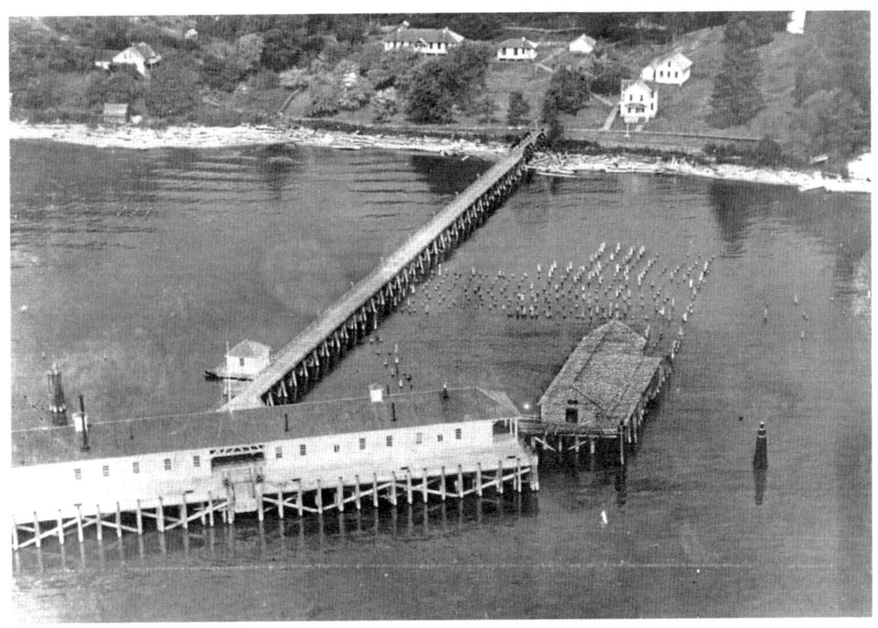

This aerial view shows the Columbia River Quarantine Station at Knappton Cove (1899–1938), a facility that dealt strictly with health matters, not with naturalization of immigrants. *KCA.*

Island of the Columbia." Oregon officials refused to have the "pest house," as it was derogatorily termed, on their side of the river, so it was located on the north shore in Pacific County.

Interestingly, though, the percentage of foreign-born residents of Pacific County at the end of the nineteenth century was considerably lower than the high jail figures might indicate. In 1887, in preparation for its bid for statehood, Washington Territory did a thorough population census, county by county. At that time, there were a total of 2,312 inhabitants in the county, 496 of whom were listed as "foreign born."

Corroborating population figures for specific areas in the county are difficult to come by, especially because many of the 1890 federal census records were destroyed by fire in later years. However, other documentation makes clear that numbers of Chinese workers were employed in the canneries and on the railroad, a large Finnish and Nordic population worked in the fishing and logging industries and numbers of German and Polish immigrants were beginning to settle and farm in the Willapa Valley.

The logging and fishing industries of Pacific County depended heavily on these newly arrived, hardworking residents, but as in other areas of the

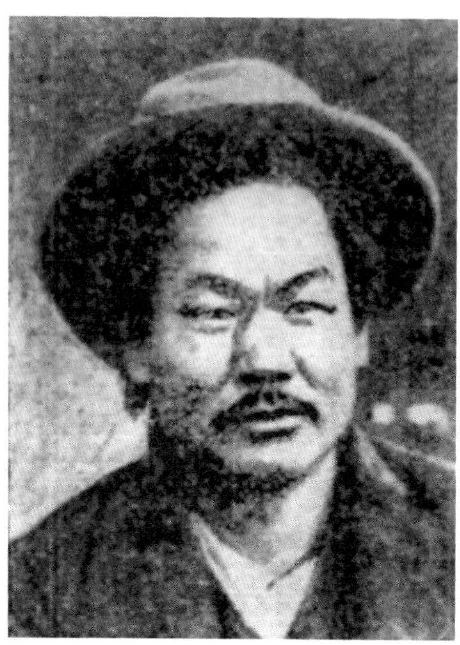

According to contemporary accounts, Lum You was a "jolly sociable fellow" and was well liked in the community, especially by children. *PCHS.*

state, misunderstandings and outright discrimination occurred. Unfortunately, the old jail book is silent on the back stories of the men imprisoned.

The four prisoners booked into the jail during the last seven months of 1894 were Matt Anderson from Finland, Lum You from China, Adolph Johnson from Sweden and Andrew Mandel from Germany. They were twenty-two, thirty-four, forty and forty-two years of age, respectively.

Anderson, booked in June, and Johnson, booked in October, were each jailed for reasons of insanity and transferred to the asylum at Steilacoom.

You (pronounced "e-ow") was booked on July 29 for assault and Mandel on November 10 for assault and battery. In You's case, he was found guilty of assault by a jury and sentenced by the court to six months in the county jail and a five-dollar fine. There was no hint in the jail book or elsewhere that Lum would one day become one of Pacific County's most notorious prisoners. As for Mandel, the only notation for him was: "In Jail until his release on December 10."

Crimes and Times

On January 10, 1895, five arrests were made simultaneously. Randolph Gilberg (34) of Norway, Lewis John (30) of Greece, L.B. Olsen (30) of Norway, Samuel Sweningson (25) of Norway and John Williams (35) of New York were all booked for violation of Section 4597, U.S. Statutes (desertion.) This law had to do with crew members "jumping ship" in U.S. ports. All five men were discharged by a justice of the peace on

January 12. It was further noted that Gilberg and Olsen each had an anchor tattooed on his left hand.

Twenty-nine days into 1895, young Len Shumway of Indiana was jailed by Justice of the Peace Henry Kayler, of Ilwaco, for housebreaking. Shumway was sixteen years old and five feet, six inches tall, with light hair, blue eyes, a fair complexion and a slight build. It is noted that he was released from prison on February 14, 1895, and taken to reform school on December 14, 1895, by Sheriff Roney. There is no indication of Shumway's whereabouts during the time between his release from jail and his transport to reform school. It is possible that he was sent home or placed with a foster family for a time, especially if the judge was inclined to be forward thinking about the rehabilitation possibilities for young offenders.

Apparently, the jail and courthouse were often a focal point in the daily lives of South Bend citizens—and not only to those who were breaking the law or struggling to enforce it. For an article in the autumn 1975 *Sou'wester*, Mary Frances Bale Hunt reminisced about how things were when her family arrived there in April 1895:

> *What a sight to see the wide, high streets built of wood planks over the tide flats. My father built a large house near good schools and the Congregational church; we were also near the old court house, so we attended many trials, including the Gates and Olson one and that of Lum You…We played on planks in the water, and on the porches of the Willapa Hotel. Then we owned a farm across the river from Eklund Park, and furnished produce for the Nettleton Store which was near the depot. We delivered milk for 5 cents a quart, picked wildflowers to sell to Stuart's Restaurant when mother sold butter there. Once I remember that Uncle George Bale rowed down the river to the South Bend post office. It was closed. In disgust he said, "It must be some fool's birthday!" Well, it was February 22nd—George Washington's birthday, as well as his own!*

On April 5, 1895, Isaih [*sic*] Robinson (45), of Iowa, was arrested and bound over to Superior Court for concealing stolen goods. "Smokes cigarettes, has weak voice, parents live in Whatcom County," according to the jail book. Although Mr. Robinson was sentenced to thirty days in jail and fined $100 by the Superior Court on May 1, 1895, he was not discharged until July 11.

The next three listings—"A.W. Louderback (25), William Lamely (26) and Elmer Louderback (29)"—all indicate that the men were from Pacific County and were booked for the crime of burglary. Lamely gave a bond of $1,000, was found guilty by a jury and a new trial was ordered. He was acquitted on July 11. The Louderbacks, however, were taken by Sheriff Roney to the state prison in Walla Walla, where they were to serve out a year-long term.

Two arrests were made for assault in December 1895. Jack Gardner (35), of Missouri and Mike Meehan, (40), of Ireland were both tried in Superior Court. Gardner was discharged in April 1896 on the recommendation of the county commissioners. Meehan, on the other hand, was discharged on February 27, 1896, having served his sentence in full: sixty-seven days.

Bookings Continue

Only three men were booked into the jail in 1896: Harry Adams (43), originally from Indiana; Charles Anderson (27), born in Denmark; and Thos. Robinson, (24), birthplace Kansas. They were all accused of crimes involving theft.

Adams, the eldest of the three, was listed as a banjo player. He was five feet, ten and a half inches tall, with blue eyes, light hair, a fair complexion and lumps on his neck under his right ear. He was arrested and charged with grand larceny on May 16, bound over to Superior Court and, on June 1, taken to the state penitentiary in Walla Walla for a term of one year.

Unlike Adams's booking for grand larceny, the charge against Charles Anderson was petit larceny. He was fined $90.25 and served his sentence of thirty-eight days in the county jail. He was discharged on July 4, 1896.

The record in the jail book is incomplete for Thos. Robinson. It is noted only that the five-foot-ten Kansan had light hair, brown eyes and a fair complexion and was booked into jail on November 16, 1896, by the authority of Justice of the Peace Kayler on the charge of burglary. He was bound over to Superior Court, but concerning the outcome of his trial, there is nothing recorded.

By 1897, South Bend, like towns all across the country, was beginning to recover from the Panic of 1893. Jobs were opening up, and there was a feeling of optimism in Pacific County. In 1897, for the first time in several years, jail bookings were fewer, and even the county commissioners' meetings that year seemed to reflect a more lighthearted spirit. "Believe it or not," their minutes noted, "on August 18, 1897, an undertaker presented a claim for the burial of a man by the name of George Coffin."

Only two arrests were made that year. About the first young man, Lincoln Lewis, there is more information than is usual. Lewis was twenty and was booked into jail by Justice of the Peace G.G. Hicks on the charge of rape. He was bound over for trial in Superior Court, found not guilty and was discharged by the court on March 12. Lewis was described in the jail book as five feet, seven inches tall, with dark hair, dark eyes and a dark complexion; he also had a scar on his left leg above the knee from a cut. He was listed as Indian, born in Washington, was a musician who played the violin and mouth organ and belonged to the Shaker Church.*

The only other arrest that year took place on March 18. No descriptive information is noted for Peter Mohr—only that he was jailed on the authority of Justice of the Peace Geo. Holton, for assault and battery, was fined $5.00 and costs of $23.90 and served nine days in jail. He was discharged on March 27, 1897.

The Century Ends

The last five arrests of the nineteenth century would all take place in 1898. If there was crime in Pacific County during 1899, it did not come to the attention of the county authorities, or at least not in a manner that caused action to be taken or notations to be made in the jail book.

James Downey (30), and Richard A. Leonard (29), were both arrested on May 24, 1898, on the authority of H.F. Long, justice of the peace. They were booked into the jail on the charge of burglary, bound over to Superior Court and both pleaded guilty. On July 16, they were sentenced to two years in the state penitentiary in Walla Walla.

The personal information about Downey and Leonard is fairly detailed. Downey, with black hair, gray eyes and fair skin, was from Australia. He had tattoos on his left forearm, clasped hands and a star with the letters CSRI; a

* Perhaps Lincoln Lewis lived in Bay Center and was a member of the Indian Shaker Church there. According to current-day members of the Chinook tribe, many Bay Center Indians belonged to the church, which was established there in the late 1880s. Since the early Indian Shakers rejected the Bible and other forms of written scripture and instead relied on communicating directly with God, it was a belief system that dovetailed smoothly with American Indian tradition. Through shaking and ringing bells, they received messages straight from heaven. Many stories persist of experiences that supported that belief.

tattoo of a bird on his left hand at the base of the thumb; a tattoo of a star on his right hand at the base of the thumb; a shield on his right forearm; three scars on his left temple; and had been a sailor. Leonard had dark hair, light blue eyes, a fair complexion and was from Illinois. He had a circular scar over his right eyebrow, very plain; a sandy mustache; a low, narrow forehead; a long, narrow face; and full chin. He was a carpenter.

On August 18, 1898, Mike Janousek, a native of Bohemia, was booked for assault on the order of G.G. Hicks. He was sentenced to seven days but was discharged on August 23, also by the order of Hicks.

Oregon native S.F. Lockwood, (41), was confined on October 14, 1898, by the authority of Superior Court and held to answer to the charge of embezzlement. He was found not guilty and discharged by the court on November 2.

The last county jail booking of the century was by order of Andrew Olsen, justice of the peace. Charles Anderson, (28), described as having light hair, blue eyes, a fair complexion and a weak mind, was from Washington. He was held to answer for the crime of burglary, was found guilty and was sentenced to three years at the penitentiary in Walla Walla, where he was taken by Sheriff Z.B. Brown on November 24, 1898.

By the turn of the century, twenty-eight men had been arrested and booked into the county jail since South Bend had become the county seat. Only one of those men would ever be listed in the jail book again. In 1901, seven years after he was first arrested, Lum You would be confined once again in "the cage," as the iron jail cell was known. His story would become legend, and his ultimate fate would make history in Pacific County and Washington State.

8

THE HANGING OF LUM YOU

You are cordially invited...

"Hear Ye! Hear Ye! Hear Ye! You are all cordially invited to a hanging!" Thus began the Shoalwater Storytellers'* dramatized version of *The Hanging of Lum You*. Even though the performance was scripted nearly a century after the actual event, the facts were not far off. Sheriff Thomas A. Roney (pronounced "Rooney" despite the spelling) did, indeed, send five hundred personal invitations to the citizens of Pacific County for the execution, scheduled for 9:00 a.m. on Friday, January 31, 1902.

The hanging was not the only big event to take place during Tom Roney's two terms as Pacific County sheriff. He had first been elected in 1892, which gave him the distinction of being the county's first sheriff following Washington's admission to the Union as the forty-second state. Just two months after he took office, the infamous "kidnapping" of the county seat occurred. The publicity and excitement surrounding the event may have influenced Roney to not seek reelection in 1896.

However, by 1900, things had calmed down a bit in Pacific County. The dreadful aftermath of the 1890 Frederiksen murders was fading from memory, and South Bend was settling into its role as the seat of the county and the business center of the Willapa Bay region. Roney again sought and won the sheriff's position.

---

* Shoalwater Storytellers is a performance group founded on the Long Beach Peninsula in 1980. They specialize in dramatizing stories about southwest Washington history.

M *Chris Savins*

You are respectfully invited to be present at the execution of

LUM YOU

Friday, January 31, 1902, at the Pacific County Court House at 9:00 o'clock a. m.

Present this Card
Not Transferable

Thos Roney Sheriff

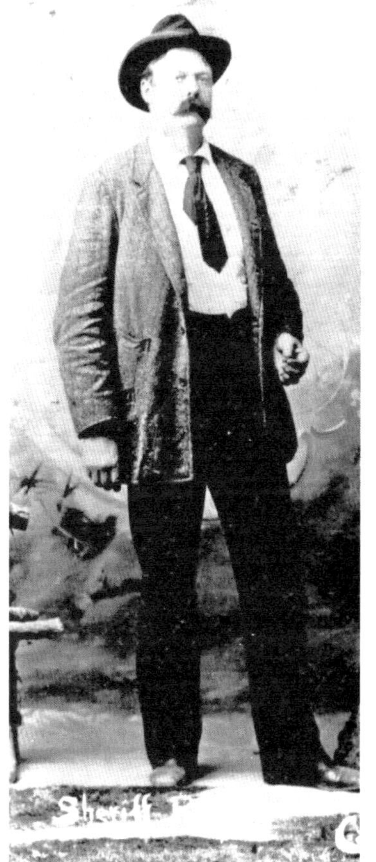

Above: Sending out invitations for public hangings was not an unusual custom in the western United States at the turn of the century. *CPHM.*

Left: Sheriff Tom Roney, known as "a man with a big heart," found the hanging of Lum You a difficult duty to perform. *PCHS.*

There had been little crime in the county during the four-year interval since Roney's initial tour as sheriff. Even after he was elected for the second term, there was "not much doing" with regard to jail activity. During the first eighteen months of the new century, only four men had been booked into the little county jail cell, now housed in the basement of the newly built courthouse on Quincy Street. Of those, the most difficult from Roney's viewpoint was the case of forty-year-old Manuel Gates.

Notations in the old jail book indicate that Gates, a native of Spain, had black hair, dark eyes and a dark complexion and was five feet, seven inches tall. He was charged with manslaughter on the authority of the Superior Court, and it became Sheriff Roney's duty to escort him to Walla Walla to the state penitentiary. A further notation states that no property was left in care of the sheriff.

Sheriff Roney had been back in Pacific County for little more than a month after his trip to eastern Washington when Lum You was booked into the jail. This was You's second arrest, and the sheriff undoubtedly remembered him well. The Chinese cannery worker had spent a goodly amount of time in the county jail seven years previously during Roney's first term as sheriff.

"Chinaman Troubles"

Although neither Roney nor You realized it at the time, his arrest for assault in 1894 would turn out to be a significant one for the Chinese man. Previously, he'd had trouble with another Chinaman and had complained to South Bend police chief Marion Egbert, who told him, rather impatiently, "Don't come to me with your Chinaman troubles."

Lum You then asked Egbert's advice on what to do to protect himself, and Egbert told him, "I don't care. Chop off his head if you want to."

Well, apparently Lum You wanted to, and Ging later had the scar to prove it. The incident amused the white people in the area and put an abrupt end to Lum's "Chinaman troubles." A number of character witnesses would later testify at his murder trial that Lum You was "peaceable unless pushed beyond endurance."

It was that incident—attacking Ging with an axe—that had landed Lum You in jail in 1894 on a charge of assault and resulted in the fine of $500 and a six-month sentence. Some accounts suggest that it was Lum's limited understanding of English that caused him to take Egbert's suggestion literally, thus leading to the great misfortune of establishing for himself a criminal record. Such a record would prove to be a great liability when more serious trouble erupted seven years later.

Lum You's second stay in jail in 1901, his trial and his subsequent fate immediately became, and has remained, the most infamous account in the chronicles of Pacific County law and order. Amazingly, there is absolutely no notation in the jail book of the crime for which You was incarcerated, the incidents that occurred during his time in the county lockup or the trial. The page is blank under the columns headed: "For What Offense and for what

Term," "Date of Leaving Prison," "Escaped or Discharged; If Discharged by what Authority" and "Remarks—Action Taken if Prisoner Escaped."

What is noted deals mainly with his description: forty years of age; five feet, five inches tall; dark hair; black eyes; fair Chinese complexion; born in China. He was booked into the jail on August 7, 1901, on the authority of the justice of the peace. The only other note, inexplicably written under the column headed "Special Marks or Peculiarities as to Prisoner History," states, "Hung January 31, 1902."

"A Jolly, Sociable Fellow"

Fortunately, at least for posterity, there was a great deal of publicity about the case in the turn-of-the-century newspapers of Pacific County. The portrait of Lum You that emerged was a sympathetic one, and accounts of the infamous murderer and his hanging have been told and retold in subsequent years. According to a 1971 article by the late Ruth Dixon, editor of the Pacific County Historical Society's quarterly magazine, *The Sou'wester*:

> *He was a distinctive, unique character, and somewhat of a "dandy." He carried himself proudly. His immaculate clothing was of English cut. He wore jade bracelets, had a large gold watch and fob, with two ornamental chains draped across his vest. He had a queue—a very long one, and for dress-up occasions it was braided with a length of fine China silk, ending in an ornate tassel.*

For this account, "Invitation to a Hanging," Dixon interviewed people who had known Lum You and had fond memories of "a jolly, sociable fellow—quite a guy." It was reported that children, too, liked Lum You and that he always had a story or exotic tidbit to share with them.

Charlie Nelson (1883–1978), for instance, remembered that when he was a youngster growing up in Oysterville, Lum You had been a resident of the barracks-like building called "China House" at the Chabot cranberry bogs in Long Beach. There, Lum You, who spoke and understood a little English, acted as agent between the workers and employers.

Charlie and his friends especially liked a fruit* Lum often gave them that "contained a pit and tasted much like a good plump raisin." According to

* These were most likely lychee (litchi) nuts.

Charlie, the boys also enjoyed looking on while the Chinese played games such as "odds and evens" and "fan tan" using curious coins, each with a square hole in its middle. And he remembered watching the Chinese men load their clay pipes with opium, which in those days was smoked openly at China House.

Must Not Complain

By the summer of 1901, Lum You was living in Bay Center and was working at a nearby cannery. On the evening of Tuesday, August 6, a large man named Oscar Bloom bumped into the smaller Asian man at a card game, tipped over his chair and knocked the cards from his hand. Witnesses later said that Bloom grabbed Lum You around the neck with one large hand while removing the valuables from his pockets with the other.

Bloom took $40.75 in gold and silver coins and made threats against Lum You's life. This was not the first time that the big man had become abusive, but Lum You felt he should not complain to Chief Egbert again. As he had understood Egbert's previous advice, he needed to take care of the problem himself.

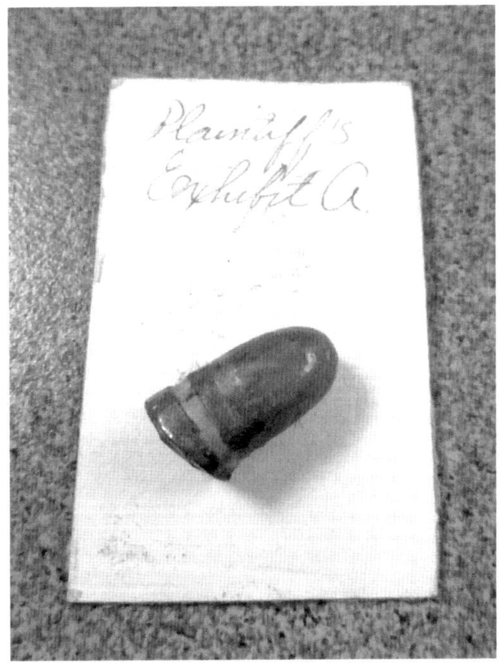

Filed with the court transcripts of Lum You's trial is "Plaintiff's Exhibit A," the bullet that killed Oscar Bloom. *Sydney Stevens Photo.*

At the time of his arrest and later at his trial, Lum You readily admitted going to his room, putting one bullet in his gun and shooting Bloom at a distance of thirty feet. He then went home. Many people in the area apparently heard the shot, but no one went to investigate.

It was not until the next morning when Bloom did not appear that someone went to find him and sent word of the shooting to police chief Egbert in South Bend. Egbert immediately engaged the steamer *Flora Brown* and made a speedy trip to Bay Center, taking with him Dr. Gruwell and county attorney John T. Welsh. They arrived "a short" twenty-three hours after the shooting.

Deathbed Statement

Notary public L.L. Bush and other witnesses were called to Bloom's bedside, and he made an affidavit that stated:

> *Last evening in the neighborhood of 9 o'clock, I was on the street and may have had some words with Lum You, a Chinaman. As to the matter of words, I however do not recall...Lum You ran to his room and I soon came to my house...The shot struck me in the abdomen...I got into my bed and was there all night before anyone came...My recollection is clear to all events of assault, though not as to what may have occurred in the street before...When Lum You shot me, he immediately ran away, and I did not see him again. I was not out of my house afterward. I am making this statement...fully believing that I am now dying.*

Those familiar with the circumstances surrounding the shooting were sympathetic to Lum You, and the incident might have been more or less overlooked, but employers of "Orientals" insisted "that action be taken against this Chinese man who had dared to harm a white man!" Accordingly, Lum You was arrested on August 7 and charged with murder, and a trial was held in October 1901.

Jurors were John Adams, Andrew Alexander, A.J. Baker, John M. Cooper, F.O. Gaither, J.W. Gamage, William Germond, Robert Johnson, Robert Marshall, Richard Stiff, J.H. Timmons and C.E. Williams. For 110 years, the story has persisted that the first ballot was eleven-to-one for acquittal. One man held out so tenaciously and was so intent on a guilty verdict that, finally, the other eleven, weary with arguing, gave up and voted for conviction. All of them seriously believed that the little Chinese man would receive a light sentence.

Although the final decree, "to be hanged by the neck until dead," was heard with disbelief and dismay, only one of the jurors later signed a petition to the governor requesting that the sentence be reduced. In the end, the petition was to no avail, and it would be the duty of county officials to carry out the order for execution.

It was all a matter of timing. Although a recent act of the legislature, effective as of September 12, 1901, required all executions to be carried out at the state penitentiary at Walla Walla, Sheriff Roney found that his responsibilities would be a bit more arduous than escorting Mr. You across the state. The murder of Oscar Bloom had occurred just a few weeks too early for the new law; responsibility for the hanging of Lum You rested with Pacific County. It was a job Sheriff Roney did not look forward to.

Cell Door Unlocked

Another enduring story is that Lum You's cell door was never locked at night and that he was encouraged, even ordered, to flee but that he feared the disgrace of deportation to China and possible beheading even more than he dreaded the hangman's noose. Presumably, he felt that beheading and the resulting separation from his sacred queue would prevent him from entering "Tian" (heaven).

Meanwhile, preparations for the hanging were underway. The execution date was set for January 31, 1902. Sheriff Roney had a number of invitation cards printed and was about to issue them to persons who had expressed a desire to witness the hanging. But before the invitations could be sent, Lum You did, in fact, disappear for a few days. How he engineered his escape has never been satisfactorily explained, but he was gone, and even as the county officials breathed an unofficial sigh of relief, a manhunt was begun in full force.

Posters were put up by the county commissioners offering a $200 reward for You's capture and return. All places having telegraph services were notified to be on the lookout. A posse was busily engaged in searching the wilderness areas around the town.

Two versions of Lum You's return to jail have been told over the decades. One is that several days after his disappearance, Lum was found by a search party in the woods south of town and was returned to jail. The other is that Lum You, hearing of the manhunt, returned of his own accord, not wanting to lose face or cause trouble for his jailers.

The excitement of the jail escape and the subsequent manhunt fanned interest in the approaching execution, and Sheriff Roney was deluged with requests for invitations. An extra supply was printed, and about five hundred,

FIRST LEGAL EXECUTION IN PACIFIC COUNTY.

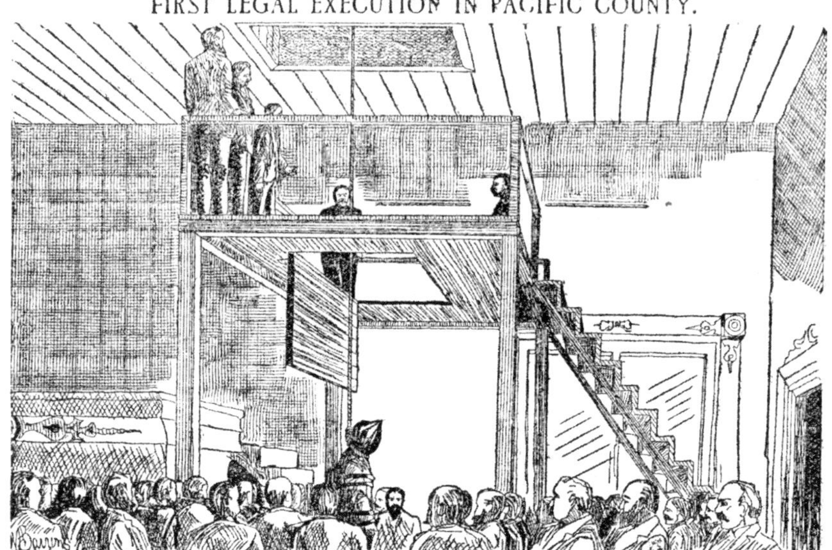

Lum You (murderer of Oscar Bloom in Bay Center, Wash., on August 6, 1901) paying the death penalty on the gallows in the courtroom at South Bend, Wash., today.

Illustrator Will Barrows sketched Lum You's hanging and rushed it back to the *Chinook Observer* for same-day publication, Friday, January 31, 1902. *CPHM.*

in all, were issued, not only to the movers and shakers of the county and to those who wanted to honor their Chinese friend but to the curious and the thrill-seekers as well.

When the time came, Roney also gathered a group of youngsters to witness the event, believing that "this way the horrible experience of being an eye-witness to a hanging will be remembered for many decades, and thus serve as a crime deterrent." Ed Wickberg (1883–1966) remembered it for the rest of his life as a "terrifying experience."

In preparation for the hanging, workmen fashioned a trap over a ventilator opening in the floor of the courthouse. Four unwilling men were chosen to manipulate the ropes, which were worked into an intricate maze so that none would know for sure which man was the executioner. It was arranged that Sheriff Roney would give three strokes on a gong, and the trap would be dropped on the final stroke, all four men handling their ropes in unison.

The Hanging

The execution took place on schedule. As custom proscribed, Lum You was given an opportunity to speak with the crowd beforehand. When he was brought into the execution room, he bowed low and said, "Goodbye, everybody, all my friends, women and men. Wish me all good luck. Me ready to die." When the hood was in place, he waved in salute and then said, "Me no can see. Kill me good." He was pronounced dead at fifteen minutes past nine.

Since Sheriff Roney had not made arrangements for Lum You's burial, Deputy Sheriff Z.B. Brown provided a grave site on his own property. It was located near the County Road, where friends could easily come to pay their respects. The Browns' son recalled in later years that Lum's Chinese friends would often purchase chickens from his mother and take them into a secluded, nearby grove, where they prepared a traditional feast to honor their unfortunate countryman.

The old South Bend Courthouse where Lum You was hanged no longer exists. The building was torn down in the 1930s, and of the original landscaping, only the stately old maple trees remain. Located on the southwest corner of Harrison Street and Montana Avenue, the area is approximately an acre in size. It is now owned by the Pacific County Historical Society, and in memory of Lum You and of the only official execution ever to take place in Pacific County, it is referred to as "Hangman's Park."

Chinese Labor on the Lower Columbia

As a young reporter in 1891, Rudyard Kipling traveled up the Columbia River on a fish-buying expedition. He wrote of his experience in his book *American Notes*. His description of the workforce employed in the canneries is considered a classic:

> *Only Chinamen were employed on the work, and they looked like blood-besmeared yellow devils as they crossed the rifts of sunlight that lay upon the floor. When our consignment arrived, the rough wooden boxes broke of themselves as they were dumped down under a jet of water, and the salmon burst out in a stream of quicksilver. A Chinaman jerked up a twenty-pounder, beheaded*

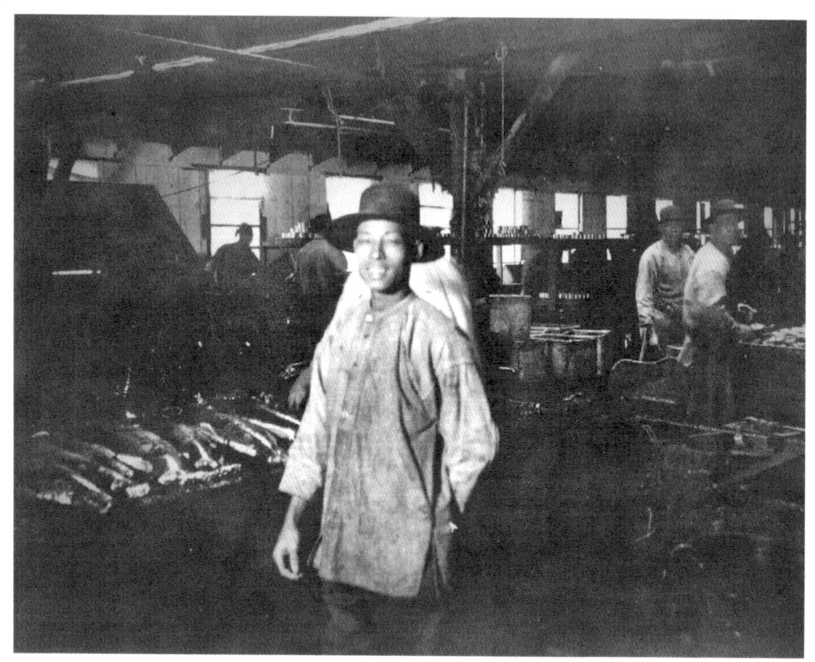

The Chinese workforce at B.A. Seaborg and Company in Ilwaco began to dwindle with the passage of the Chinese Exclusion Act in 1888. *CPHM.*

> *and detailed it with two swift strokes of a knife, flicked out its internal arrangements with a third, and case it into a blood-dyed tank. The headless fish leaped from under his hands as though they were facing a rapid. Other Chinamen pulled them from the vat and thrust them under a thing like a chaff-cutter which, descending, hewed them into unseemly red gobbets fit for the can.*

The first Chinese labor force on the Columbia had been contracted by George Hume in 1872 for his Eagle Cliff Cannery in Wahkiakum County. The Chinese, though unskilled, proved efficient and dependable and would accept low pay. Soon, canneries up and down the river followed suit, and by 1881 more than four thousand Chinese men were working in Columbia River canneries.

While many Scandinavians were also employed in the fishing industry, it was the Chinese who were confined to cannery jobs. By unspoken agreement among those of European descent, the Chinese were not allowed to fish. They were relegated to the difficult and dirty jobs in the canneries, working as fish slimers and cutters.

Toward the end of the nineteenth century, however, Chinese immigration was beginning to be looked at as a threat to the living standards of whites in North America. The Chinese were seen as invasive, and this mounting xenophobia culminated in what has since been termed the "Yellow Peril Hysteria."

In the United States, Chinese immigration was banned with the passage of the Chinese Exclusion Act in 1882. This act provided a ten-year moratorium on Chinese labor immigration but was renewed in 1892 and made permanent in 1902. For the first time, federal law proscribed entry of an ethnic working group on the premise that it endangered the good order of certain localities.

Although the early twentieth-century Chinese workforce was considerably curtailed by the Exclusion Act, there were limited provisions in the act allowing Chinese who had immigrated before 1880 to stay. In 1903, as if in answer to the growing labor problem, E.A. Smith of Seattle invented a machine that did the work of fifteen to twenty people. It could remove fish heads, fins and tails; open and clean fish; and complete all preparations for cutting—all this at the rate

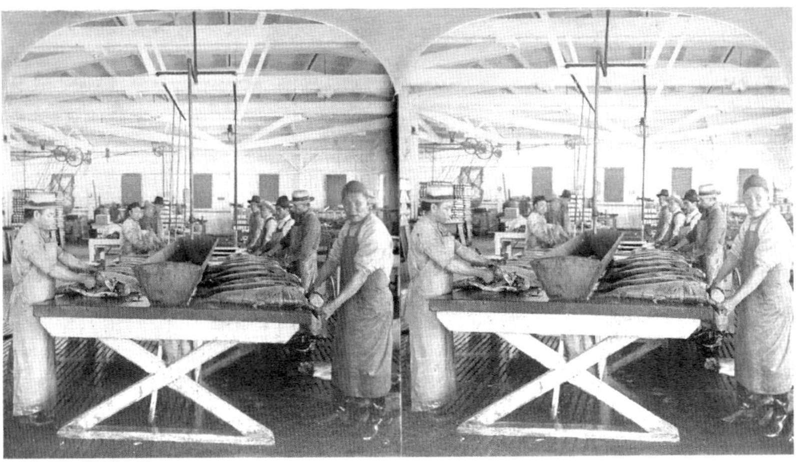

This stereopticon slide depicts salmon butchers at work at an Astoria, Oregon cannery in the 1880s, when the Chinese labor force still dominated the canneries. *CPHM.*

of twenty-two thousand fish per hour! It was offensively labeled the "Iron Chink" because it replaced much of the Chinese labor force.

Still, there were a number of Chinese workers in Pacific County well into the twentieth century. As a participant in the Washington State Oral History Project in 1975, Charlie Koe of Pacific County told about his father's experience as part of the Chinese labor force at P.J. McGowan's cannery in Ilwaco:

THEY CAME FOR THE GOLD

My father was born in Canton, China, in 1861. He came over to this country, I don't exactly know the age. But according to the 1880 United States census of Pacific County, Washington Territory, most of the Chinese came over to work in the cannery when they were about eighteen to twenty-five years old.

In those days most of 'em came over to America to become Gum San, *that means "gold hill." They figured there was gold here in those days. More opportunity for them. My father was a cannery foreman. He was working for P.J. McGowan & Sons in Ilwaco. The twenty-nine Chinese crew was contracted by season, from May the first to the end of August. Then, for the fall season, they send another contract; we had a smaller crew on in the fall season because it's only three months and there is not as much fish.*

Those days, wages were pretty low, fifty, sixty dollars a month around 1910. Most of the workers were single men; he'd get his crew from Astoria or Portland, and they'd come over and work about eight, nine months out of the year. Most of the Chinese crew would work about ten hours a day. When there was too much work, they'd generally work on Sunday overtime. They would be all tired out and have no place to go; not even go to a show or downtown. The only time they'd go downtown those days was to pick up the mail for the crew.

In those days, the Chinese was just one community by itself; they didn't stray away from the bunkhouse too much, you know. They generally worked on the garden and then went to bed. Early morning, they would go to work. There was not too much machinery there during those days. The only thing they had was a steam engine to run the crimping machine, which sealed the tops.

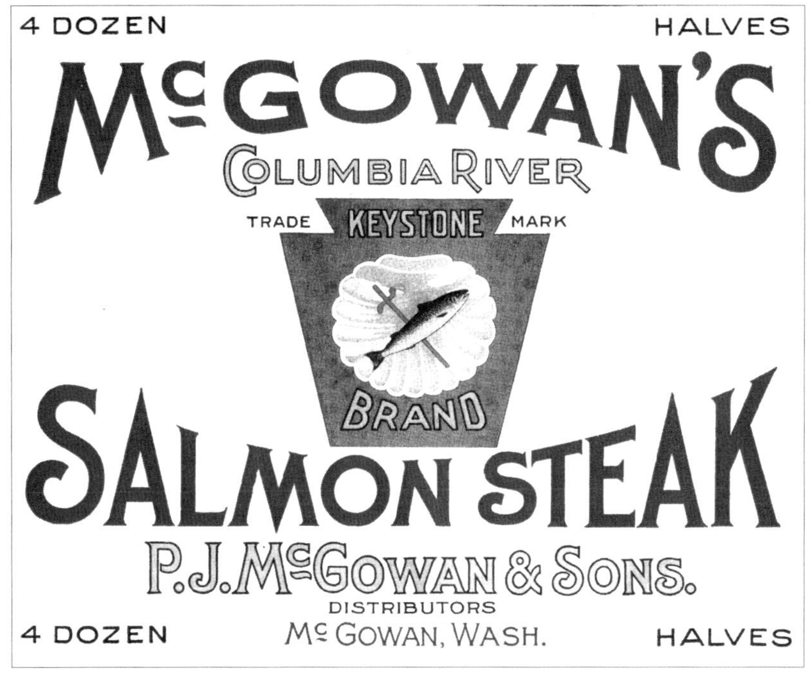

At the peak of the salmon canning industry in the 1880s, there were thirty-nine canneries on the Lower Columbia River; now there are none. *CPHM.*

It would seem from Koe's recollections that the P.J. McGowan & Sons Cannery in Ilwaco was not yet using Smith's newfangled invention to replace its Chinese workers. Nevertheless, the industry was gradually changing due in large measure to declining salmon runs rather than to immigration laws and mechanization.

As the century wore on and the number of canneries diminished, fewer and fewer Chinese were hired from the increasingly competitive labor pool. As unbelievable as it might have seemed in the early 1900s, the last major cannery on the Columbia River closed in 1980. Not only the stories of the early Chinese labor force but also the stories of the salmon canneries themselves have already become the subjects of museum exhibits and history books.

9

WOMEN IN THE JAILPLACE

A cell for each…

The old leather-bound jail book contains the names of 590 prisoners booked into the Pacific County Jail during the thirty-three years from 1886 to 1919. Of all the names listed, 31 unquestionably are those of women. There are a few others—Jessie, Litty, Ora—whose names might have been for either male or female prisoners. Unfortunately, however, among the detailed categories for providing information about prisoners, the book does not include a heading for "gender," so a best guess has to suffice.

During the first decade of the twentieth century, the jail was housed in the basement of South Bend's "new" wooden courthouse on Quincy Street. The little iron two-bunk cell, originally purchased in 1880, had been barged across Shoalwater Bay and up the Willapa River in 1893, when the county offices were moved from Oysterville.

That the cell was not commodious—it was often referred to as "the cage"—did not seem to be a matter for comment. Perhaps it was considered adequate for the number of prisoners it was required to house in the early years. Even on those occasions when three or four men were jailed simultaneously, the jail book gives no indication regarding the adequacy of the accommodations.

It was not until 1905 that the first female prisoner was booked into the county jail at South Bend. Kate Debeau was arrested and released the same day, November 22. There were no other prisoners; she had the cell to herself.

There was only one notation concerning her circumstances: insane. Was she sent to the Western Washington Hospital for the Insane at Steilacoom? Or perhaps released to the care of family or friends? The matter remains one of conjecture.

Not quite nine months later, a second woman's name was entered into the jail book. A Mrs. McMahon (40), was arrested on August 6, 1906, on a charge of petit larceny by the authority of the justice of the peace. The record is silent on the conditions in which Mrs. McMahon found herself when the jailer locked the cell door behind her.

As far as is known, her situation was exactly the same as a male prisoner's would have been. Whether special accommodations might have been made had she needed to share the space with a male inmate is left to speculation. As it turned out, Mrs. McMahon was released on October 6, having served her two months as the only occupant of the basement cell.

A Woman's Place

At the beginning of the twentieth century, the role of women in American society was still narrowly defined. Most young women were expected to get married and have children. Those who did not marry in a timely manner were referred to as "spinsters," a somewhat derogatory term implying that they were not good enough to get a husband.

Options were few for unmarried women. Those who did work were often employed as domestic servants or, perhaps, worked in factories or in service industries. Wages were low and working conditions abysmal. Teaching and nursing were considered more acceptable and appropriate occupations for single women but were usually not open to married women. Once she was wed, a woman was expected to stay at home to look after the children while her husband worked and brought in a weekly wage.

In rural areas such as Pacific County, women—married or single—often labored right alongside the men of the household. Women worked in the cranberry bogs and on the oyster beds, as well as in the fields and with the livestock. They prepared the food products to be sold at market, and some women even acted as boat-pullers for their fishermen husbands.

But because they did not work outside the home or bring home a weekly pay envelope, women were not considered part of the labor force. Their contribution to the economy was taken for granted and seldom mentioned.

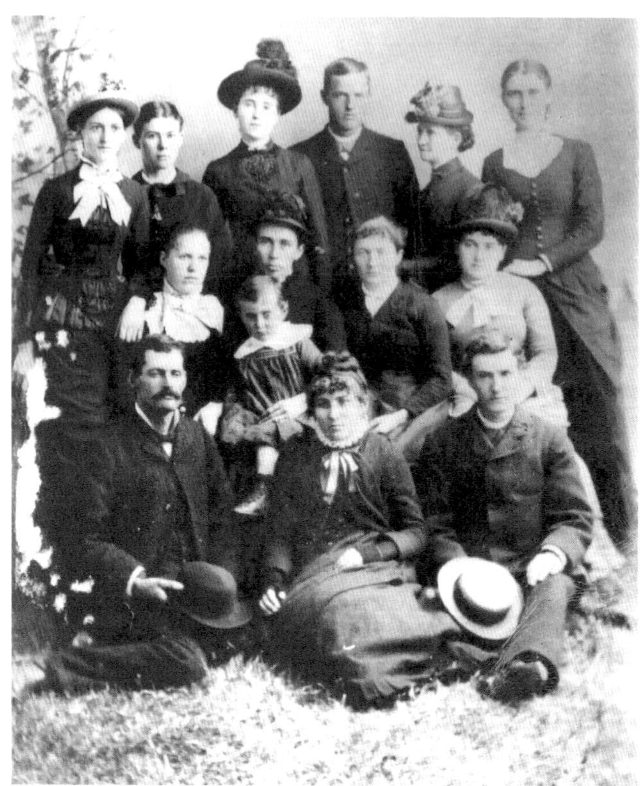

Left: In 1885, Pacific County held its first Teachers' Institute in Oysterville. Most participants were women, the main workforce of rural one-room schools. *PCHS*.

Below: On the oyster beds of Shoalwater Bay in the early 1900s, picking crews often included both women and men. *EEA*.

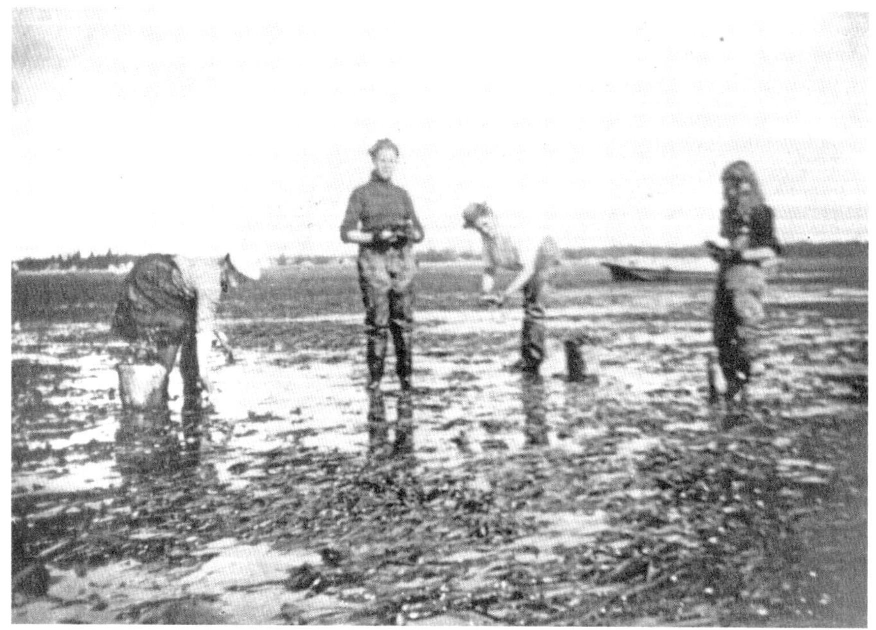

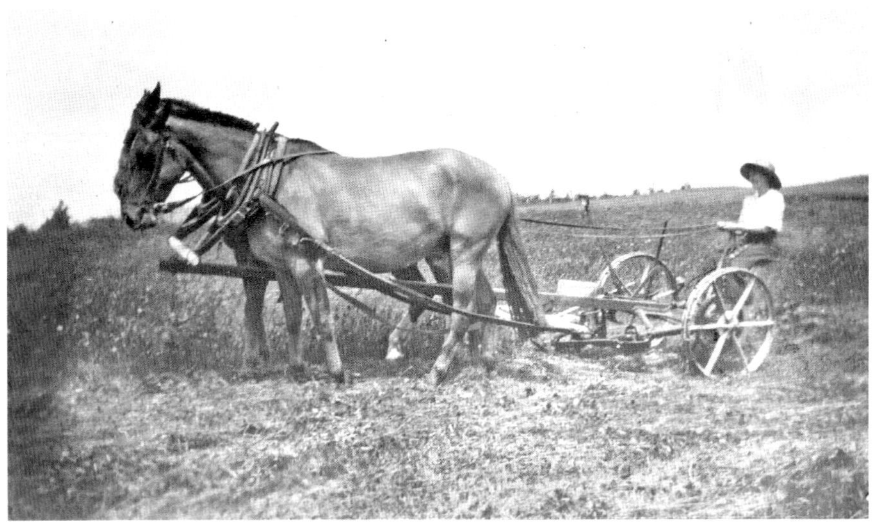

On small rural farms such as those in Pacific County, wives often participated in the day-to-day work as equal partners with their farmer husbands. *DWC*.

The age-old adage, "Men work from sun to sun; a woman's work is never done" made perfect sense to the women of early twentieth-century Pacific County—and to the men, as well.

With most people still of the opinion that a woman's place was in the home, it is probable that there was little sympathy for or attention paid to the women who were arrested and put in the county lockup. Men who went to jail were looked down on; for women, an offense serious enough to warrant an arrest was not to be acknowledged at all.

Although prison reform groups were springing up in many places throughout the United States, it would be a number of years before any substantive changes were enacted for women. In Washington State, it was not until 1971 that women were relocated from the state penitentiary in Walla Walla to their own facility at Purdy.

The Jailplace

Following the first two arrests of women in 1905 and 1906, three years would pass before another woman became a guest of the county. Jennie Nice (25), was arrested on September 10, 1909, and committed to jail by the authority of the justice of the peace on the charge of selling liquor without a license. She was released on October 4 on the authority of Sheriff T.J. Stephens after serving "25 days in the County Jale [*sic*]."

Unlike the circumstances in which Kate Debeau and Mrs. McMahon found themselves, Jennie Nice may not have had the jail to herself. Twelve days of her confinement in the county facility overlapped with time being served by Arthur Lindstrom (31), a native of Sweden. According to the jail book, from September 7 to September 18, Lindstrom was jailed for committing an assault.

This was the only occasion (at least as recorded in the jail book) that co-mingling of the sexes may have presented a challenge. It is to be assumed that in an era when Victorian sensibilities concerning roles and interactions between men and women still prevailed (indeed, where the very word "gender" was preferred to the term "sex")* separate accommodations would have been provided if at all possible. It was only a matter of time before a new, up-to-date facility would offer a solution to potential lodging problems.

The final booking into the small iron jail cell occurred on April 15, 1911, just days before the new jail would be put into use. Although Daisy Cochrane (18), had the jail to herself for the two days she was there, she undoubtedly had a few bad moments on April 17, 1911, when she was sentenced to the state penitentiary in Walla Walla for six months to fifteen years. She had been booked into jail on the authority of Raymond justice of the peace J.E. Elwood for "Burgelry [*sic*]." Ultimately, however, her sentence was suspended pending good behavior.

New County Jail

On June 23, 1911, a headline in the *South Bend Journal* announced, "New Court House Is Opened." The article described the $132,000 courthouse in detail and had this to say about the jail:

* My neighbor Tucker Wachsmuth remembers that his grandfather Louis Wachsmuth (1877–1957), who grew up in Oysterville, for all of his long life referred to "legs" by the euphemistic term "limbs." Like the word "sex," legs was considered a risqué term in Victorian times and, apparently, for long afterward in some less progressive, rural areas.

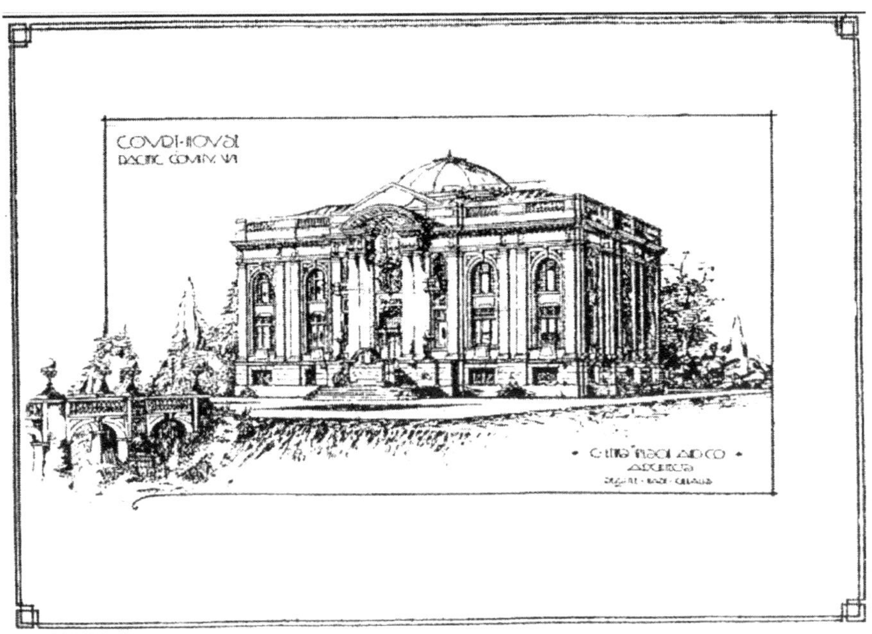

By the time the "New Stone Courthouse" was completed in 1911 at a cost of $132,000, pundits had dubbed it the "Gilded Palace of Reckless Extravagance." *PCHS.*

> *Connected with the second floor of the court house is the new fire proof jail by a bridge of sighs so that prisoners can be conveniently conducted to either the Sheriff's offices or the court room without coming in contact with the public. The jail itself is of reinforced concrete, absolutely fireproof, without any wood in its construction. It cost $10,000. In it there is a kitchen, a jailer's office, a waiting room, a cell each for women and for insane persons and three general cells. The jail is 33 feet wide and 44 feet long and of two stories.*

Perhaps the new facility with its substantially increased capacity explains the immediate increase in the number of prisoners booked into the county jail. It had been twenty-five years since the first entry in the jail book. By the time of Daisy Cochrane's jail stay, 142 persons (only 4 of whom were women) had spent time in the iron cell.

Prisoners had been booked into the jail on an average of six or seven a year. It is easy to speculate that the lack of jail space severely affected the dispensing of law and order in Pacific County. In the following eight years, until December 1919, which is as far as the jail book entries go, 448 additional persons would be booked into jail—an average of 56 per year. It does not seem reasonable that crime in Pacific County would so dramatically increase in such a short time. Other factors certainly influenced the number of entries placed in the jail book.

The years from 1910 to 1919 were a time of great change—worldwide, nationwide and statewide. Historic events would include the sinking of the *Titanic* in 1912 and the beginning of the first moving assembly line in 1914. In 1915, the one-millionth Model T ($345) would be produced.

In 1919, the National Park Service would begin, as would Prohibition. Jim Thorpe, an American Indian, would win gold medals at the Olympics, the first parachute jump would be made and the Girl Scouts of America would be formed.

But overriding every other facet of life would be the beginning of the First World War in 1914. Its effect on women and their role in society forever changed the Victorian notions of a "woman's place," and shortly after the war ended, the Nineteenth Amendment was ratified, at last giving women the right to vote. Altogether, it would be a decade to remember. As for law and order in Pacific County, the new courthouse and jail were just the beginning.

Numbers on the Increase

It would seem from entries in the old jail book that the plaster had barely dried on the walls of the new jail, opened in June 1911, when the number of women arrested and booked began to noticeably increase. Undoubtedly, the fact that the small two-bunk jail cell had now been replaced with five separate cells, one of which was expressly for women, had a bearing on the rate of arrests.

In 1912 alone, eight females were arrested—twice as many as had been arrested in the previous twenty-five years. It is difficult to believe that women had suddenly become less law-abiding during that single year. On the other hand, suffragettes and their sympathizers had been busy changing attitudes toward women, and perhaps that sword cut both ways. Responsibilities beyond home and hearth carried with them the liabilities of the greater society. Sometimes that could mean time spent in "the Jailplace."

From the time the new jail opened in 1911 until entries in the jail book ceased in 1919, a total of 27 women were arrested—nearly seven times as many arrests in that seven-year period than in all the years that the old jail was in use. Still, it was a small number in comparison to the 420 men arrested during the same period, though the rate of male arrests had only increased threefold during the same time span.

Women and the Vote Washington on the Cutting Edge

In November 1910, nine years before the Nineteenth Amendment to the U.S. Constitution extended the vote to all the nation's women, Washington became the fifth state to give women the right to vote. The amendment to the state constitution carried by nearly two to one.

The early enfranchisement of women in Washington State followed a pattern that had begun in 1854, when at the first meeting of Washington's territorial legislature Seattle's founder, Arthur Denny, proposed women's suffrage. His suggestion lost by an eight-to-nine vote, but in 1883, the territorial legislature did give women the right to vote, passing the legislation by a good majority. The victory was short-lived, however, and in 1887 the territorial Supreme Court ruled that Congress had not intended to give territories the power to enfranchise women.

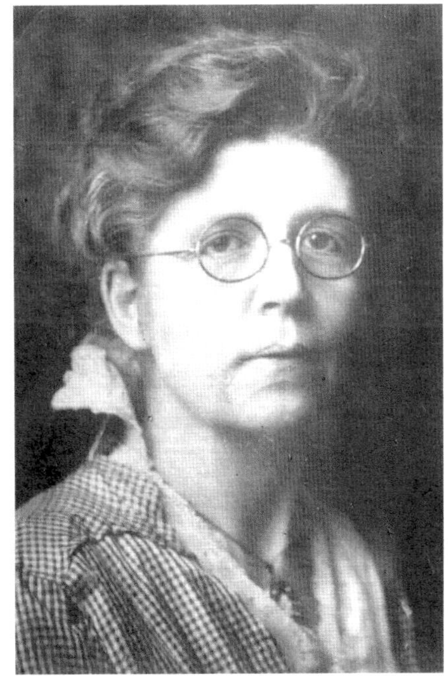

Senator Harry Espy's wife, Helen, a modern helpmate in most regards, was uncertain that election polls were a suitable place for women. *EEA.*

The women of Pacific County, like women in other parts of the state, had mixed feelings about the privilege of voting and its attendant responsibilities. Helen Richardson Espy of Oysterville, the wife of a state senator and well acquainted with the necessities of voting, expressed her frustration in a letter to her eldest daughter who was away at school:

> *Tuesday, November 3, 1914*
> *Dear Daughter:*
> *This has been Election Day and some way it has been strenuous. Papa, Mr. Stoner and Mr. Goulter have charge of the polls. Mrs. Stoner took the men up their noon meal and I sent dinner tonight. Our stove has been smoking to beat its record, and I had an awful time getting anything cooked. To top it off, your three year old brother went off with little Albert Andrews today and had an undress parade right down Fourth Street. I was so provoked. They were not together fifteen minutes. This happened while I was off voting. Willard has been threatened with dire results if he went ever since their last "undress parade" so I punished him this time and think he is duly impressed. It just goes to show that women belong at home and not at election polls.*
>
> *Much love dearie. Take care of yourself, for remember nothing in the world could take the place of mother's first born.*
>
> *Devotedly,*
> *Mama*

Four years later, Mrs. Espy would work at the polls herself, in Oysterville. It was her first (and only) paying job.

10

EQUAL OPPORTUNITY FACILITY

Incorrigibility, Vagrancy, Insanity

As the new century marched along, there began to be other changes in the clientele at the jailhouse. Even as more women's names were being entered into the jail book's pages, increasing numbers of under-aged lawbreakers were being listed right along with those who were considerably older. No longer could the Jailplace be considered the exclusive domain of male transgressors in Pacific County.

Just as the place of their mothers and older sisters began to shift in the early twentieth century, so were the expectations for children changing. In order to protect child welfare, compulsory education laws were enacted in the United States around 1900. By 1918, every state had some form of a compulsory attendance law on the books. Even in Pacific County, school attendance—at least through eighth grade—became the norm. Some legal exemptions* were allowed, but in general, failure to send children to school could result in fines or, more often, community censure.

As long-established traditions changed in families and in the workplace, the stresses began to manifest themselves in the halls of justice. However, women and children still seemed a bit of a conundrum to the dispensers

---

* In 1924, my mother's eighth grade classmate Les Wilson had to drop out of school when his father was drowned in a boating accident on Willapa Bay. Rather than attending Ilwaco High School, young Les went to work to help support his mother and himself.

of law and order. Notations in *Prison Record No. 1 Pacific County* frequently disclosed the distress and concern felt by compassionate clerks and jailers as they booked women and young offenders into the jail system.

Out of Sight, Out of Mind

Apparently, loathe to be explicit concerning particular offences, jailers and judges often used euphemisms in an effort to retain some sense of Victorian propriety. In contrast to the forthright declarations concerning male offenders, there was a hesitancy on the part of arresting officers in describing behaviors of women and children. Judges, too, were apparently uncomfortable in dispensing justice in the "usual manner" and, increasingly, prisoners (if they were women or children) were quickly sent on to other institutions—facilities away from Pacific County entirely.

Except for one seventeen-year-old boy arrested in 1910 for "petit larson [petit larceny]," there had been no arrests made for boys or girls under the

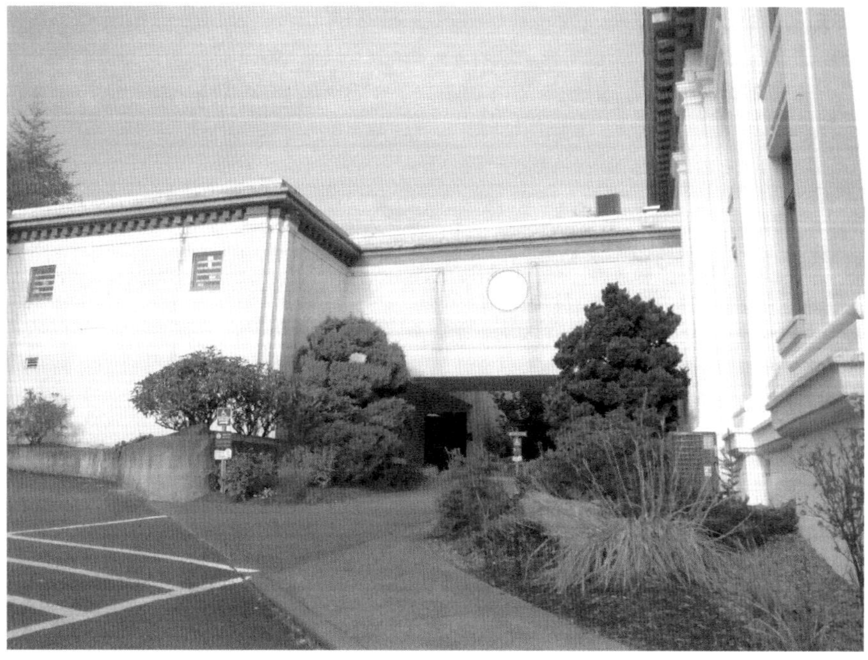

The enclosed, second-story passageway from jail (right) to courthouse (left) is still called the "Bridge of Sighs" after its Venice, Italy namesake. *Sydney Stevens photo.*

age of eighteen up until that time. Two years later, children would begin to enter the Jailplace in earnest, no doubt due to the expanded facilities at the new jail.

Of the eight underage women arrested between 1912 and 1919, Effie Shriver was the first and the youngest. She was thirteen years old; stood five feet, three inches tall; and had light hair, light eyes and a light complexion. Effie was from Washington and was booked into jail on the authority of Justice of the Peace Goodell for incorrigibility on February 15, 1912. "Incorrigible" was the most common listing for most of the teenaged girls.

On the other hand, only three of the seventeen underage boys were listed as incorrigible. Their other offences included forgery, burglary and breaking parole. The youngest of the boys was Arnie Duke (11), whose weight was about ninety pounds. After one night in jail, Arnie was sent home with J.M. Tanner, who brought him back after a trial of one week. A further notation states that Arnie was placed "Under care of Gordon, Jailer, Pacific County Jail." There are no further notations regarding young Arnie.

Those who entered the data into the jail book (perhaps a clerk, perhaps the jailer) seldom made subjective comments. However, whoever entered the information about thirteen-year-old Kenneth Downing apparently could not resist these remarks: "This is a bad boy. Always looks under his eyebrows. Has a mania for traveling and stealing."

Training in Morality, Temperance, Frugality

The Washington State Reform School opened in Chehalis on June 10, 1891. It was both an orphanage and a reformatory for boys and girls ages eight to eighteen. Prior to its opening, there were no options for punishing young offenders or for assisting children abandoned by their parents.

According to the mandate from the state legislature, students were to be "taught and trained in morality, temperance and frugality, and...also be instructed in the different trades and callings of the two sexes, as far as possible, in the scope of the institution."

Additionally, the school was to teach the regular school curriculum through grade eight. The school's facilities included a farm, workshops, living quarters and classrooms. Students learned farming, tailoring, shoemaking, carpentry, laundering, machine work, dairy operations and hog raising. They also received nonsectarian Christian religious instruction.

In 1907, the school's name changed to Washington State Training School and, still later, to Green Hill School. In 1913, Maple Lane, located near Grand Mound, was created for girls. Still later, orphans and younger children were sent elsewhere, as well.

In general, youth being booked into the reformatory were listed as "incorrigible," no matter what their offense might have been. It was a charge often made against young offenders in the jail book, particularly if they were being sent to the institution in Chehalis.

It was felt that charging a young person with a specific crime and making it a matter of record was not "in harmony with the spirit of work which should follow such a commitment." The term "incorrigibility" was thought to carry less stigma for the offender in later years.

The school is now a medium/maximum-security fenced facility that provides older, male offenders education and vocational training. Green Hill School is administered separately from the state correctional system, as part of the Department of Social and Health Services. The school's goal continues to be training and reforming youth. The school offers academic classes and vocational training and works to help the boys gain new skills for living in the community.

Most of the teenaged offenders, both boys and girls, were sent to one of the state facilities for young offenders: the State Training Facility at Chehalis or the Grand Mound Training School or Maple Lane. Occasionally, as in the case of fifteen-year-old William Hedrick of Oysterville, youngsters were sent home with their parents. The one notable exception to this "usual outcome" occurred on July 12, 1918.

On that date, fourteen-year-old Hazel Lovelace and fifteen-year-old Serena Luby were booked into the jail, "Held for Investigation for Army Officers" and discharged with no complaint filed. By the date of their arrest, of course, the United States had been involved in the Great War (World War I) for more than a year, and there were military personnel stationed throughout Washington, including several Pacific County locations. According to evidence supplied by the jail book, Pacific County authorities cooperated fully with the military police in matters of law and order. Perhaps Hazel and Serena had also been cooperating (a little too fully?) with military personnel. Hazel was arrested again in May 1919, this time for juvenile delinquency. She was sent to the Pacific Coast Rescue and Protection Home.

White Slavery

The Mann Act

"White slavery" was a term used in English-speaking countries in the eighteenth, nineteenth and early twentieth centuries to differentiate the slavery of European descendants from that of African descendants. The term was used regardless of the specific type or nature of the slavery enacted and could be applied to indentured servants, to criminals in penal colonies or to those in debt bondage.

By 1880, however, the term had become linked to enforced prostitution, especially of young women of European descent. Agitation concerning "traffic in women" rose to such a pitch in Victorian England that "white slavery" became a target for crusading journalists and defenders of public morality. The subsequent outcry led to the passage of antislavery legislation in Parliament.

In the early twentieth century, a similar scare occurred in the United States when Chicago's U.S. attorney general declared that an international crime ring was abducting young girls in Europe, importing them and forcing them to work in Chicago brothels.

These claims, largely unsubstantiated, inflamed public opinion and led to the passage of the White-Slave Traffic Act of 1910. It also banned the interstate transport of females for immoral purposes. Its primary intent was to address prostitution and immorality. The act is better known as the Mann Act, after American lawmaker James Robert Mann.

One of the most intriguing situations among the youthful offenders was that of Marsha Mossman (14), who was booked into jail on April 25, 1919. For almost a month, Mossman was held as a witness in the Cora Langland case, until May 23, 1919, when she was sent to the Rescue Home in Seattle on order of the court.

Besides the notations about Mossman's personal characteristics—she was five feet, three inches tall with dark brown hair, blue eyes and a fair complexion and from Kansas—there is no other information. It is necessary to look at the entry for Cora Langland for clues about Mossman's stay in jail.

Langland was booked into jail on the same day as young Miss Mossman. No personal details are written about her. Under "By What Authority Committed" is written "Information" and in the column headed "For What Offense and What Term" is written "White Slavery." Ultimately, she was sentenced to nine months in county jail.

One scenario might have been that young Marsha Mossman had been held or housed by Langland for purposes of prostitution and was kept by the authorities in the county jail for an extended period so that she could testify at Langland's trial. Unfortunately, there is no indication in the jail book that there *was* a trial, though logic would indicate that Langland's subsequent

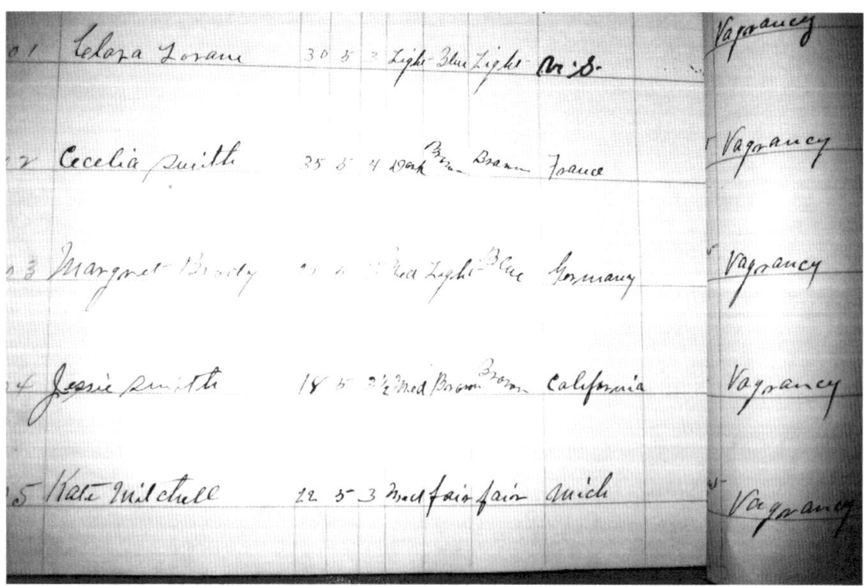

On November 9, 1912, five women with disparate backgrounds were charged with vagrancy and released two days later without further commentary. *Sydney Stevens photo.*

nine-month stay in the Jailplace as a guest of the county was, indeed, a determination made by a judge at a trial.

Just as the crimes of young offenders were disguised by the term "incorrigible," women eighteen years and older who were booked on a charge of "vagrancy" were usually not vagrant at all but were working women in the world's oldest profession. It is clear from later entries in the jail book that "vagrancy," as it applied to women in those years, was a euphemism for "prostitution."

On November 9, 1912, five women were booked into the jail: Clara Losane (30), United States; Cecelia Smith (35), France; Margaret Brady (25), Germany; Jessie Smith (18), California; and Kate Mitchell (22), Michigan. They were a disparate group, yet they were all booked into the jail on the same day on a criminal warrant. In the annals of the jail book, this was the first group of women arrested at the same time and for the same offence, which gives rise to serious speculation that "vagrancy" was a euphemism for an entirely different sort of transgression.

Working Women

That there were houses of questionable repute in Pacific County there can be no doubt. The women arrested on November 9, 1912, may even have worked for the very establishment in a neighboring town that would become big news the following year. In a 1913 court case that would result in a prison term for the city attorney of Raymond (the municipality adjacent to South Bend), testimony was introduced to the effect that one Maggie Rose ran a house of prostitution and thus could not be trusted to tell the truth. "A woman's reputation for truthfulness could not survive a life of immorality," the Supreme Court opined in its decision on the appeal.

The only booking even vaguely reminiscent was many years previous, when a Mr. George Vincent was accused of running a bawdy house back in 1888. He was discharged by order of the court after paying a $100 fine. The five "vagrant" women of 1912 fared somewhat better, however. All were discharged by order of the court on November 11, and there was no further notation concerning any of them—for the time being. But within two weeks, Cecelia Smith was back again. The familiar charge, vagrancy, kept her in the county lockup for five days this time, from December 1 to December 6.

The women had only one other jail mate during their sojourn at county expense. Peruvian native Ridia Estinagh (21) had been jailed on September 25, 1912, by the authority of Justice Fred Colbert on the charge of misdemeanor. According to the badly smudged notation in the jail book, she was "Taken to Seattle and turned over to the Immigration Commission on January 14, 1913." There is no indication concerning the disposition of her case in the interim. Presumably, she remained in the county jail at South Bend for three and a half months before being transferred to Seattle.

Personal information was not noted for Daisy West, who was booked into jail on September 20, 1913. Nor was her offense listed as "vagrancy." Still, one wonders. She was charged with lewdness by Justice Rhodes and released two days later. There were no notations under "Remarks" by the keeper of the jail book. Of the thirty-one women listed in the jail book, Daisy West's is the only name with "lewdness" written after it.

The term "prostitute" is used only twice* in the jail book. On May 17, 1917, twenty-five-year-old Della Miller, native of Washington, was booked with the charge of vagrancy. "She is a prostitute," noted the clerk. It is the first definitive link between the terms "vagrancy" and "prostitute."

Ordered to Leave

Miller was described as five feet, five inches tall, with light brown hair, blue eyes and a fair complexion, and was arrested under the authority of Justice Wright. She was released the following day. Her thirty-day sentence was suspended providing she stayed out of the county for one year.

Nellie Imus, too, was told to quit the area, though the reason for her arrest was not stated. Nellie (20), was five feet, three and a half inches tall and weighed 120 pounds. She had brown hair, brown eyes and a medium complexion and was from Spirit Lake, Iowa. Booked into jail on March 6, 1918, on the authority of Justice Wright, she was released the same day. The notation concerning her discharge: "$10 fine paid; costs omitted provided leaves town."

* Della Miller (in 1917) and Grace Walkowsky (in 1919) were the only two women listed in the jail book using the term "prostitute."

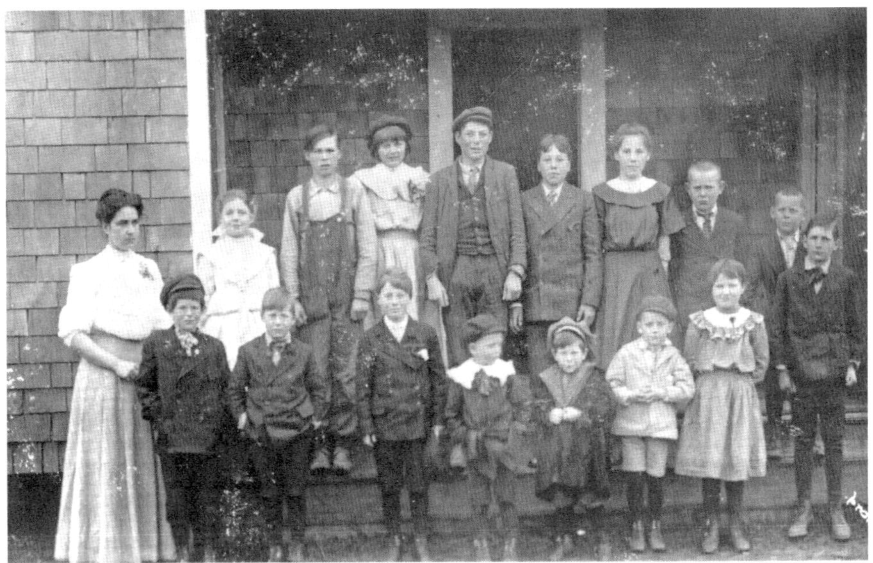

Students attending Oysterville School in 1909, here with their teacher Miss Butler, included Grace Walkowski, third from left in the back row. *EEA*.

The requirement that an offender leave town was apparently a solution only in the case of female prisoners. Certainly such a directive is not noted for any of the male inmates of the Pacific County Jail between April 1886 and September 1919. The fact that women were being treated differently from men is undoubtedly a reflection of the changing times, not only in the Jailplace but also in society at large.

By late 1919, the ratification of the Nineteenth Amendment was imminent. The number of women in the workforce had increased by 25 percent, partly because World War I necessitated women working. Clothing styles changed radically; corsets and long skirts gave way to clothing more convenient for an active lifestyle.

And even in Pacific County, the "Flapper Era" was beginning. Young women danced the new dances, smoked in public and were sexually liberated—or at least to a degree that would shock their Victorian mothers. Times were certainly changing, and the keepers of law and order in Pacific County were hard pressed to keep up.

On February 1, 1919, Tena Martin was booked on a charge of larceny. She was one of the few women to serve time in the county jail for anything other than "incorrigibility," "vagrancy or prostitution" or "insanity." Tena was discharged with the notation: "paid cash appropriately and all costs."

The last female name in the jail book is that of Washington native Grace Walkowsky,* age eighteen, with black hair, black eyes and a dark complexion. She was booked on July 17, 1919, by the authority of a police judge, the charge being vagrancy and prostitution. Her sentence: thirty days in jail.

A Place for Insanity

In addition to "vagrancy" and "incorrigibility," the third large category under which female inmates in the Pacific County Jail were booked was "insanity," and though men, too, had been judged insane and dealt with accordingly over the years, a far higher percentage of women arrested were so listed. Furthermore, although many of the women labeled insane in the jail book were, indeed, transferred to the Western State Hospital for the Insane at Steilacoom, some were simply released from jail, presumably able to resume their lives as law-abiding citizens. "Insane" may have been a catch-all term used for those who were disturbing the peace or otherwise not acting according to the accepted norms of female behavior.

The year 1913 was a busy one in the jailhouse—particularly for those so afflicted. On February 14, 1913, sixty-six-year-old Mrs. Mina Linn was jailed. Described as five feet, four inches, with brown hair turning gray and a large mole on the right side of her neck, she was taken to Fort Steilacoom Hospital for the Insane two days later.

Though the year 1913 was only six weeks old, Mrs. Linn was the third person listed as "insane" in the jail book that year. (In all of 1912, there had only been six insane persons listed—every one a man.) On the date Mrs. Linn was put into jail, February 14, 1913, one other inmate, a man, was also being held for insanity.

Presumably, he and Mrs. Linn were placed in separate cells now that such a luxury of jail space existed, but which was in the cell designated for the insane is not noted. Mrs. Linn could have been put in the woman's cell, or she could have been the first female prisoner to occupy the new

* Grace Walkowsky's name is the only one of the many listed in the jail book that is familiar to me. She was the fourth daughter of John Walkowsky and his wife—the fifth of their ten children. The Walkowskys lived just south of Oysterville, and Grace was a schoolmate of my mother's eldest sister, Medora. After Grace finished eighth grade, she did occasional housework for my grandparents. My grandmother said that although Grace did good work, she eventually had to let her go as she was too easily distracted by her many siblings, who could not be convinced to leave her to her chores.

cell that had been earmarked specifically for the insane. The record gives no indication.

Elsie Takkenen, a native of Finland, was also listed as insane when she was booked into jail on April 14 on the authority of the Superior Court. She was released the following day without further commentary.

IN AGAIN, OUT AGAIN

Under "Special Marks or Peculiarities as to Prisoner History" for Ida Waldon is written: "Sent to the asylum for the second time." This was recorded on December 27, 1913, and just to make sure that it was duly noted, a little farther along on the line, under "For What Offense and for What Term," is written: "Sent to the Asylum." A few categories later, under "Escaped or Discharged; If Discharged by What Authority," the notation is made for the third time: "Committed to Hospital for the Insane at Fort Steilacoom, Wash."

Waldon, twenty-five, had dark eyes, dark hair and a dark complexion and was from Kentucky. She was booked into jail on November 29, and despite the very clear notation that this was to be her second stint in the asylum, there is no mention of her previously in the jail book. However, she does show up again later.

This time, she is listed as Ida Wallon, still with a dark complexion, still from Kentucky, and now, on March 16, 1915, she is "Committed to Asylum Third Time after spending one day in jail." Again, there is a second notation: "Sent to the Hospital for the Insane at Steilacoom."*

In those years, it was with some difficulty that patients could be released from Steilacoom, so it is curious, indeed, that Ida Wallon shows up *again* on the pages of the jail book—this time on October 29, 1918. The jailer has apparently given up on her personal information. None is listed. Under "For What Offense and For What Term" is one word: "Insanity." On November 1, 1918, there is an order of discharge by the court commissioner, "Insanity

* To further confuse the various reappearances of Ida Waldon/Wallon in the pages of the jail book, records from Steilacoom indicate that Ida Waldon of Kentucky was admitted twice to the asylum for manic depression—first in December 1913 and second in July 1915. She was released in 1917 and listed as "recovered." There is no indication that she was in the state hospital prior to 1913, despite the notation in the jail book on page 26 on November 29, 1913: "Sent to asylum for the second time and the further notation on page 30 (when she was listed as Ida Wallon) that she was Convicted [sic] to the Assilum [sic] for the Third time."

Charge Dismissed," and Ida Wallon's name never shows up in the pages of the jail book again. (Nor does Ida Waldon's, for that matter.)

During the four-year time period that Waldon/Wallon was in and out of the asylum and in and out of the Pacific County Jail in South Bend, five other women were jailed in Pacific County for reasons of insanity.

Very little is written about these women, leading to speculation about whether they were able to speak for themselves or whether there was anyone to speak for them. Or were the sensibilities and expectations concerning a "woman's place" still so imbued with Victorian morality that those who could speak with some authority were hesitant to do so?

Few advocacy groups of any kind existed in the early twentieth century—especially for women and even more especially for women who were in difficulty with the law. It's a story that has little documentation and can be known only by reading between the lines.

11

PRISONER LOGISTICS

A long journey…

At the turn of the twentieth century, there were only eight thousand registered automobiles in the whole of the United States. Whether any of them were in Pacific County, Washington, is open to conjecture.

It is a matter of record, though, that by 1906, J.J. Haggerty had purchased Raymond's first car, and five years later, Bert Andrews of Oysterville had a new 1911 Winton—probably the first automobile on the North Beach Peninsula. Where they traveled in their "machines" is another matter open to conjecture.

Roads were scarce, and those that existed were primitive by today's standards. Few were paved or even "improved" beyond their beginnings as rutted wagon tracks through forest and marsh, and though many counties were working on their own "road projects," communication and cooperation between counties was not the norm.

Even so, county business often involved traveling from one part of the county to another or even beyond the county line. One of the duties of the sheriff, for instance, was to escort prisoners to the state penitentiary in Walla Walla or to the State Insane Asylum at Steilacoom or, perhaps when necessary, to the Washington State Reform School at Chehalis. Usually, it was a one-time transport per prisoner.

In the case of Manuel Gates, however, Sheriff Thomas Roney needed to make several round trips between the Pacific County seat in South Bend and the state prison facility in Walla Walla just a year or so after the turn of the

A Movement for Good Roads

It was a group of bicyclists from the League of American Wheelmen in the 1880s who began a movement toward better roads. Under their leadership, good road associations sprang up in several states. However, in the Pacific Northwest, a system of roads and highways did not evolve easily.

In Washington and Oregon, even by the turn of the century, there were few improved roads and, though many counties were beginning to plan road projects, they were not coordinated with one another. A 1904 survey in Washington showed that just 1 percent of the roads in the state were paved, and most of those were within cities.

In those days, county commissioners were responsible for building roads, usually just graded tracks, within their counties, with little attention paid to how the networks interconnected. Property owners could either pay for roads through poll and property taxes or work off the obligation with their own labor.

The good roads movement in Washington began in earnest in 1899 when Great Northern Railway executive Sam Hill (1857–1931) invited one hundred men to Spokane to discuss improving the state's highways. They formed the Washington State Good Roads Association and named Hill president. For the next thirty years, he spent much of his energy and a million of his own dollars on the campaign.

By 1905, the legislature had created a state highway department headed by three commissioners—the fourteenth such agency in the country—and during the next ten years, the number of motor vehicles in Washington increased almost one hundred times, to seventy thousand.

Still, there were many segments of the population who did not yet agree fully with the goals of the Good Roads Association. Washington farmers, for instance, felt that the automobile was just a means of recreation for the urban elite. It was not until the railroads became overburdened during World War I and more farmers were spurred into hauling their produce to market by truck that the value of better roads became clear. Even the state Grange rallied to the movement.

When the Federal Highway Act of 1921 focused funding on an interstate system of highways, a boom in road construction began. At first, priorities were given to the needs of recreational drivers and

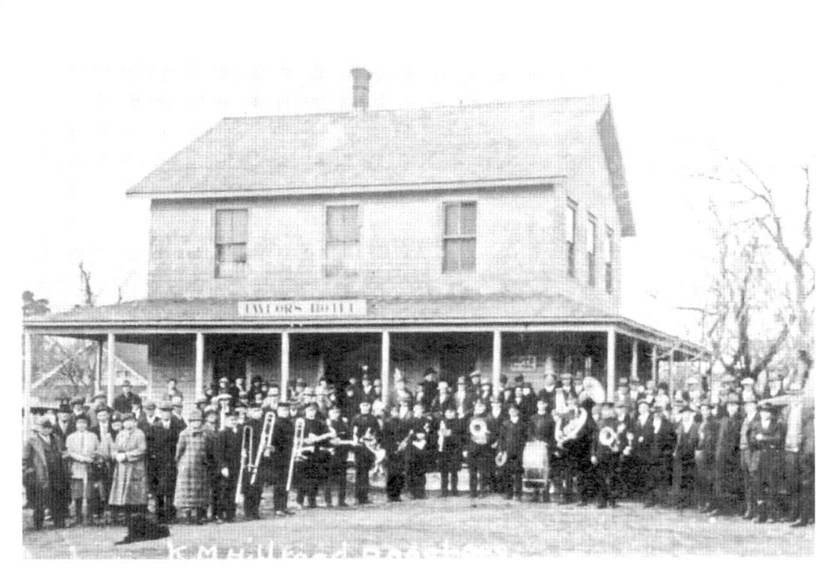

K.M. Hill Boosters and Brass Band promoted the first automobile caravan to traverse the Ocean Beach Highway (WA State Route 4) on May 29, 1925. *PCHS.*

farmers, but by the 1950s, the priorities shifted to moving residents between the cities and their new suburban homes.

Three highways of particular importance to the Washington Good Roads Association were the Pacific Coast Highway from Vancouver, British Columbia, to Tijuana, Mexico, the Inland Empire from Spokane to Ellensburg by way of Walla Walla and Pasco; and the Sunset Highway between Spokane and Seattle over Snoqualmie and Blewett Passes.

Of greater immediate importance in Pacific County were "The Highway around the Bay" (now part of Highway 101), which finally, in the 1920s, provided a land connection between the Long Beach Peninsula and the rest of the county, and the Ocean Beach Highway (now Washington State Route 4) from Kelso to Long Beach, completed in 1925. Until that time, connections both within and beyond county borders depended almost completely on water and rail connections.

Today, the organization is known as the Washington State Good Roads and Transportation Association and still fosters construction, maintenance and general improvement of good roads and transportation infrastructure throughout the state.

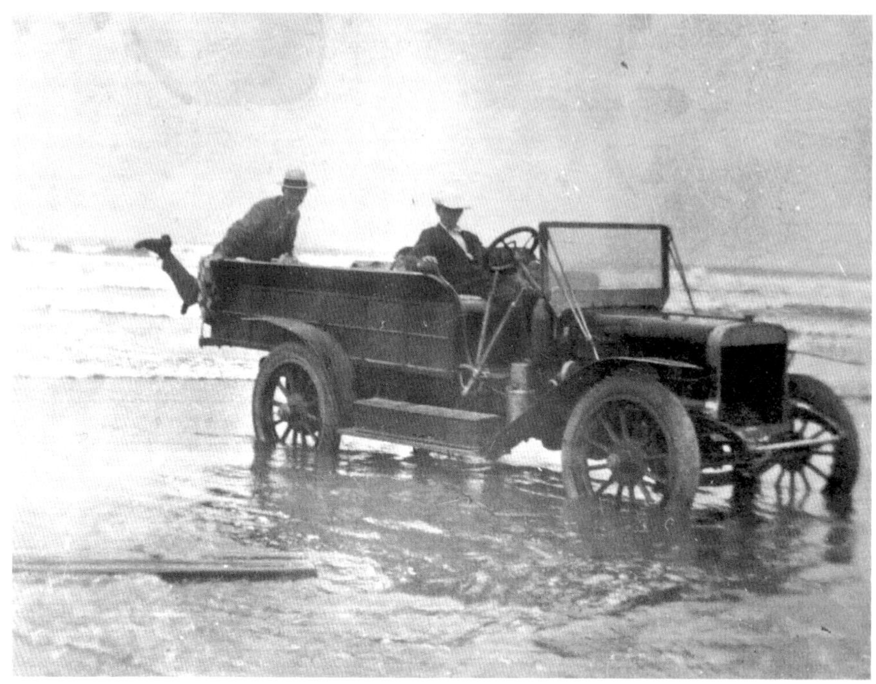

With few roads available to them, early Peninsula drivers often took to the hard sands of the twenty-eight-mile-shoreline for a bit of joy riding. *EFA.*

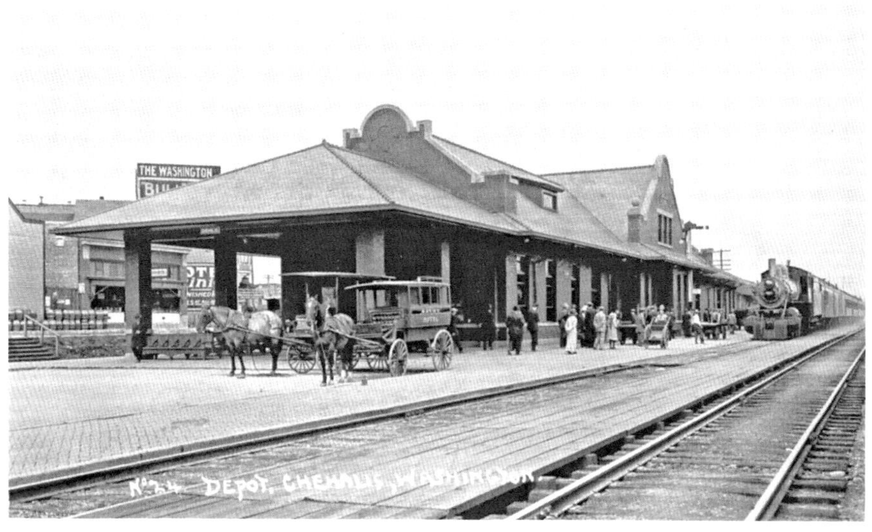

The Northern Pacific Railroad Depot in Chehalis established a transportation hub between Puget Sound and cities to the south, including South Bend. *PCHS.*

century. Such a trip could have involved both train and water transport, but considering that the sheriff had a criminal in tow, it is likely that they went by the fastest, most direct method.

Conveniently, the western terminus of the Northern Pacific Railroad system had been located in South Bend since 1893, and the depot was just a stone's throw from the old jailhouse. In July 1901, when Sheriff Roney escorted prisoner Gates, the first leg of the trip to Walla Walla would have been by rail to Chehalis, fifty-eight miles away.

At Chehalis, there would have been another change to a train bound for Wallula, almost three hundred miles distant. There, the third and last train change of the trip would be to another rail line, the Walla Walla and Columbia River Railroad, to board a train headed the final seventeen miles for Walla Walla. It was a long journey.

Prisoner Manuel Gates

The initial entry concerning Gates in the old jail book reads: "Manuel Gates, 40, 5'7", dark eyes, dark complexion." It was further noted that he was from Spain and was booked into the jail cell in South Bend "on the authority of the Superior Court." The charge, according to the log, was "manslaughter." He was "taken to Walla Walla by Sheriff Roney" with "No Property left in care of the Sheriff."

Although the jail book was silent on all other aspects of the case, the *South Bend Journal* was not. In fact, on August 31, 1900—nearly a year before that first jail book entry—the newspaper's front page proclaimed:

> *DISAPPEARED.*
> *Probable Drowning of Captain Beeson*
> *Of Launch Leonore.*
> *Craft Found Without a Master*
> *Ran into a Net*
> *Captain W.A. Beeson is supposed to have been drowned by falling off the naphtha launch* Leonore while coming up the Willapa River Wednesday*

* A naphtha launch, sometimes called a "vapor launch," was a small open motorboat powered by a naphtha engine. These boats were developed as an alternative to steam launches, which, in America, required as a safety precaution that all steam boats carry a licensed engineer at all times.

night about 11 P.M. The story told by James Gates a gillnet fisherman, and his boat puller Lauritz Olson, is that while they were drifting in the neighborhood of beacon No. 6 below Sea Haven that night, the launch came up the river and her wheel caught in the net. They yelled to the captain and the boat turned partially about. They gathered in the remnant of their net which had been torn by the wheel and then, seeing no light on the boat and getting no response to their calls, they boarded the launch, which had stopped, but found no one. The wheel was set hard a-starboard, which had swung the launch about, and the captain's coat and vest and some personal belongings were found in the cabin. It is supposed that when the launch struck the net Captain Beeson set the wheel and then ran out to either cut the net or disentangle it from the wheel and fell overboard. The fishermen declare they heard no outcry.

A search is being made for the body. There is a bare possibility that Beeson swam ashore but it is hardly possible, as he would have turned up ere this. The fishermen brought the launch to town and claim salvage.

The launch is the property of McGowan & Sons and was carrying fish.

Captain Beeson was little known here. His home was in Astoria, though his wife and two children are at present stopping at the Hotel Beverly. Mrs. Beeson refuses to believe that her husband is lost.

The headlines in the next week's paper took a dramatic turn. Things were not as they had first appeared:

MURDER MYSTERY
W.A. Beeson Undoubtedly Murdered,
But Who Did It?
Body Found with a Deep Gash
in the Neck and Contusions
on the Head.

A continuance of the history of the case of the finding of the launch commanded by Captain Beeson is as follows: Thursday night, after consultation with the county attorney, Judge Egbert issued warrants for the arrest of James Gates and Lauritz Olson, the fishermen who brought the launch to town. They were taken to the city and county jails respectively and held until the next morning, when a searching party in the launch Leonore, under Attorney Stratton, went to the place was said to have been found, Gates being taken along to identify the location. The searchers returned in the evening unsuccessful. Saturday and Sunday like attempts to find the body of the missing man proved abortive, and the matter remained quiescent in the belief that nothing more could be done until the body came to the surface from natural causes. In the meantime the arrested men were discharged.

Monday evening as Herman Martz and his brother-in-law, Chas. Kirsch, who were going to the fishing grounds off Toke's Point discovered Beeson's body afloat abreast of beacon No. 8, and after securing the same to a nearby willow bush, came back to town and informed County Attorney Welsh, who at once notified Justice Marion D. Egbert to take the preliminary steps toward holding an inquest…

The inquest was opened at 2 p.m. Tuesday, when Manuel Gates, his boat-puller Olson, Dr. Vickery, Dr. Gruwell and Chris Korkan were examined.

In his testimony Gates said he started in his boat from South Bend with his partner at 7 o'clock on the evening of August 29, and it was 8 o'clock when they got below Sea Haven. Near beacon 6 "I saw a boat below me and told my partner to tie to the beacon and let the other boat get away before we put out our net. We stayed at the beacon a short time and then we put out our net and started to the north side. Heard the sound of a launch approaching and told my partner that the launch would run over our net; he asked me if I had a light in the boat; I said "no, I use matches." I saw two lights below me. The launch was still approaching, but I told my partner it would miss us the way it was then coming. Then all at once, when abreast of us, it swung around and did not move again and the propeller stopped about 600 feet from us. I knew it was McGowan's launch by the sound. Then I pulled my boat along the cork line and when I got near the launch I saw that my net was bunched. I asked the launch, "Why don't you clear the net?" but received no answer. Then I went back and picked up the net, this taking about twenty minutes; then I spoke again and said, "What kind of a cuss are you, anyway?" I thought that perhaps he did not clear the nets for meanness. I then boarded the launch and said, "Where are you?" and lit some matches on the stern of the launch. I looked in the cabin through the glass and did not see anyone. I said to my partner, "I'll bet he has fallen overboard," but he said, "He is probably sleeping." I said, "This is no place to sleep, where we are all drifting, in the middle of the night." Then I went to the anchor and found it had no line, so I took a rope from the scow and tied it to the anchor and then anchored the launch. My net was tangled in the propeller and I cut it loose. At 11 o'clock I started for South Bend with the launch and scow in tow, and arrive there at 3 o'clock Thursday morning, August 30...

Drs. Gruwell and Vickery, who held the autopsy, testified that they found an opening two inches wide in the neck made by a sharp instrument, which severed the windpipe; there was a bruise on the forehead and a punctured wound on the left hand; the apex of the skull was also bruised. The crabs had attacked the wounds. The lungs floated, showing that they contained a normal amount of air and it was Dr. Gruwell's opinion that Beeson did not drown, as there was but little water in the lungs…

H. Jackson and Louis Johnson, testifying to the same point, said that on the evening of the 4th of September, on the sidewalk in front of Rose's hotel, James Gates said that "He didn't kill Beeson; but knew who did, and that there was blood on the launch when he went aboard." Johnson then told Gates "to speak up and save himself."

At 2 p.m. the jury rendered their verdict, which is that William Beeson was unlawfully killed on August 29, 1900, by some person or persons unknown, with a cutting instrument and also with a club or blunt weapon.

The Astoria correspondent of the Oregonian says that Beeson was a very careful man, but did injure some nets and incurred the enmity of several fishermen on the Columbia. The latter part of the season he would not go out on the river in the launch at night, as several shots had been fired at him and there was an evident intention to take his life. He states that Gates had been suspected of some shooting on the Columbia. In the present instance, however, the evidence cannot be said to be strong enough against him to warrant his detention.

The funeral of the unfortunate William Beeson was held Wednesday morning at 9 o'clock in the city wharf building, the services being conducted by Rev. Mr. Cort. A goodly number of people were present. The coffin was covered by the American flag and decorated with beautiful flowers. The body was deposited in the city cemetery for everlasting rest.

Mrs. Beeson and children will remain here temporarily, the guests of Mrs. Clarence Green. She possesses a little house at Warrenton and that is all, but she has a brave heart and faces the world amid these unfortunate circumstances hopefully and in the firm belief that He who notes the sparrow's fall will also deal kindly with her and her children.

Discrepancies

The fact that Gates was taken to the city jail may clarify the discrepancy in dates between the time the murder was initially reported in 1900 and the first notation of Gates's name in the county jail book in 1901.

However, as indicated in the *Journal*'s account, the name of Gates's boat puller and alleged accomplice, Lauritz Olson, does appear in the jail book. It was noted that he had dark brown hair, gray eyes and a fair complexion and was born in Norway. Although there was no date entered under the "When Committed" column, it was noted that he was "Discharged by Order of Court October 20, 1900." That information concurs with subsequent newspaper reports of the trial.

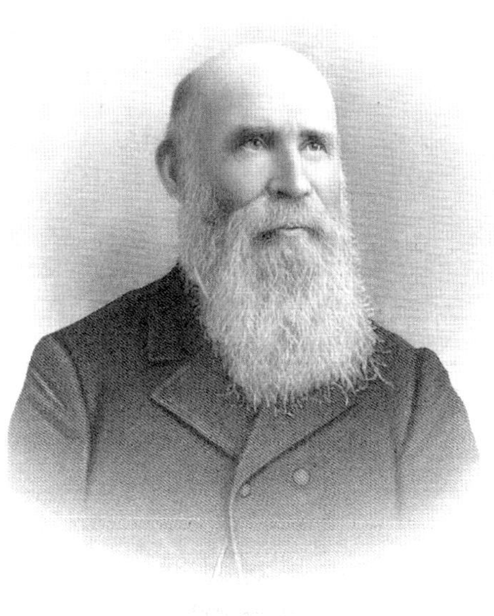

Patrick "P.J." McGowan began the first salt salmon packing company in Washington Territory, switched to a canning operation in the mid-1880s and established a company cannery town. *EFA*.

Mention of the city jail in the newspaper may also help to explain why there so few inmates in the county jail during the early years—the years before 1910, when the new, roomier jail was finally built. Perhaps the city lockup was used for "overflow" prisoners. Or perhaps, when two inmates were involved in the same crime, putting them in separate facilities was an expedient method of limiting their communication and potential collaboration on their stories.

Another inconsistency between the *Journal* and the jail book is in the matter of Gates's name. In the first several news articles about the Beeson murder, Editor Hazeltine reports Gates's given name as "James" but changes it to "Manuel" in subsequent reports. A mistake? Or was Gates known in the community as "James," though his legal name was Manuel? Perhaps that would explain why he is entered in the jail book as "Manuel."

RE-ARRESTED

Gates and Olson Again in Custody as a result of some detective work
Sensational evidence promised at the Examination Tomorrow

As soon as the coroner's jury had rendered their verdict in the inquest upon the body of the late William Beeson, P.J. McGowan, in whose employ Beeson was at the time of his untimely end, employed Sam Simons one of the best of Portland's detectives to ferret out the murderer. Mr. Simons set to work at once with such definite results, that affidavits, based upon information obtained, were prepared by County Attorney Welsh, and properly sworn to before Justice Marion D. Egbert, who on the evening of September 15, issued warrants for the re-arrest of Manuel Gates and Lauritz Olson for the murder of William Beeson on the night of August 29, 1900. The writs were placed in the hands of Deputy Sheriff McDonald, who, with Deputy Marshal Cornelius, served the same on Olson about 9 p.m. on the street, and on Gates about 1 a.m. Sunday, down on the river near beacon No. 1 where he had placed his net. They were taken to the county jail. Both took the matter of their arrest coolly, accompanying the officers with every show of willingness.

Monday at 8 p.m. Gates and Olson were arraigned before Judge Egbert, who read the charge to them, which was that of murder in the first degree. They pleading not guilty thereto, Mr. Welsh, on the part of the state moved the court for a continuance on the ground of inability to obtain material witnesses before Saturday morning…

Sam Simmons [sic], *the well-known Portland detective who solved the mystery connected with the robbery of the late William M. Ladd's* body from the grave, claims to have ample evidence to convict. Certainly both Sheriff Brown and his deputy, A.B. McDonald, have been busy summoning witnesses.*

The First Trial

During the preliminary examination on Saturday, September 29, 1900, seventy-five witnesses were examined on the part of the state. The investigation resulted in both defendants being held to answer, without bail, until the next term of the superior court.

* Millionaire William S. Ladd (1826–1893) of Portland, Oregon, was known for his business acumen, his philanthropy and his civic involvement. Four years after his death, three unsavory (and perhaps unstable) men robbed Ladd's grave and removed his well-preserved body from its coffin. Detective Sam Simons was involved in recovering the body even before the ransom demand could be made and, ultimately, leading authorities to the grave robbers.

Subsequently, at a special session, Gates and Olson were charged with the murder of Captain Beeson. Both pleaded not guilty and chose to be tried together.

The trial opened on Monday, November 12, 1900, and as the *South Bend Journal* reported later that week, evidence against the two men was piling up. The paper also noted that difficulty was had in several instances in bringing some of the witnesses to a comprehension of even the simpler forms of speech, notwithstanding many years' residence in this country.

Something of a sensation was caused when Deputy Sheriff A.B. McDonald testified concerning Gates's knife, which had been presented as physical evidence. After examining it in the courtroom, McDonald testified that it was not in the same condition as when it was offered to the justice of the peace at the preliminary hearing. The bloodstains now on it had not been there previously.

Testimony concerning the whereabouts of the knife during the interim period was then given by several witnesses, including the stenographer, the county clerk and the county attorney. No conclusion about the bloodstains was reached.

Perhaps most damning of all the testimony was that given by two witnesses, Joe Howard and Alfred Miller, who said that on the night of the murder they were on their way down the river to Miller Bros. logging camp on the Dobie place, and when off the mouth of Johnson's slough, they heard the launch coming up the river. They heard it stop and recognized Gates's voice, who demanded of Beeson what he was doing. Beeson replied that he couldn't help it. They heard Gates say, "I'll kill you."

Their report seemed to be backed up by Charles Stevens, who testified that a year earlier, Gates had told him he intended to kill Beeson, and by fourteen-year-old Benny Corwin, who testified that in August or September at Ilwaco, Gates told him that if any man ran his launch into his nets, he would kill him.

On Tuesday, November 20, 1900, the verdict was rendered: "Guilty of murder in the second degree" for Gates and an acquittal for Olson. According to the final paragraph in the newspaper's report:

> *Many are wondering why Olson was acquitted when Gates was convicted. It is understood that a large majority of the jury favored Olson's conviction for at least manslaughter, but it either meant the verdict rendered or a disagreement. After the first ballot the jury stood 11 for murder or manslaughter to 1 for acquittal, and the twelfth man held out for 11 ballots, when the verdict was agreed to as a compromise.*

At this point, it can be assumed that the sheriff transported Gates from the South Bend city jail to the state penitentiary in Walla Walla.

Two months later, on January 11, 1901, newspaper headlines declared:

A NEW TRIAL
NEW Evidence and Olson's Acquittal
Give Gates Another Chance
Petition to Be Circulated to Dismiss the Gates Case.

Although the trial began on June 24, 1901, Gates's name was not entered in the *Pacific County Prison Record* until July 1. Perhaps he had been returned to the city jail at first. Certainly, he was present at his arraignment on June 19, 1901, at which time he again pleaded "not guilty." In his report of the proceedings, Editor Hazeltine wrote:

> *Gates is apparently enjoying good health and appears more confident of an outcome favorable to him than before, though he is naturally very uncommunicative about the matter.*
>
> *...Star witness for the defense is Lauritz Olson, who was pulling boat for Gates on that memorable night when Beeson was murdered and who was acquitted at the first trial of any complicity in the crime, arrived on the steamer Rival this week from San Francisco. Since last November he has been working as a sailor on coasting vessels holding himself in readiness to respond to the summons to return here to serve as a witness.*
>
> *He has thus disappointed many who predicted that he would never come back, even though his own life could not be placed in jeopardy again.*

Alone in the Docket

There were several major differences between Gates's first and second trials. Now he was at the docket alone, and his erstwhile boat-puller, Lauritz Olson, was a witness on his behalf rather than a fellow defendant. In addition, witnesses Miller and Howard, who had testified at the first trial that they had heard Gates cursing Beeson and proposing to kill him, were not called on. Nor was reference made to Gates's knife with its controversial spots of blood.

Nevertheless, the outcome of the trial differed little from the first one. According to the *Journal*, the defense counsel immediately launched an appeal

> *on the grounds that the court did not permit the defense to impeach the testimony of Charles Stevens by asking him incriminating questions when he was on the stand during the trial, and for the further reason that the testimony is insufficient to convict.*

The same article pointedly commented on the effect to taxpayers that would result from the costs of the Gates case:

> *In all about $6,000. Of this, about $2,000 will be refunded by the state, being the amount of all witness fees in the trial and the witness fees for the prosecution in the preliminary examination. But for this trial, the county current expense fund would be way ahead and a reduction in the tax levy for next year might be expected.*

By July 4, 1902, the headlines concerning Gates had the ring of finality about them:

> *HIS FATE SEALED*
> *Gates Must Serve His Sentence in the Penitentiary*
> *Supreme Court Denies Appeal*
> *Holds that Trial Was Fair*
>
> *Gates wept some on the receipt of the news of the decision adverse to his cause but he rather expected it. The news was broken to him by Mr. Gudgel and Gates thanked him for his hard fight in his behalf. Sheriff Roney has kept Gates pretty closely in the steel cage much to Gates' disgust though he has been treated well. Nevertheless, life in the penitentiary Gates thinks, would have been preferable and he frequently told his jailer, John Shipper, that he would have chosen the penitentiary had he known that he was not to have the liberty of the jail. His health is not of the best and a little hard work may do him good.*
>
> *As to his sentence, the law allows him rebate from his sentence for good behavior for each of the first two years, four months from each of the second two years, and five months for each year thereafter so that he will be able to shorten his sentence to a little less than five years if he is a good prisoner which he probably will be.*

On September 1, 1902, Manuel Gates was returned once more to Walla Walla. This was the second round trip Thomas Roney would make on behalf of Mr. Gates and the eleventh train trip during his tenure as sheriff, thus far, to escort a prisoner out of the county. But it would not be his last.

Honor Among Prisoners?

It was Manuel Gates who shared the prison cell in 1901–02 with Lum You, the Chinese cannery worker who would subsequently be hanged for murder—the only hanging to ever take place in Pacific County. The two men had been in the little jail cell together for more than ten weeks when, on Friday, January 17, 1902, the front-page headline of the *South Bend Journal* proclaimed: "LUM YOU ESCAPED!"

The cell, frequently described as an "iron cage," was just large enough for two bunks. When it was located in Oysterville, it was often left unlocked, giving prisoners access to the jail itself and to the warmth of the woodstove that was located there. They could also make use of a frying pan, coffee pot and a few dishes kept near the stove. Presumably, the outer door was kept locked.

During the first decade of the twentieth century, when the jail was located in the basement of South Bend's new wooden courthouse on Quincy Street, between Montana and Oregon Streets, the arrangement of the unlocked inner cell door and locked outer door apparently continued, although the cell door was locked at night. However, during the months that Lum You was housed there, sympathies for "the little Chinese" ran high, and it was said that both doors were often left unlocked. Lum You, so the story goes, was even encouraged to leave.

On the day he disappeared, the last sighting of Lum You was, according to the *Journal*, "a little after nine a.m., when Amon Markham, the deputy sheriff, built a fire in the jail stove. Mr. Markham says he then saw him in his bunk, and Gates says that after the deputy sheriff left, Lum went out to the stove with his trousers in his hand and dressed and then went back to his cell."

The news article went on to say: "Gates professes to be totally ignorant of how or when Lum escaped though it seems hardly possible, and so small is the jail that it would not be possible for one prisoner to escape unseen by the other."

12

DOING TIME IN THE WAR YEARS

Deserters, Slackers, Wobblies**...*

On August 6, 1914, just ten days after war had been declared in Europe, fifteen-year-old Medora Espy of Oysterville wrote in her diary: "Everybody seems quite excited over the war. They predict the end of the world."

It's difficult to tell who is included in the "everybody" that Medora refers to. Perhaps they were her teenaged friends from the Portland Academy who were visiting in Ocean Park that week, for a few sentences later she wrote: "Foster McGuire dropped in about eight and talked war with me." Foster McGuire was one of the "Ocean Park crowd" whom Medora entertained with boating on the bay and who reciprocated with tennis parties on the courts in Ocean Park.

Elsewhere in Pacific County, the citizens watched and waited as America maintained a stance of nonintervention under President Woodrow Wilson's policy of "armed neutrality." On August 14, the *Chinook Observer* reported that "Miss Eleanor Gile, who is in Europe and on account of the outbreak of

---

* "Slackers" in World War I parlance was synonymous with "draft dodgers."

** "Wobbly" was a derisive term used to describe members of the International Workers of the World (IWW). Established in 1905 in Chicago, the union advocated the overthrow of the wage system and putting workers in control of their own work lives through industrial organization. Many of its members were against American participation in the Great War.

war was causing anxiety to her friends, has been heard from…she is either on her way home or safe in [London]."

A year or so later, on September 3, 1915, there was a report about former Chinook fish-trapper Louis Hauffe, who had returned to his native Germany in 1912:

> *Louis Hauffe…in writing to friends forgets that a great big war is on and that the censors of all nations are busy. We saw one of his effusions this week and all we could make out was: "I am well, tell the boys that they can go." The rest of the letter was blurred out with a rubber stamp.*

"As Usual" at the Jail

As for the county jail in South Bend, life was pretty much as usual. The numbers of prisoners continued to increase each year now that the new, spacious jail was up and running. During 1914, three years after the old two-bunk cell had been abandoned by the county, a record-breaking forty-one names had been entered into the jail book, officially still known as the *Prison Record No. 1 Pacific County*.

The offenses for which people were confined ran the gamut, as they had for many years. In 1914, even while many people were focused on the news from "over there," bookings for grand larceny, petty larceny, insanity, murder, forgery and drunkenness were recorded. The next two years, 1915 and 1916, were much the same.

But in 1917, things began to change. In January, when the Germans resumed unrestricted submarine warfare, there was persistent talk of the United States entering the war after all. On March 30, 1917, the front page of the *South Bend Journal* declared:

> *WAR IMMINENT*
>
> *Therefore we want you to come to the Commercial Club Friday evening March 30 and show your patriotism by endorsing the President in his stand for the integrity and the honor of our country.*
>
> *Also take up the matter of the formation of a Home Guard.*
>
> *C.A. Coulter, Mayor*

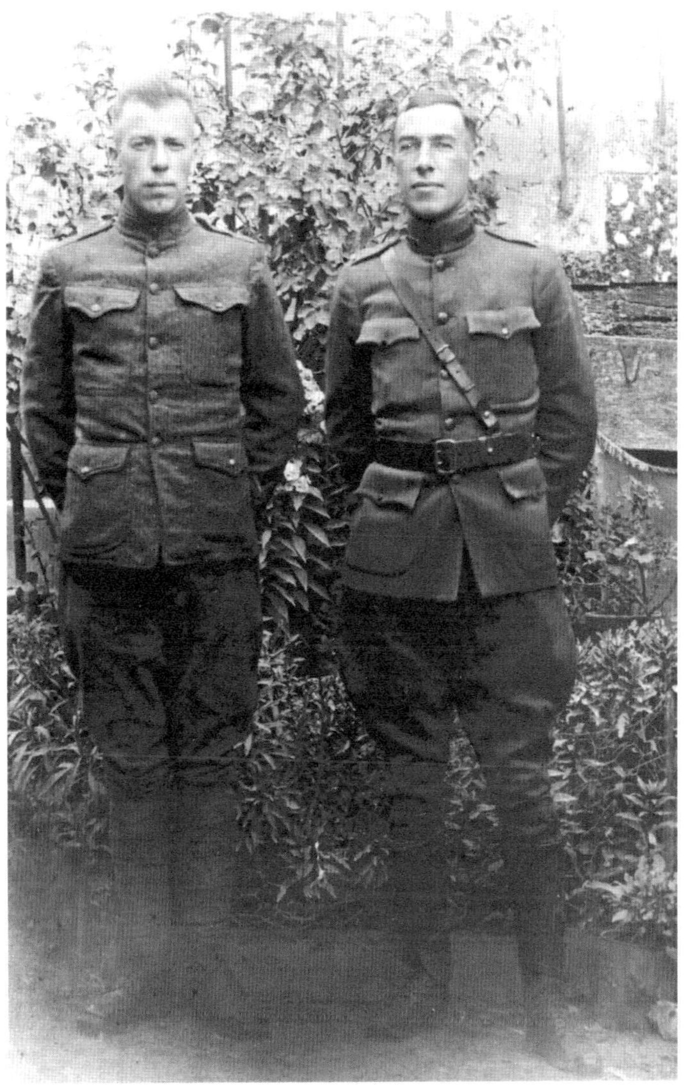

Brothers Rees and Lew Williams of Ilwaco both served during the Great War. They are pictured here in France in 1917. *EEA*.

Exactly one week later, on April 6, 1917, America entered the war on the side of the Allies. President Wilson's administration decided to rely on conscription rather than on voluntary enlistment to raise military manpower for the war. All male citizens and noncitizens between twenty-one and thirty-one (later, between eighteen and forty-five) years of age were required to register at local draft boards.

Rising Patriotism

In the following months, the headlines in Pacific County newspapers concerned "Home Guards" and "Red Cross." Drill schedules were given, and lists of needed bandages and sewing instructions were provided to the women on "the Homefront."

HOW TO STAY AT HOME AND GO TO WAR
Following is a condensation of a stirring patriotic appeal issued last Monday by President Wilson to the people of the United States:

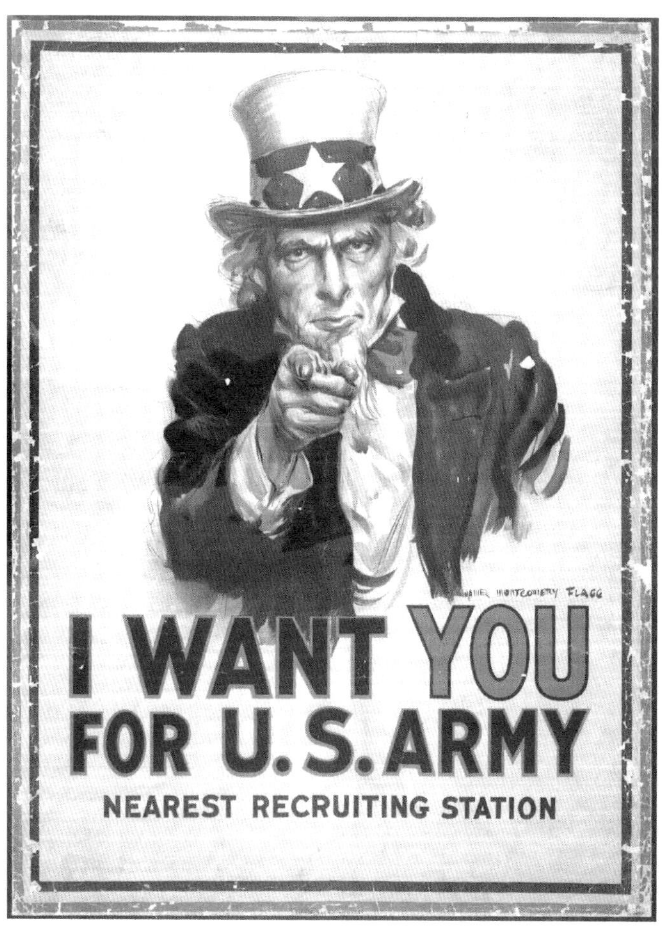

As the United States entered the Great War, four million copies of this iconic poster by James Montgomery Flagg were printed. *Tucker Wachsmuth.*

Supply abundant food for ourselves, our army, our navy and the nations with whom we now have made common cause.

Supply ships by the hundreds to carry to the other side of the sea, submarines or no submarines, what will every day be needed there.

Supply abundant materials out of our fields, and our mines and our factories to clothe and equip our own men and the armies with which we are co-operating in Europe.

Keep the looms and factories there (in Europe) in raw materials.

Provide coal to keep the fires going in ships at sea and in furnaces of hundreds of factories across the sea.

Provide steel out of which to make arms and ammunition, both in America and Europe.

Provide rails for worn out railways back of the fighting fronts.

Provide locomotives and rolling stock.

Provide mules, horses, and cattle for labor and for military service.

Provide everything with which England, France, Italy and Russia have usually supplied themselves.

The men and the women who devote their thought and their energy to these things will be serving the country and conducting the fight for peace and freedom just as truly and just as effectively as the men on the battlefield or in the trenches.

The supreme need of our own nation and of the nations with which we are co-operating is an abundance of supplies, and especially of foodstuffs.

Registration for the draft was to begin on June 5 in Pacific County. The newspapers were full of dire warnings:

SLACKERS TO BE SENT TO PEN

Failure to Register Constitutes a Crime

...A willful neglect or refusal of anyone between the ages of 21 and 31, inclusive, to register on that date is a crime punishable by imprisonment for one year and all "slackers" will be duly prosecuted.

On a more positive note, it was reported that thousands of automobile owners through the state of Washington were tendering the use of their "machines" to carry young men to and from registration sites. In addition, banks and mercantile establishments were lending their entire clerical staffs for service on June 5—a date which had been declared a holiday by Governor Lister, set aside for the purpose of registration.

The following week's *Journal*'s headlines reflected the county's growing patriotism:

1316 MEN REGISTER FOR SELECTIVE DRAFT
THREE AUSTRIANS DECLINE TO REGISTER.
NO OTHERS OBJECT.
Twenty-Three Listed as Alien Enemies. One Colored Man of Military Age in the County.
Aliens Register. Conscription Day Passes with No Sign of Trouble.
So far as known there are no slackers in Pacific County and, except in the

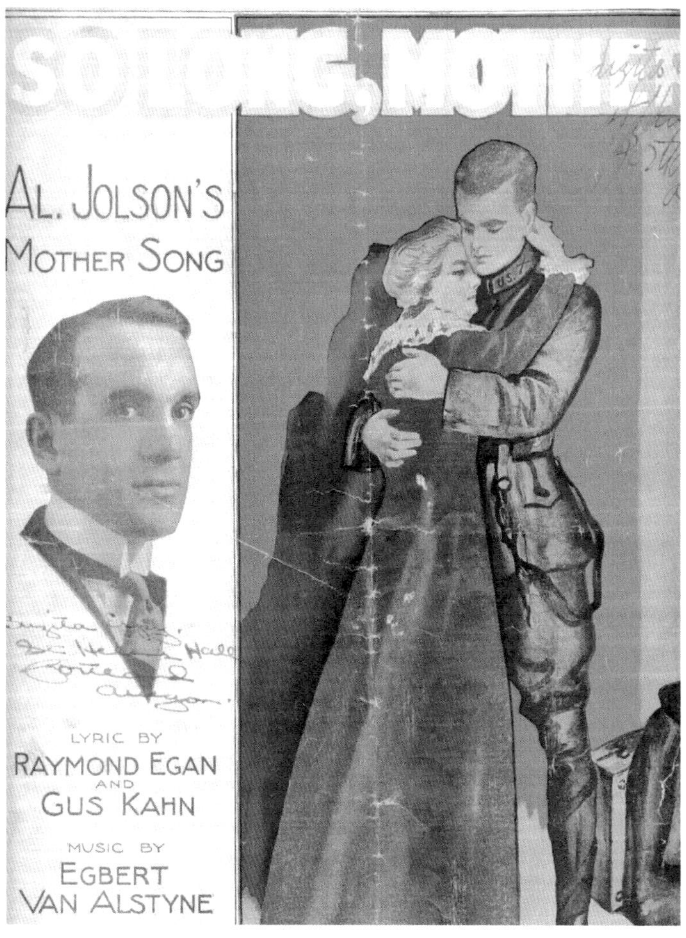

The sheet music business flourished during World War I with almost ten thousand patriotic songs published and sung in family parlors and music halls. *EFA*.

> *case of three Austrians in Brix logging camp, no man of military age under the conscription act objected to registering. There are 1316 registered and the whole matter did not cost the government one cent thanks to the public spirit and patriotism of the volunteer registration officers and others who gave the free use of their autos etc. Of this number the registration cards indicate that 635 are not entitled to exemption on any ground and 681 may possibly be exempted on account of government service, physical disability or on account of dependent relatives. There is just one colored man of military age in the county and he lives in Raymond. There are 341 aliens besides 23 Germans not naturalized who are classified as alien enemies. As for the Austrians who declined to register, Sheriff Turner has reported them to the federal authorities in Astoria where their cases can be more conveniently handled...*

In July, it was announced that Pacific County had to furnish 142 soldiers. By September, Company M of the Third Provisional Regiment, Washington State Guards, had formed, and the first quota of 57 "soldier boys" were given a farewell reception at the Commercial Club in South Bend. They were then treated by the management of the Lyric Theater to see Mary Pickford in *The Poor Little Rich Girl.*

War-Related Offenses

The first jail book notation regarding a war-related offense was on October 23, 1917. "Arthur Stevens, 26, five feet, eight inches, brown eyes, light brown hair, weighing 140 pounds" was from Hudson, New York. He was charged with "vagrancy" and was put in jail on the authority of Judge Wright. After serving five days of a fifteen-day sentence, Stevens was "turned in [to] Camp Lewis* as deserter on October 18, 1917. Deserted from Columbia Co. New York."

* Camp Lewis, located south of Tacoma on the Nisqually Plain, opened on September 1, 1917. Immediately, the Ninety-first Division, under commanding officer Major General Henry A. Greene (1856–1921), arrived and launched into rigorous training. The Ninety-first served with honor in France, and as they fought, the Thirteenth Division trained at Camp Lewis, but then World War I ended and the division dissolved. Construction of the permanent Fort Lewis began in 1927, and in 2010, it merged with neighboring McChord Air Force Base to form Joint Base Lewis-McChord.

About the same time (though no date was entered), one Go. Gun from China was also booked as a deserter from the National Army. He was described as "30, short and stout, with black hair and black eyes." On November 4, he was taken to Camp Lewis as a "deserter from Pacific County Local Board Quota."

The next five men to be booked as deserters were also foreign born. Constandenos G. Leffas and Panagis Agelopulos were both from Greece; Frank Brano and Mike Padalok were from Austria; and Walter Baltus was from Russia. All were deserters from the Pacific County Local Board, except for Padalok, who was from Ontonagon County, Michigan. Their ages ranged from twenty-three to thirty years, and each was taken to Camp Lewis by Justice W.C. Wright or by another officer of the court.

On December 17, twenty-two-year-old Henry Hamreus, a San Francisco native, was booked as a deserter from Grays Harbor County. The next day, Otto Nykanon, a Finland native, was listed as a deserter from Pacific County. They, too, were escorted to Camp Lewis.

The last two entries for 1917 in the old jail book were made on December 27. Rudolph Chouble, alias John Raine, from Russia and Frank Berger from Austria were both held "for investigation as slackers." Both men were twenty-one years of age, and on January 22, 1918, they were taken to federal authorities in Seattle by W.C. Wright.

In addition to the eleven men who were actually found to be deserters or slackers, twelve men were picked up for investigation and immediately released on advice that "[they] had not been called for serving." About half were foreign born, but there is no indication of whether they were U.S. citizens.

What does seem apparent is that the Pacific County sheriff and his deputies were practicing due diligence with regard to seeking out those who were not doing their patriotic duty.

Wobblies Jailed

During 1917, a record one hundred names were entered in the jail book—the greatest number of any year recorded in *Prison Record No. 1 Pacific County*. The year 1918 would be the final full one reported, and until November 11, when the armistice was signed, transgressions related to the war effort continued to dominate the book's pages.

On February 12 and 13, respectively, Peter Williamson, alias Peter Williamson Merta [*sic*], and Emil Jaki, both natives of Finland, were arrested for posting IWW cards in public places. Williamson/Merta was sentenced to fifteen days from February 18, 1918. On March 5, 1918, he was "taken by Geo. N. Patterson, Immigration Inspector for deportation." Jaki, on the other hand, was held until March 3 for investigation with regard to his registration. No notation was made in the jail book concerning his subsequent fate.

The February 22 issue of the *South Bend Journal*, however, had this to say:

> *MURTI, IWW LEADER JAILED*
> *15 Days Under Vagrancy Charge. Had Seditious Literature.*
> *Justice Dorrien of Raymond last Monday sentenced Peter Williamson Murti, the IWW leader, to fifteen days in jail for vagrancy though it was really for the seditious literature he was distributing. His associates Emil Jaki and Edward Bradbury, were continued under $100 bail. Mark Litchman of Seattle, the IWW attorney, defended Murti, is a Finn and was refused citizenship on account of his anarchistic utterances.*

Perhaps the two men were lucky. The IWW (International Workers of the World) was a union whose members were sometimes called "Wobblies." Many IWW members opposed United States participation in the Great War, as it was then called, and some of their propaganda was considered seditious under the Espionage and Sedition Acts of 1917 and 1918. Worst case scenario situations could lead to prosecution and punishments of up to twenty years' imprisonment and a $10,000 fine.

On February 19, German-born Theodore F. Simbill was arrested for failure to register as an alien enemy. In the jail book column headed "By What Authority Committed" was written: "On investigation by Federal Authorities." About Simbill, the *Journal* reported:

> *SIMBALL ARRESTED AS ALIEN ENEMY*
> *F.T. Simball First Claimed American Citizenship, Now Australian*
> *F.T. Simball the local manager of the McCormick Lumber Co.'s yard is now in the county jail having been arrested by Sheriff Turner as an alien who had failed to register. Mr. Turner says that he called Simball's attention to the fact that he had failed to register last week and Simball said he had taken out citizenship papers in South Dakota and Mr. Turner wired back to the address he gave but got no reply. Later Simball phoned Postmaster Smith and said that he wanted to register but it was then too*

late as the registration period had closed and he had sent the books into headquarters. Simball's desire to register did not fadge [match] *with the claim that he was a citizen and he was arrested.*

According to his story he went to Australia some thirty years ago from Germany and there renounced allegiance to Germany and became a citizen of Australia. Twenty years ago he had located in Lake Preston S. Dakota and says he thought that he had completed his citizenship there. He has retained John T. Welsh to defend him.

Simball is reputed to have shown his German sympathies very strongly early in the history of the war but has been more discreet of late. He tried to give bail but the law provides no bail for the offense of being an alien enemy and he then argued that he ought to be let out because of his connection with the McCormick Lumber Co.

Much will depend on the report of County Attorney O'Phelan as to whether he is released or interned.

Apparently, O'Phelan's report did not bode well for Simball. According to the jail book, he was "Taken by U.S. Marshal Fleetwood on February 27."

Patriotic Fervor

In March 1918, patriotic fervor continued unabated in Pacific County, at least as reflected in the jail record. Diligent attention was paid to "deserters and slackers," and full cooperation was given to military personnel and to other agencies that might have jurisdictional authority over a draft dodger or runaway.

On March 6, Verner Holms, a native of Finland, was "held for investigation as slacker. Registrar Juab County, Eureka, Utah Local Board there advise certificate is forgery." Holms was taken to a court commission in Chehalis, Washington, on March 13.

Three days following Holms's arrest, W.J. Christian was "jailed on the authority of Meredith Jones, 1st Lt. Sig. R.C.A.S. Comdg. Sq. Christian was "Put in at the request of Lieut. Swanson to be held until trial by U.S. Army." On March 12, he was "taken by Military Authorities."

The even more serious-sounding charges of "Criminal Anarchy" were brought against two men arrested on March 24. Chas. Brown of Brookfield, New York, and Fred Lowry of San Francisco, California, were both described in great detail.

Brown (37), was five feet, ten inches tall, with dark brown hair and eyes and of medium complexion. Further information given: "Weight 140; Slender; Teeth—poor, decayed, badly discolored. Red Beard. IWW—joined [in] Centralia 8 months ago. Index and middle finger off."

Lowry (32), was five feet, five inches tall, with light brown hair, blue eyes and a fair complexion. Additionally: "Weight 155, square shoulders, well built, Eyes blue, nose been broken, Teeth good, two gold crowns in front. Laborer. Iron work, logging camps—arrested at North Yakima and Pasco 1917." Both Brown and Lowry were "Bound over to next term of Superior Court $500 bail."

Meanwhile, in Ilwaco, April 2 had been declared "Patriotic Day" by the mayor. All businesses and schools were to be closed from noon on. The *Journal* reported:

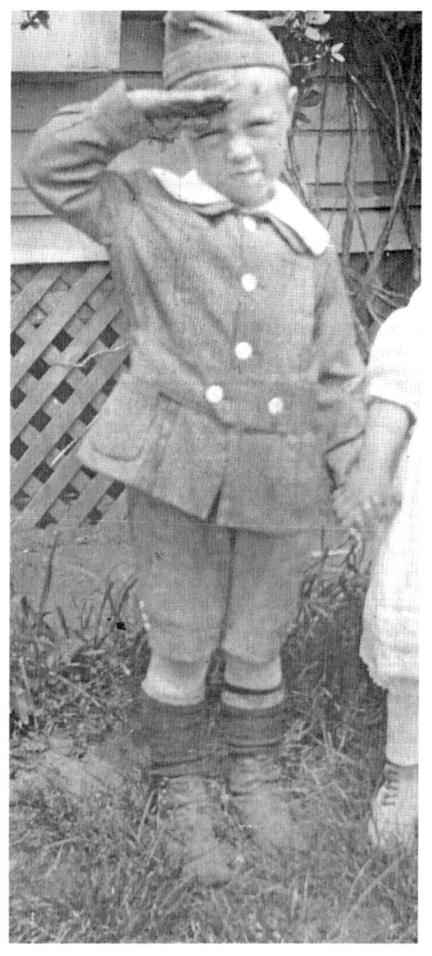

Five-year-old Brongwyn "Bronk" Kahrs Williams salutes passing soldiers at the Armistice Day Anniversary Parade in Ilwaco on November 11, 1919. *EEA*.

> *Col. Ellis commander of the Coast Artillery will be over from Ft. Stevens with a band and will make an address. Col. Leader has been invited also. There will be a parade, a flag raising, and all citizens will be asked to salute the flag.*
>
> *The Council of Defense has appointed a vigilance committee and today this committee, assisted by loyal Finns, are making the rounds of the town and asking every person to sign a declaration of their allegiance to the U.S. Flag. They mean business.*
>
> *Disloyal utterances principally by Finn socialists and secret meetings have aroused the loyal citizens. Refusal to help in patriotic work and refusal to permit children to wear Red Cross buttons have stirred up a strong*

feeling. The best citizens in town are on the committees. They include J.D. McGowan, L.D. Williams, Mayor Hanson, Cap Beyer, E.M.E. and P.L. Sinclair, Ed Wood, E.T. Hawkins, Matt Saarela, Mose Lugnet, Eric Hilley and many others.

Quick action has been advised as some socialists are said to be leaving town. More than 100 men met Monday night and organized a vigilance committee. They will tolerate no slackers. Well known socialists attempted to enter the meeting last night and were asked to leave.

Two arrests were made in May with specific reference to war-related concerns. Mike Reason was held for investigation and taken to Camp Lewis as "delinquent on draft U.S. Army." Aloyzy Pierog was held "for Federal Authorities" under a "Presidential Warrant" with the notation that "U.S. Marshal Fleetwood received this prisoner on Presidential Warrant in June 1918."

The presidential warrant referred to in the case of Aloyzy Pierog allowed the arrest and internment in army camps of suspicious enemy aliens. These arrests were done under the authority of U.S. marshals rather than through the U.S. court system. The notation in the jail book concerning Pierog is the only specific reference to the presidential warrant, although a number of foreign-born men were taken to Camp Lewis or other military bases after a short stay at the Pacific County Jail, an indicator that the presidential warrant had been in use.

During the final six months of the war—from June until the war's end—seven more war-related arrests were made. Sometimes, very little information was noted in the register other than the eventual transfer of the prisoner from Pacific County:

Napoleon Bowles—Held for Local Board.
Geo. H. Smith—Held for California Authorities on Warrant of Arrest. Taken by H.R. Youngblood, Undersheriff Stockton, San Joaquin County, Cal.
Sheldon Frank Cordell—Held for Department of Justice—waiting for Induction Papers—Taken to Camp Lewis for Army.
Mike Gerow—Held for investigation regarding draft.
Robert Smith—Held for investigation regarding draft.
Louie Marich—Held for investigation with regard to disloyal remarks—Released on request by Department of Justice.
August Suaze—Failing to file Questionnaire. Sent to Camp Lewis.

Joyful News

The Armistice, agreed on at 5:00 a.m. on November 11, 1918, came into effect at 11:00 a.m., Paris time. Citizens of Pacific County, like those throughout the state and nation, were jubilant. The November 15 *South Bend Journal* gave an account of the celebration at the county seat:

> *CITY CELEBRATES A WORLD'S PEACE*
> *Confirmed Report of Peace Brings Joy Unlimited to Everyone*
> *GREATEST EVENT IN HISTORY*
> *Streets Crowded with Elaborately Decorated Autos—Speeches Made*
> *Kaiser Hung and Burned in Effigy—Memorable Event*
> *Sunday, Oct. 13th, at 3:39 a.m. witnessed the first demonstration for peace. Whistles blew, bells rang and generally everyone made demonstration. Everyone knew that it was about time peace came even though it was later learned that the report was false.*
>
> *Then on Thursday, Nov. 7th, the report came that seemed so authentic that all over the nation there was rejoicing and great demonstration, even though the governmental heads gave no confirmation.*
>
> *Again on Monday, Nov. 11th came the word, this time confirmed from Washington that the armistice had been signed...So on confirmation of the report, the employees of the Willapa Harbor Iron Works, who have been employed on government jobs for a long time, making logging jacks and blocks and other logging tools, started out in force upon the street with cans and a circular saw, making all the noise possible. People generally were afraid to enter into the process lest it might prove another hoax, but the report being confirmed, the town fell into line. Whistles blew, bells rang, blanks were fired and every other exhibition of joy entered into...*
>
> *...The streets were filled. Flags were everywhere. Everyone was rejoicing. The South Bend division had a coffin on a small wagon, labeled "For the Kaiser." The men had their hats off all through the march and if any forgot they were promptly knocked off for them...*
>
> *...The city had the appearance of a great carnival. Children were dressed in various costumes and draped with the national colors, flags were carried, confetti thrown, sparklers burned, firecrackers and revolver blanks were fired.*

Except for two arrests unrelated to the war—for larceny on November 20 and for bootlegging on December 10—there were no further notations in the jail book until January 10, 1919, and none at all that referred to the nation's or the state's or the county's recent preoccupation with the war effort. The Great War was over. The world was once again safe for democracy. And if the jail book is to be believed, there was no crime in Pacific County for an entire month!

Wobbly Aftermath of War

On November 11, 1919, during a parade celebrating the first anniversary of Armistice Day, a violent and bloody incident occurred in Centralia, Washington, in the county adjacent to Pacific. The conflict was between the American Legion and workers who belonged to the Industrial Workers of the World, the union also called the "IWW" or "Wobblies."

Known as the Centralia Massacre, it resulted in six deaths, a number of wounded, multiple prison terms and an ongoing and bitter dispute over motivations and events that precipitated the occurrence. The

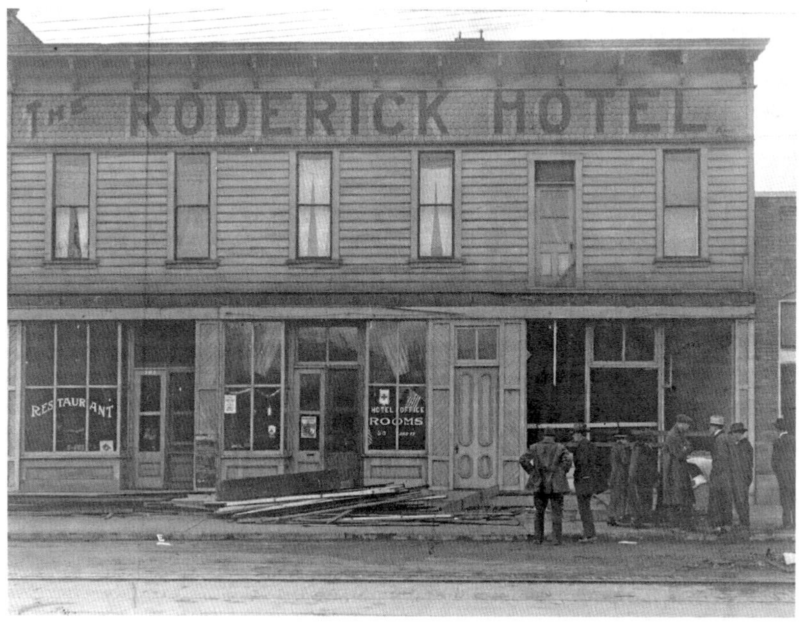

Six died in the Centralia Massacre. It began at the Roderick Hotel during the Armistice Day Parade in November 1919. *Walter P. Reuther Library.*

ramifications included a trial that attracted national media attention and a deep-rooted enmity between the local American Legion and the Wobblies that has persisted into the twenty-first century.

The massacre was the culmination of years of bad blood between the two groups. Both Centralia and the neighboring town of Chehalis had a large number of World War I veterans with robust chapters of the legion, as well as a large number of IWW members, some of whom were also war veterans.

The trouble had started as early as 1914 with low-level harassment on both sides. When the IWW attempted to open a hall for the use of its members, it was stopped by the vigorous objections of the legion. The situation between the two groups continued to worsen, and when the IWW hall was finally situated in the old Roderick Hotel, it vowed never to be evicted again.

A Centralia lawyer, Elmer Smith, a pacifist and sympathetic to the IWW, tried to broker a peaceful arrangement between the two groups. He was unsuccessful in his attempts at mediation.

Sides Disagree

To celebrate Armistice Day, the town leaders of Centralia planned a combined parade with the neighboring city of Chehalis, to be followed by festivities. The full contingent of both Centralia and Chehalis American Legion Posts, along with other civic organizations, were to march in the parade. As the parade unevenly wound its way through the town, the Centralia contingent, which was beginning to press up on the Chehalis group, paused just before reaching the site of the hall. As the gap began to open back up, legionnaire Warren Grimm turned to address his Chehalis troops and uttered the command, "Halt. Close up." At which point the front ranks began to mark time. From that point, there is no agreement between the sides about what transpired next.

According to the American Legion, this realigning of ranks presented Wobbly Eugene Barnetta opportunity for a direct shot at Grimm. The bullet from Barnett's high-powered rifle caught Grimm in the chest, passing through his body and eviscerating him where he stood. Legionnaire Arthur McElfresh, standing nearby, was next. Hit in the brain by a .22-caliber bullet allegedly fired from Seminary Hill over five hundred yards away, he was killed instantly. As the mortally wounded Grimm was dragged to the sidewalk, additional shots rained down on the unarmed legionnaires. At this point, caught between dying in the open and charging their ambushers, the legionnaires stormed the Roderick and surrounding buildings.

In contrast, the IWW claims that, as the legionnaires paused, a small group, possibly with Grimm's complicity, broke off and charged the Roderick with the intent to repeat the events of the previous year. When this initial group broke down the doors, the Wobblies, fearing for their lives, fired in self-defense. As the first group of legionnaires fell back in disarray, Grimm was gut shot in the entrance of the hall leading a second group of attackers. McElfresh was then shot by John Doe Davis, one of the few Wobblies never to be captured.

Evidence seemed to support both sides. Most of the witnesses supporting the IWW's version of events were members of various unions. Most of those supporting the American Legion's version were war veterans and local businessmen sympathetic to the legion.

By the time the Wobblies were captured and taken to the local jail, four American Legion members had been killed, and five had been wounded. Elmer Smith, who did not participate in the actual massacre, was also rounded up and incarcerated. As evening fell, a vigilante mob began to form outside the jailhouse.

Wobbly Martyr

Suddenly, the power grid at the municipal electric power plant was turned off, plunging the town into darkness. Whether this was accomplished by a lone individual supporting the growing mob or was someone acting under the direction of Centralia's sheriff remains another disputed issue.

Under cover of darkness, the mob seized Wesley Everest. Although Everest's personal identity was unknown, with some believing him to be IWW leader Britt Smith, he was "positively recognized" as the Wobbly who had shot and killed legionnaires Ben Cassangranda and Dale Hubbard. Everest was the only Wobbly taken from the jail. The subsequent details surrounding the death of Everest are as hotly and violently contested as the death of Warren Grimm.

The IWW claims that the mob proceeded to beat Everest, caving in his teeth with a rifle butt and castrating the helpless man. They then carried him to the bridge on Mellon Street, tied a noose around his neck and threw him over the edge three times, the final toss breaking his neck and killing him. That bridge was subsequently known as the "Hangman's Bridge."

Centralia's town records make no mention of the beating, let alone any castration. The coroner's report lists the cause of death as "suicide." Centralia's prosecutor, Herman Allen, claimed that he would prosecute the lynching if any evidence was brought forth. However, none of the vigilantes was ever charged.

Unfortunately, the coroners of Centralia or nearby Chehalis did not examine Everest's body. As a consequence, there was no physical evidence to support either position. However, considering the mood of the mob that night and what Everest had done, Everest was almost certainly beaten and hanged. He was eventually buried in an unmarked grave. Everest became one of the union's best known martyrs.

Then, as the hunt for escaped Wobblies continued over the next few days, deputy sheriff John M. Haney was killed on November 15. This final fatality was thought to have been caused by friendly fire. The captured Wobblies were charged with murder, and the resulting trial was held in Montesano, Grays Harbor County. After a trial that received national coverage, eight Wobblies were convicted of second-degree murder, two were acquitted (including Elmer Smith) and two had all charges against them dropped. Those convicted were sentenced to prison terms of twenty-five to forty years, far in excess of the standard ten-year sentence of the day.

As time passed and passions cooled, a public campaign spearheaded by Elmer Smith was eventually able to secure the release of those Wobblies still in prison. Although their convictions were never overturned, all of the remaining Wobblies, save Ray Becker, were paroled in 1931 and 1932. Continuing to maintain his innocence, Becker refused parole and was eventually pardoned in 1939, with his sentence commuted to time served.

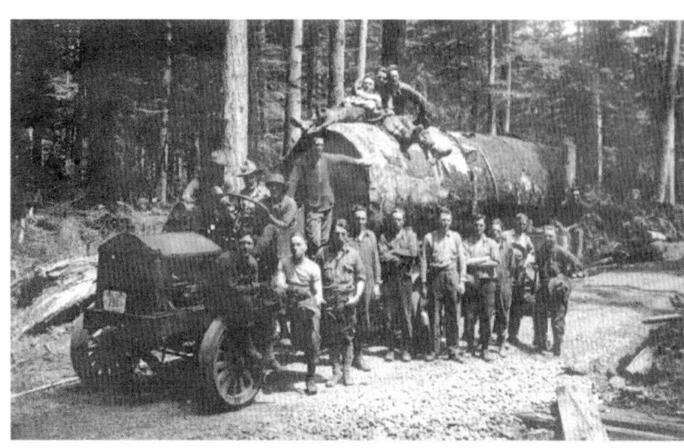

Spruce Division soldier-loggers pose with a spruce log being trucked to a nearby mill in Pacific County, Washington. *Courtesy Bob Swanson.*

The Spruce Division

Sitka spruce (*Picea sitchensis*), the fourth-largest conifer in the world, grows in an approximate fifty-mile strip along the Pacific Coast from Northern California to Kodiak Island, Alaska. It grows best on moist, sandy or even swampy soils, thriving in areas of heavy rainfall and attaining a height of two hundred feet with a fifteen-foot diameter. Spruce trees are as familiar to Pacific County residents as sword ferns and salal.

At the turn of the twentieth century, spruce was used primarily for items such as berry boxes, pleasure boats, ironing boards, caskets and refrigerator wood. During World War I, it was discovered to have the necessary properties of toughness, lightness and resiliency to make it ideal for building airplanes.

With that end in mind, Brigadier General Brice P. Disque was assigned the job of increasing the production of spruce lumber. He set up headquarters in the Yeon Building in Portland, Oregon, and immediately organized the U.S. Army Spruce Production Division—his answer to the wartime shortage of loggers due to IWW strikes, the draft and the lure of better wages in other wartime industries.

In most instances, Spruce Division soldiers were employed by civilian companies. These companies had contracts to supply the government with spruce, some of which went to Great Britain, France and Italy to help finance the operation. Spruce Division soldiers earned a standard industry wage, though each man actually received only his army pay; the private employers paid any difference to the government.

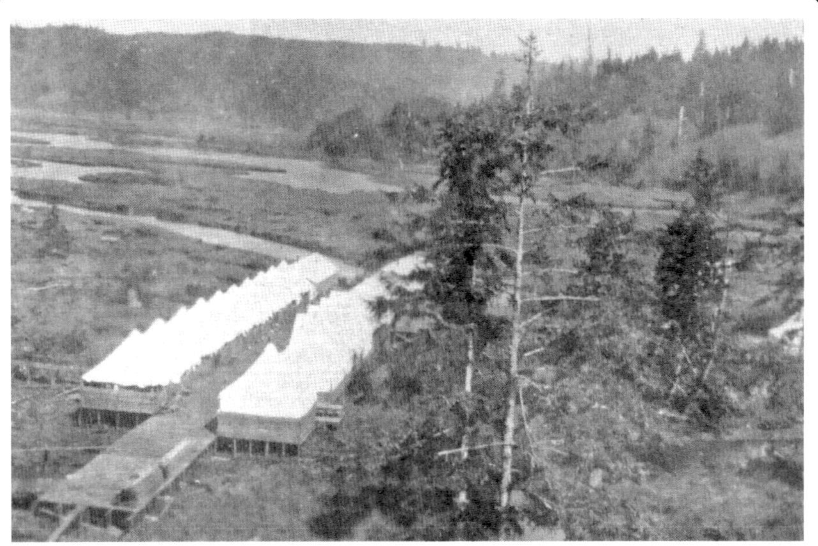

Above: With its rows of wooden-based tents, Camp 4A on the Naselle River was typical of the U.S. Army's Spruce Division logging camps. *Appelo Archives Center.*

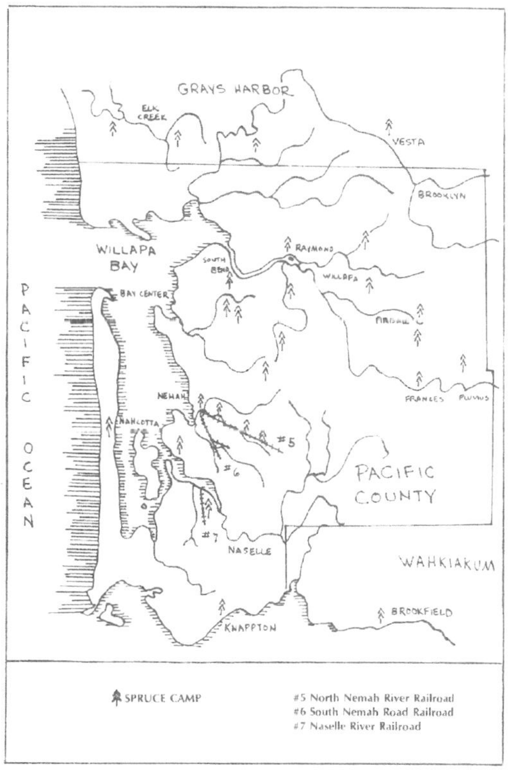

Right: At peak production, 234 Spruce Camps were established in the Northwest, with 21 scattered across the Willapa Hills in Pacific County, Washington. *Larry Weathers Drawing, PCHS.*

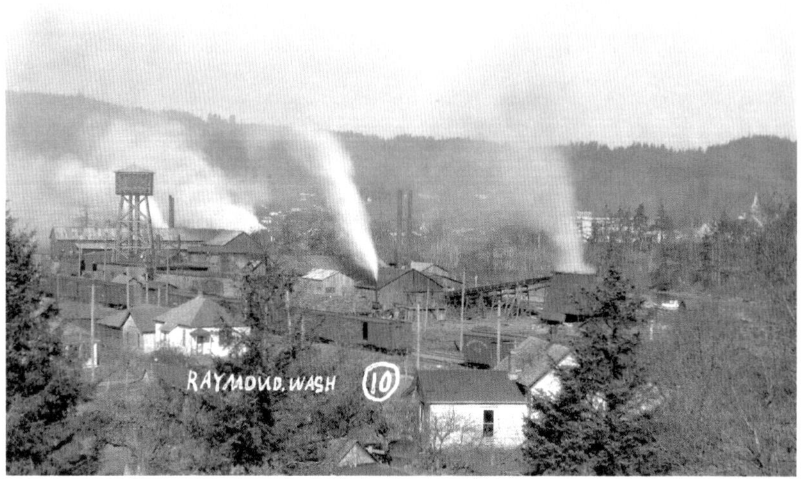

The Case Shingle and Lumber Company, Raymond, was one of six Pacific County mills producing perfect, straight-grained, long-length lumber for the Spruce Division. *Murfin family collection.*

Using Civilian Camps

Under orders from the army, the civilian camps were "cleaned up." Poor latrines were condemned, cookhouses were inspected and bathing facilities were built. A hospital was maintained at Vancouver, but elsewhere civilian hospitals were used as the men were scattered throughout the Northwest.

General Disque established five production districts in Washington and Oregon: Yaquina Bay, Lewis and Clark, Aberdeen, Clallam and Raymond. A total of 234 camps were opened, and at the peak of production, 26,122 enlisted men and 1,027 officers lived in them. There were approximately 1,700 support personnel attached to the division, including chaplains, motor transport drivers, medical corps, field clerks and supply quartermasters.

The twenty-one camps in Pacific County were spread out across the Willapa Hills. There were four on the Nemah River, two on the Palix, two near Firdale, two on Church Road and one each in Frankfort,

Nahcotta, Naselle, South Nemah River, Pluvius, Frances, Willapa, South Fork, Raymond, Ward Creek and South Bend.

Perfect, straight-grained lumber of long lengths was required in the manufacture of airplanes. After studying the best ways to saw spiral-grained spruce, instructions were given to local mills. Six mills in Pacific County and ten in Grays Harbor County were put to work, but eventually it was decided that their progress was too slow and the process too costly.

The dilemma was solved by erecting what was known as the "Cutup Plant" at Vancouver Barracks, Washington. Some four thousand soldiers were employed there, working three eight-hour shifts. A twenty-four-unit dry kiln was also added.

Delivering logs to the mills was another problem faced by the Spruce Division. Roads near the camps were poor or nonexistent, and the ever-present rain slowed the progress of logging shows. It was too difficult to get full-size logs out of the forest, so it was decided to rive (split) them into quarters using mauls and wedges. Horses could then haul them to an existing county or newly constructed road, where they were loaded on trucks and delivered to the mills or taken to the nearest railroad spur.

The Answer: Railroads

Ultimately, the division decided that many of the transportation problems between the woods and the mills could be solved by the construction of a system of railroads. By this means, whole logs could be transported from the woods to the sawmills. The construction program called for the completion of seven railroads in western Washington and six for coastal Oregon.

In the spring of 1918, as soon as the weather allowed, the project began. The first railroad was built in Clallam County and the next in Grays Harbor County on Elk River. Three more railroads were built in Pacific County.

No. 5 on the north Nemah road was started in June 1918 and had eight miles of main line with a short spur. Its terminus was the town of Nemah. Work was proceeding on an extension when the armistice halted it.

No. 6 on the south Nemah road was started in August and consisted of two miles of main line and a one-and-a-half-mile spur.

No. 7 on the Naselle River had two miles of narrow-gauge rail and was also started in June.

The U.S. Army Spruce Production Division operated for only one year from November 15, 1917, to November 11, 1918, and is considered an "anomaly unique in the annals of American history." During that time, spruce production jumped from 2,887,623 to 22,145,823 board feet monthly, the largest percentage being from Washington. According to some estimates, that was a 5,000 percent increase in the production of aircraft lumber in a little less than a year.

On November 12, 1918, the day following the armistice, tree falling on all government operations ceased. Soldiers were shipped to Vancouver, where they reverted to regular army life. Mills, railroads, camp supplies and downed timber were all liquidated. The Spruce Division had accomplished exactly what it set out to do by providing millions of board feet of needed wood for the war effort, and now that the war was over, its job was done.

13

OF TEMPERANCE AND PROHIBITION

Drunk and disorderly…

As far as is known, the first "ardent spirits" in Pacific County were brought by HMS *Chatham* under the command of Lieutenant William Broughton. On October 20, 1792, the ship was stranded on Peacock Spit near the mouth of the Columbia. Although the crew was able to get it away with the next tide, it was apparently in the area long enough to offer a tot or two of rum to the friendly Chinook Indians.

At least, this was surmised by pioneer author/historian James G. Swan in his 1857 book, *The Northwest Coast, or Three Years' Residence in Washington Territory*. In January 1853, while he was living on Shoalwater Bay just north of Stony Point, he had a visit from a group of Chinooks, including Carcumcum, sister of the famed Chief Comcomly. She told him of a girlhood memory:

> *They drank some rum out of a wine-glass—how much she did not recollect; but she did recollect that they got drunk, and were so scared at the strange feeling that they ran into the woods and hid till they were sober. The rest, who did not get any rum, thought they had gone crazy or had turned foolish…Old Carcumcum said they had but a very little rum from the traders until the settlement of Astoria* [1811, by Americans], *when they began to get a little more used to it…*

Wet versus Dry

By the time of Swan's stay and the beginnings of settlement in Pacific County, the procurement of alcohol seemed to be no problem. Within a year or two after its founding in 1854, for instance, Oysterville was reputed to have three saloons. There wouldn't be a school or church for some years, but alcohol, seemingly, was a necessity in the lives of the men who converged on the "oyster treasure" in Shoalwater Bay. Predictably, where there were drinkers, there were also those who preached abstinence, and Oysterville, like other burgeoning pioneer settlements, had its share of both imbibers and teetotalers.

Just two years after Swan's visit with Old Carcumcum, the second session of Washington's territorial legislature circulated a petition among the four thousand people of Washington Territory proposing a law to prohibit the manufacture and sale of liquor. The proposed legislation failed, but Pacific County's vote was eighteen in favor of prohibition, fourteen against. The citizens of the county would remain divided on the issue for many years to come.

Arrests related to liquor are few and far between in the first twenty years of the jail book listings, with none at all recorded until February 27, 1888, two years after the record began. Twenty-eight-year-old Chu Chu Lee, described as an "opium fiend," served ten days for selling liquor to an Indian. By then, the territorial legislature had passed a local option law. It allowed residents of a town or precinct to petition for elections on the licensing of liquor sales within their own community. On June 28, 1886, a local option election had been held in seven precincts of Pacific County, The total vote was 274 for licensing and 116 against. North Cove, Bay Center and Oysterville were unanimously for, South Bend was 31 to 3 for, Springbrook was 17 to 2 for and Willapa was 70 to 26 for. Only Wallicut was against licensing of liquor, with a 57-to-35 vote. By the time of Chu Chu Lee's arrest, the wets were clearly in the ascendency in Pacific County.

No doubt, Lee's arrest was indicative of the continuing concern over "wild Indians and liquor" and was the same issue that had prompted the territorial legislature's attempted action thirty-three years previously. Though that 1855 proposal had not become law, the legislature did pass a law against selling intoxicating drink to Indians. However, no jail sentence was required for that offense, an oversight many believed showed that a significant part of the territorial economy was involved in the liquor traffic with Indians. It is curious that Lee was arrested at all—unless, of course, there was more to the story than the jail book indicates.

Many are the stories about the imaginative ways people got around the law. A Bruceport merchant, for instance, was said to have amassed a fortune of more than a quarter million dollars by selling pencils for a dime! There was, of course, a gimmick connected with the sales. The purchaser of every pencil was entitled to a trip to the back room, where a barrel of "tanglefoot" was kept—the concoction so named because a beginner could handle only a sip. Customers included Indians, of course, since the law did not forbid the sale of pencils.

Another old story concerned a cannon located near Stony Point. When it boomed, many men within hearing distance paused in their work to do some counting. Each shot indicated that a barrel of whiskey was ready and waiting. Despite such elaborate ruses, however, arrests were occasionally made.

On June 13, 1889, John Doe (47), from Sweden, described as a hard drinker, was arrested for being drunk and disorderly. His was the twelfth name entered into the jail book. He served one week as a guest of the county and was discharged by the authority of the committing magistrate.

The controversy between "wets" and "drys" continued unabated into the twentieth century. The "Sabbath Law," which prohibited the sale of liquor on Sundays, was routinely overlooked in towns and cities that were predominately anti-prohibition. National temperance organizations such as the Woman's Christian Temperance Union (formed in 1874) and the Anti-Saloon League (formed in 1893) had a strong presence throughout the county. Local newspapers, too, got into the act.

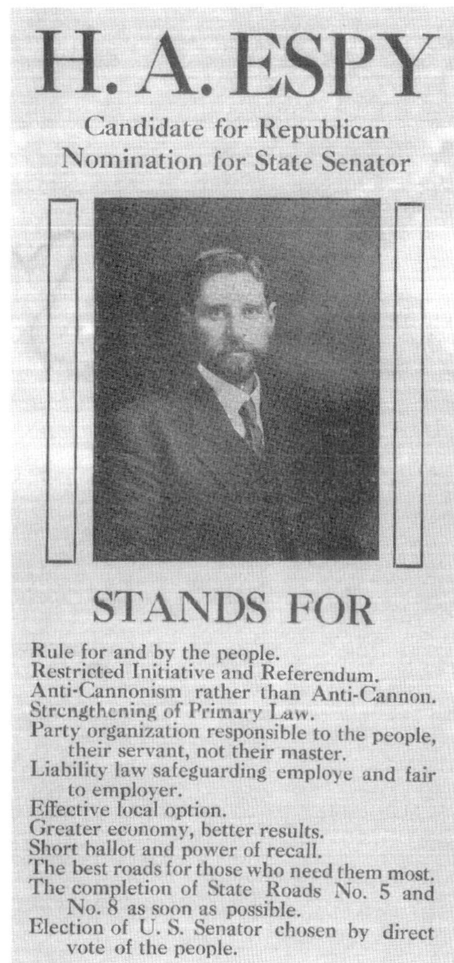

H.A. Espy, representing Pacific and Wahkiakum Counties, won handily as the "local option" candidate in the 1910 election for Washington State senator. *EEA*.

A Matter of Emphasis

In 1907, the Pacific County Bartender's Union held its first annual picnic at Tokeland. Referring to the bartenders as "Knights of the White Apron," the South Bend *Willapa Harbor Pilot* reported that the event was held on a Sunday, when saloons were closed by state law.

The boats *Shamrock* and *Reliable* transported the bartenders to and from the picnic site, the weather was pleasant and everyone reputedly enjoyed the day-long barbecue. Among the activities that day was a baseball game between teams from Raymond and South Bend. The South Bend team won 6–3. No mention was made of alcoholic beverages or of any other liquid refreshment, but a picture of the event in the summer 1983 *Sou'wester* shows that beer was not only available but also being enjoyed.

The story was buried on page seven of the *Pilot*. On the other hand, earlier in the year, an article concerning the Sixth Annual meeting of the Pacific County chapter of the Woman's Christian Temperance Union (WCTU) at the South Bend Methodist Episcopal Church was given a prominent front-page location, making it obvious where the sentiments of the newspaper lay. By running the WCTU story two columns wide, the full length of the page and naming every good lady in town who had participated, publisher C.A. Heath and editor Val Heath made their "dry" sentiments well known.

During the same period, George Hibbert's *Chinook Observer* was taken to task by F.A. Hazeltine of the *South Bend Journal* for running so many saloon ads. "Wet" proponent Hibbert and prohibitionist Hazeltine sparred continually in the pages of their respective newspapers, backing politicians who agreed with them and playing up or playing down the booze news, according to their beliefs.

With adjoining wet and dry districts, there was much "visiting about" and, predictably, there were those who became "confused" about whether they were in wet or dry territory. In 1915, for instance, three arrests were made, all related to illegal liquor sales and all during the month of August. Selling liquor in dry territory without a license was the offense of Olinto Tonini and also of Robert Crawford, placed under arrest on August 20 for the same offence.

When Tonini, a Greek, went before P.W. Rhodes at Justice Court, he was held for trial for want of a bond. It was noted that he served time in full, four days. His name was reentered in the jail book on August 9 (apparently just one day after he had been released) for the same offense, and this time he was sentenced to twenty days in county jail and twenty-five dollars, the cost of the suit. A final notation says Tonini was released on September 18, 1915, a full forty days after his second arrest. Discrepancies such as this one are unusual in the jail book. Was Tonini unable to pay the court costs and for that reason held for more than the original sentence? Or did the clerk simply make a mistake in the ledger?

No personal details are given for Robert Crawford except that his complexion was "Black," the only such notation in the jail book, although there were many listings of "Ruddy," "Sandy," "Light," "Chinese," "Medium," "Dark," "Florid" and "Fair." Crawford went before Justice of the Peace Dorrien, and so few details are given in the jail book that it is difficult to determine why his sentence was so different from Tonini's. "Fine $50.00, Cost $12.50" is the only information noted. Apparently, Crawford did not serve any time in jail.

State Prohibition

On November 3, 1914, after vigorous statewide Anti-Saloon League lobbying, Washington voters approved Initiative Measure Number Three, prohibiting the manufacture and sale (although not the consumption) of liquor. Any saloons that had weathered local option closed as of midnight on December 31, 1915.

From that date forward, it was legal to drink only imported liquor that had been manufactured out of state. Individuals with permits could import up to two quarts of hard liquor or twelve quarts of beer every twenty days. Among those without permits (or those who lacked the means to prepay and ship alcohol), illegal drinking surged, largely via illegal sales. Immediately, arrests for breaking the liquor laws increased dramatically in Pacific County.

In the twenty-seven and a half years from April 15, 1886, when the entries in the jail book began, until midnight on December 31, 1915, when the state law went into effect, fourteen arrests had been made relative to liquor. By contrast, in the four and a half years from midnight on January 1, 1916, through July 18, 1919, when the last name was listed on the pages of the ledger, forty-one alcohol-related arrests were made.

In 1916, the first year of the statewide Prohibition mandate, five arrests concerned with alcohol abuse were made, two in October, two in November and one in December. Ole Taraldson (50), from Norway, and Pat Abarnicle (53), from Illinois, were both arrested on October 23, 1916. They went before Justice Dorrien's court, and each was sentenced to thirty days and served time in full.

On November 18, Victor Fischer went before Justice Dorrien for unlawfully selling liquor and was released from jail on December 14 without further comment in the jail book. John Wickland from Finland was arrested for the same offense on March 20, also appeared before Justice Dorrien and was sentenced to sixty days, a seventy-dollar fine and forty-seven dollars in court costs. There is no explanation for the relative severity of Mr. Wickland's sentence—just that he served time in full.

The last liquor-related entry for 1916 was on December 19. Oscar Anderson was charged with being drunk and disorderly, and Justice Dorrien sentenced him to fifteen days. He served time in full.

Evils of Drink

During 1917, lawmakers in our nation's capital were busy haggling over wording and drafting a resolution that would contain the language for the Eighteenth Amendment. Temperance groups escalated their activities, and newspaper and magazine editors increasingly focused on the evils of drink as the country geared up for the amendment's passage.

In 1917, too, Pacific County's jail book reflected a sharp increase in alcohol incidents, especially the "drunk and disorderly" entries—a curious situation since the state already had been "dry" for three full years:

January 23, 1917, Alley Roop, 55, Warrant of Arrest from Superior Court, Selling or giving away liquor.
April 3, 1917, Marion Samples, 21, Drinking Liquor in a Public Place, Released—not guilty.
April 3, 1917, Everett Samples, 26, Drinking Liquor in a Public Place, Released—not guilty.
May 4, 1917, Ed Smith, 35, Giving away Liquor on the Streets, Thirty Days in County Jail—Sentence Suspended.
May 12, 1917, Wm. Gibson, 49, Drunk and Disorderly, Was fined $30 including costs and given 40 days to pay fine.
May 19, 1917, Wesley King, 20, Excess Amount of Liquor (3 Quarts Whisky), paid fine of $39.60.

May 21, 1917, M. Swanson, 54, Drunk & Disorderly, 30 days & $10 fine.
May 21, 1917, C.G. Hector, 56, Drunk & Disorderly, 30 days & $10 fine.
May 21, 1917, Emil Peterson, Drunk & Disorderly, 30 days & $10 fine.
May 21, 1917, Bob Weiss, Drunk & Disorderly, 15 days & $20 fine.
May 21, 1917, Roland Charlie, Drunk, Fined $29.
June 25, 1917, Robert S. Smith, 33, Giving Away Liquor, 35 Days.
June 25, 1917, Andy Willis, 35, Selling Bulldog Cider, Paid fine and costs $117.
October 24, 1917, Oiva Wiitala, 24, Drunk & Disorderly, Fined $14.
October 24, 1917, Johnar Pulkkinen, 21, Drunk & Disorderly, Fined $14.

Despite the state prohibition on the sale and manufacture of liquor, alcohol continued to be readily available in Pacific County. Drugstores did a big business in patent medicines, many of which contained alcohol as the main ingredient. Additionally, doctors were known to freely write prescriptions for the whiskey stocked by druggists "for medicinal purposes," and rumors circulated that certain drugstore owners were making their fortunes on the legal sales of illicit beverages.

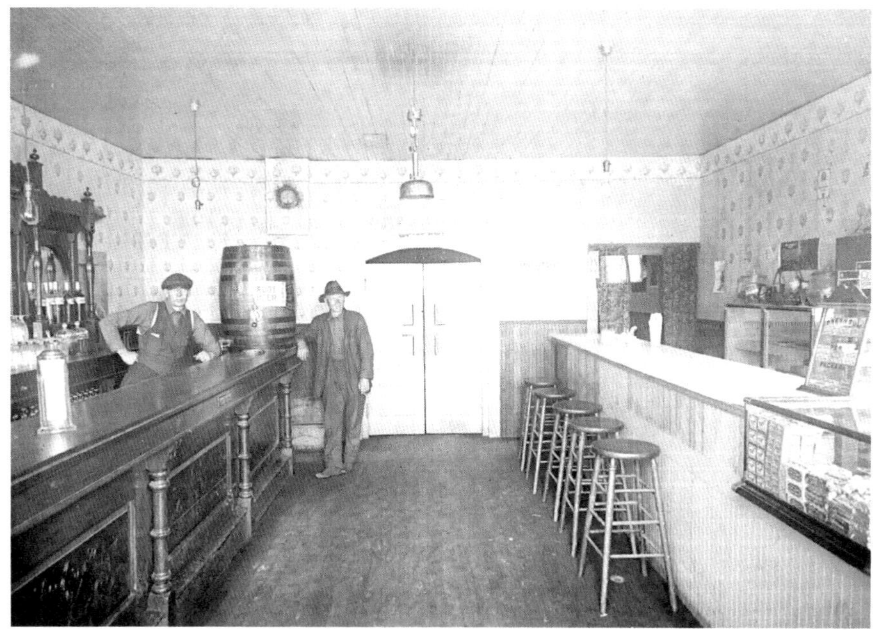

During local option in Washington, the keg of root beer at this Ilwaco establishment could have been hard or soft, depending on the decision of voters. *CPHM.*

About Those Snake Oil Salesman

By virtue of 150 years of hindsight and education, a present-day discussion of "patent medicines" conjures up visions of charlatans and fraud, snake oil salesmen and traveling medicine shows. But from the mid-nineteenth century until World War II, patent medicines were a staple of most American households, particularly in rural areas such as Pacific County.

Although the term "patent medicine" originally referred to medications whose ingredients had been granted government protection against imitation, by the 1870s, most were not patented at all. Small manufacturers, often family enterprises, did the bulk of the business, but even ethical and well-known pharmaceutical companies such as Bayer sold their share of patent medicines.

The basic recipe of most nineteenth-century elixirs included vegetable extracts laced with ample doses of alcohol. Many concoctions were also fortified with morphine, opium or cocaine. They were medicines with questionable effectiveness whose contents were kept secret, and since

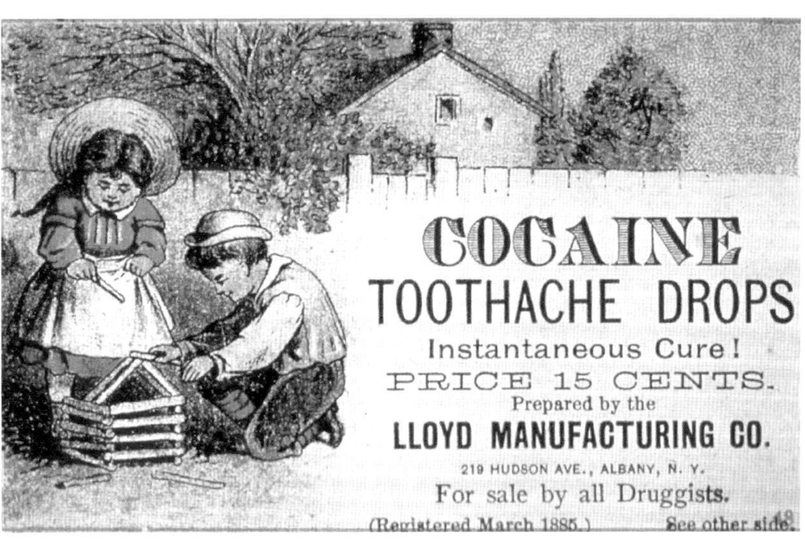

Ingredients listed on patent medicine labels of the early twentieth century seem outrageous by today's standards, but they were popular, especially during Prohibition. *National Library of Medicine.*

there was no regulation on ingredients or dosages, their use could prove fatal.

Patent medicines were among the first products to be highlighted by the advertising industry. Exotic ingredients were played up, often as a panacea for all manner of ailments. Remedies claimed to cure or prevent tuberculosis, indigestion or dyspepsia, arthritis, venereal diseases, baldness, cancer and "female complaints"—even bust developers and manhood restorers were promoted.

William Radam's Microbe Killer, a product sold widely on both sides of the Atlantic in the 1890s and early 1900s, had the bold claim "Cures All Diseases" prominently embossed on the front of the bottle. In Britain, Ebenezer Sibley ("Dr. Sibley") advertised that his Solar Tincture was able to "restore life in the event of sudden death." And one memorable group of liniments, allegedly containing snake oil, made "snake oil salesman" a lasting synonym for a charlatan.

Sales and distribution by traveling medicine shows flourished in the United States, particularly in the Midwest and rural South. The showmen hucksters went from village to village by horse and wagon, often with an entourage of musicians and actors. Entertainment might include a freak show, a flea circus, musical acts, magic tricks, jokes or storytelling. Their "miracle cures" and other products were sold between acts.

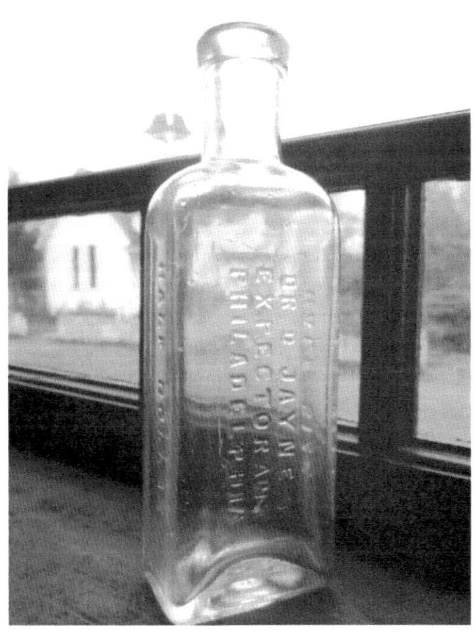

Dr. Jayne's Expectorant, an over-the-counter product sold during Prohibition, contained as much as 18 percent alcohol. *Sydney Stevens photo.*

Some physicians and medical societies objected to the sale and promotion of patent medicines from the beginning. They argued that the remedies did not cure illnesses, discouraged the sick from seeking legitimate treatments and caused alcohol and drug dependency. Finally, in 1906, Congress passed a Pure Food and Drug Act, paving the way for public health action against unlabeled or unsafe ingredients and misleading advertising. In 1936, the statute was revised to ban such ingredients entirely.

In addition, there was the problem (or the advantage, depending on viewpoint) of Washington's proximity to Canada, where alcohol was legal and plentiful. Pacific County, with its big bay and many isolated coves, sloughs and inlets, provided untold opportunities for camouflaging the mysterious barges and boats that arrived under cover of darkness. Although the manufacture and sale of alcohol was shrouded in secrecy, there were continual "whisperings" among "those in the know" and county residents who had friends in Canada or who knew a ship's captain and were thought to have an "in."

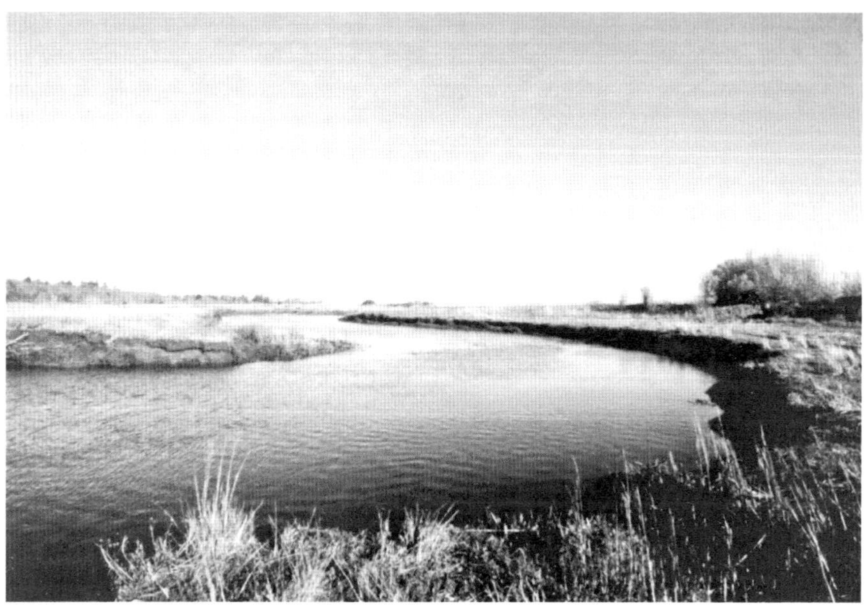

The numerous rivers and sloughs leading to secluded coves around Willapa Bay made Pacific County a rumrunner's paradise. *Lisa Farnham photo.*

According to John "Jack" G. Williams Sr. (1897–1988) in his book *Johnny Stories, Scenes from My Boyhood in Old Ilwaco*:

> *This country here was a great place for running in whiskey. In the fall of the year when the salmon season was over, it was no trick to take your boat and run up to Vancouver, BC, load two or three hundred cases of good whiskey, and come down here off the mouth of the Columbia River. Then you could sell it out at sea to the local bootleggers, or you could run it in here yourself. All of these rivers—the Nemah, the Naselle and the Columbia—were a natural set-up for running in whiskey.*

By 1918, as citizens geared up for nationwide Prohibition, it seemed inevitable that liquor-related arrests would continue to escalate and would continue to be recorded in the pages of the old jail book.

14
"THE NOBLE EXPERIMENT"

Bootlegging, Moonshining, Rumrunning…

The wording finally decided on for the Eighteenth Amendment specified a national ban on the manufacture, sale, transportation, importation and exportation of intoxicating liquors "for beverage purposes." It was approved by Congress and proposed for ratification on December 18, 1917. The law was to take effect one year after the ratification by three-fourths of the forty-eight states was achieved.

As 1918 progressed and state after state ratified the amendment and it became apparent that it would soon become law, alcohol-related arrests in Pacific County increased once more. Curiously, even though Washington State had been "dry" for four years, the words "bootlegging," "moonshining" and "drunk and disorderly" began to appear more regularly in the *Pacific County Jail Book*:

> *May 6, 1918, Andrew Beck, 40, Drunk & Disorderly, Paid $25 Fine.*
> *June 20, 1918, Ether Crum, 25, Bootlegging, $50 and 10 Days.*
> *September 13, 1918, Everk Frederickson, 23, Drunk & Disorderly, Fined and Released to go to work.*
> *September 13, 1918, Henry Hill, 37, Drunk & Disorderly, Fined and released to go to work.*
> *September 14, 1918, John Alto, 43, Bootlegging, Suspended Sentence—left County.*
> *December 2, 1918, William Martin, 40, Bootlegging.*

There were few details noted in the jail book, but teetotaling editor/publisher F.A. Hazeltine's *South Bend Journal* often headlined the interesting cases. The arrest of William Martin, for instance, was front-page news in the December 20, 1918 issue:

> *IS CHARGED WITH SELLING LIQUOR TO THE SOLDIERS*
> *Raymond Man Arrested Last Week and Taken Before U.S. Commissioner McIntosh Here—Puts Up $1,500 Cash Bond—Trap Set*
> *William Martin Cavitsch, alias William Martin, a Pole, was arrested last week at Raymond and brought to this city and had a hearing before United States Commissioner McIntosh on a federal charge of selling intoxicating liquor to soldiers. Martin plead* [sic] *not guilty but the evidence was sufficient for the commissioner to hold him to the federal grand jury in $1,500 bonds, which the prisoner put up in cash.*
>
> *Martin was caught with the goods according to the evidence brought out at his hearing before the commissioner. The federal authorities suspicioned* [sic] *for some time that he was the man who had been selling liquor in such quantities to soldiers of the Spruce Division stationed at some of the Raymond mills as to incapacitate them for work. So a trap was set for the man.*
>
> *Two soldiers went to Martin's house and asked if he had any liquor for sale. He professed not to understand what they meant by liquor, but when they asked for whiskey he readily produced a quart bottle and was paid $12 for it. As soon as the soldiers had the liquor and Martin the money, the soldiers stepped outside the door and blew a whistle which summoned the Raymond marshal who had been hiding around the corner of the building.*
>
> *At the hearing before the United States commissioner the attorney for the prisoner sought to raise a doubt as to whether the contents of the bottle in evidence contained whiskey, but this was quickly settled by Prosecuting Attorney John O'Phelan pouring out a couple of fingers and, after swallowing the fluid, pronouncing it whiskey and of a very good brand. The federal authorities think, with the arrest of Martin, they have secured one of the principal men who have been dispensing so much liquor among the soldiers stationed at Raymond and South Bend.*

Ratified!

The Eighteenth Amendment, also known as "the Noble Experiment," was ratified by more than the required three-fourths majority of states on January 16, 1919, but would not go into effect for a full year. Even though Washington had been "dry" for four years, the imminent prospect of a nationwide ban on booze seemed to further embolden the county law enforcement officers, and arrests increased rapidly.

On March 15, 1919, Mike Seuko was arrested for "Bootlaking [*sic*]." He was listed as fifty-nine years old and five feet, nine inches tall, with light hair, gray eyes, "a Swarthey [*sic*] complexion and a Polack [*sic*]." He was fined $100 and given thirty days in jail.

A few weeks later, on April 8, 1919, fifty-year-old James Hurley was arrested for moonshining. The *South Bend Journal* took the opportunity to poke a little fun:

MOONSHINER CAUGHT IN "BENEVOLENT ACT"
JIM HURLEY OF ASHLOCK FEARED "DRY AS DUST" FUTURE AND PREPARED

So, He Boiled Some of "Mike's Special" and Ran the Steam Through the Pipe and Finally Got a White Liquid Which He Barreled for His Own Private Use

Jim Hurley of Ashlock is in trouble "plum up to his brows." His case is something like this: With so many of the states going dry and so many of the whiskey factories being forced to quit business, it occurred to him that eventually the supply of "liquor sauce" would diminish to the tiniest drop. So he attempted a remedy. For his own use he began making it.

He procured a big milk can and a copper worm—regular moonshine outfit. Into the can he would put a quantity of "Mike's Special" and boiled it, and through this worm the steam would work its way and when it arrived at the outlet it was white and liquidy and stout. Jim had a more respectable idea of what a man should put in his stomach than Mike had. He had more respect for himself, too.

Tuesday Deputy Sheriff Stevens of Pacific County and Sheriff John F. Berry of Lewis County "dropped in" to his place and told him that he was wasting his time, and he finally was persuaded. His outfit was brought to the sheriff's quarters here. Jim also came along with them. He is nicely quartered at the court house now and the jailer is acting as his valet…

One barrel of distilled whiskey is Jim's contribution toward preventing a real liquor famine.

No doubt the kind judge and court will have something to do with him before long and convince him that raisins were made to put in mincemeat pies and raisin bread and the countless dishes that make us live till we die.

Mr. Hurley was released on bond on April 14 and on May 5 was tried and acquitted, according to the jail book.

Some Jailed; Some Not

By all accounts, it wasn't only the county jail that was busy hosting those who violated the prohibition laws. According to the names listed on the pages of the local newspapers, city jails and perhaps other facilities were also doing a booming business in alcohol-related arrests. On April 18, 1919, for instance, the *Journal* listed nine cases set for trial, but except for James Hurley, none of those in the docket had been placed in the county jail:

NINE CRIMINAL CASES UP FOR TRIAL AT MAY TERM OF COURT

State Charges all the Defendants with Having Violated the Prohibition Statutes—Jurors Given Notice to Appear for Duty May 1

The following named persons, all charged with violating the prohibition law in this county will be tried in the superior court which convenes on May 1: Frank Sorini, T.J. Sooter, Louis Pippi, Charles Pearson, Frank Mestrovich, Jack Daugherty, Charles W. O'Berg, Joe Gaston and James Hurley. Judge H.W.B. Hewen will preside.

The article concludes with a list of forty-eight potential jurors. Several weeks later, on April 25, the *Journal* reported:

Eight bootlegging cases and one in which the manufacture of liquor is charged, head the docket for the May jury term of the Pacific County superior court which opens next Thursday. Each of the nine defendants is scheduled for a separate trial, but where more than one action has grown out of alleged transactions occurring at the same time, failure to convict in one case may mean the dismissal of one or two other actions. Taking this possibility into consideration, Judge H.W.B. Hewen has set the cases close together, that there be no time lapse between trials…

The outcome of the nine trials was reported in the May 9, 1919 issue of the *Journal*:

> *In the bootlegging cases tried, one conviction was obtained in the most minor of the nine cases set, three defendants were acquitted, one changed his plea to guilty, two cases were dismissed and two were continued to the next term of court. The last case tried, that against Jack Dougherty* [sic], *a seaman from the steamer Avalon, charged with bootlegging, resulted in an acquittal after the jury had been out five hours and had returned to court once for further instructions.*
>
> *In preceding cases, Charles W. O'Berg was acquitted of the charge of being a bootlegger. Charles Pearson was convicted on a charge of having liquor in his possession. James Hurley, in whose home the officers of Lewis and Pacific Counties testified they seized a still and about 50 gallons of raisin mash in the process of fermentation was found not guilty of manufacturing liquor. T.J. Sooter, charged with having liquor in his possession, changed his plea to guilty when his case was called for trial and was fined $100 and costs.*
>
> *The charges against Louis Pippi of having unlawful possession of liquor were dismissed. The case of the State against Joe Gaston, charged with being a bootlegger, State against Frank Mestrovich, charged with being a jointist* and city of Raymond against Mestrovich charged with unlawful sale of intoxicating liquor have been continued over the term.*

Following James Hurley's April 1919 arrest, a whopping fifteen more liquor-related arrests were made before the jail book entries were discontinued five months later. Those fifteen arrests amounted to one-third the total arrests for illegal use of alcohol recorded in Pacific County during the entire thirty-three years the book was kept. Pacific County law enforcement personnel were taking the matter of illegal alcohol very seriously indeed:

> *April 18, 1919 Robt. Watson, 38, Having booze in his possession, Paid fine and costs amounting to $191.00.*
> *April 27, 1919, Bernard Anderson, 37, Liquor in Possession, Bootlegging. One to Five Years, Walla Walla.*
> *May 2, 1919, Bernard Flanagan, 65, Booze in possession, bootlacking* [sic], *served $100 fine in county jail.*
> *May 2, 1919, Charles W. O'Berg 36, Liquor, Released on order of U.S. Marshall at Tacoma.*

* A person who operated or frequented speakeasies or other unlawful "joints."

May 4, 1919, Jack Dougherty, 37, Liquor, Released on order of U.S. Marshall from Tacoma.
May 30, 1919, A. Soldato, 45, Moonshining and Selling Liquor, Released on $1,000 bond.
May 30, 1919, Nick Cavada, 28, Moonshining and selling liquor, Released on $1,000 bond.
June 27, 1919, Louis Pippi, 36, Selling Intoxicating Liquor, Paid Fine $150.
June 27, 1919, T. Gugliomo, 44, Selling Cider Intoxicating, Plead Guilty to Charge, Paid Fine $150.
June 27, 1919, Pete Freeman, 24, Selling Intox, Paid Fine $150.
June 27, 1919, Pete Kroge, 37, Selling Liquor, Plead Guilty to Charge, Paid Fine $150.
June 28, 1919, Frank Mestrovich, 25, Selling Liquor Intoxicated, Plead Guilty, Paid Fine $150.
June 30, 1919, John McQueen, 38, for Selling Intoxicating Liquor, Plead Guilty, Paid Fine $150.
July 8, 1919. Ed Blasfield, 32, Plead Guilty, payed [sic] *Fine of $100.*
July 27, 1919, M.B. Arsiff, 27, Selling Intox Cider, Paid Fine $150.

Off the Record

For years, the good citizens of Pacific County remained closed-mouthed concerning the era of Prohibition—the days when speakeasies and stills, bootlegging and rumrunning reached a fever pitch in the United States, in Washington and right close to home. During those years and for many years afterward, folks

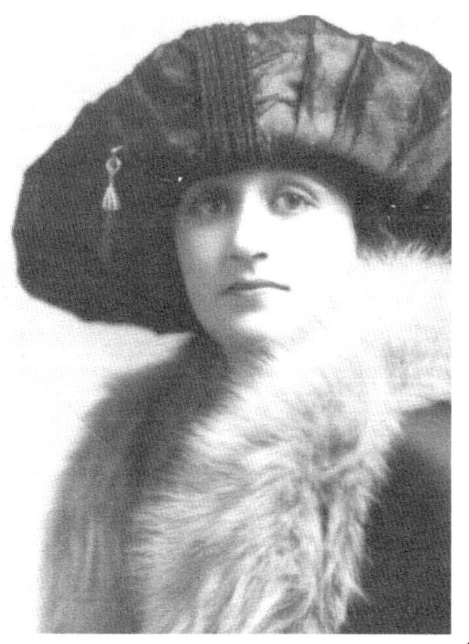

Suzita Espy (b. 1903) became the quintessential flapper and, in 1922, married Portland rumrunner Wallace Pearson, much to the chagrin of her Oysterville family. *EFA.*

spoke only in whispers about the mysterious goings-on, especially in the watery parts of the county. But gradually, some stories have emerged.

In the summer/autumn 1978 issue of *The Sou'wester*, Seattle journalist Har Plumb wrote about his adventures as a boy in Chinook. In 1920, the summer he was eight, he lived with his family aboard a scow on Peacock Spit and helped his father troll for salmon:

> *Early in my happy summer, I learned two new phrases which were rapidly becoming an essential part of our language–"rum runner" and "rum chaser." The Volstead Act became federal law January 16, 1920, making the nation officially dry under the Prohibition Amendment. Washington had been already dry for several years.*
>
> *Almost every day we could see one of the rum chasers–30 to 40-foot cabin cruisers, fast for those days at perhaps 10 or 12 knots–lying at anchor in the quiet backwater between our scow and the rock ramparts topped by the Cape Disappointment Lighthouse. Prohibition, which was rapidly becoming a leading topic of the times, was pretty fuzzy in my mind. But one night Durk and Joe[+] gave me an on-the-spot clarification I'll never forget.*
>
> *Even in those very earliest months of the national agony over liquor, smuggling the stuff into the Columbia from Canadian ships cruising just outside the three-mile limit had become a form of profitable moonlighting for a number of Ilwaco, Chinook and Astoria fishermen, particularly the deep-sea trollers. One night, near my bedtime, Joe and Durk and I were walking the inner beach when we noticed one of the rum chasers getting under way. Joe and Durk started loping toward the outer beach. Trying hard to keep up, I misjudged my jump over a piece of driftwood and filled one ear with sand. I commented on this in a manner never learned in Sunday School. "Shut up," whispered Durk. "If they hear us, they'll think we're helping them."*
>
> *Long afterward, I figured out he meant that the government men might think we were signaling the fishermen, and they in turn might think the opposite–that we were spies for the law. It was, as*

+Durk and Joe were teenaged boys from Chinook who were also working on Peacock Spit that summer.

Joe and Durk knew, and I later had made clear to me, a splendid time to remain neutral.

As we crouched behind a drift log, we could just barely make out the shape of the lightless rum chaser coming around the upstream end of our spit and out of the Ilwaco channel into the main Columbia. In a few minutes we heard the chug-a-chug of an equally unlighted troller and glimpsed her tall fishing poles, racked erect to the mast, against the dark sky. It was passing close inshore along our beach, and soon it swung southeast up the Columbia along Sand Island. The two boats were dim shadows.

Ilwaco fishermen coming across the bar cut around our spit into the Ilwaco channel. Chinook trollers continued upstream to the head of Sand Island and then took their own channel eastward a mile or so to the Chinook cannery dock. Astoria boats stayed on the south side of the river. So the fisherman we spied on was taking the Chinook way home, and I wondered which of our friends was running whiskey.

"That's not a Chinook boat," Durk murmured. "I know her; she's one of the trollers from Ilwaco. Now, you watch, and you'll see why she's taking the long way home." In a few minutes, we saw the lights blaze on the rum chaser, and faintly heard the sounds of a horn and shouting as the government men tried to stop the troller off Sand Island. Almost immediately, we heard the engine purr and saw the shadow of a second troller as it hurried along our beach and into the Ilwaco channel. It was out of sight or sound while the rum chaser and the first troller still jockeyed around far upstream.

"He's fooled them again," said Durk. "They won't find any booze on that first troller, and by the time they know that, the second one will have cases unloaded and stashed away someplace. And tomorrow there'll be some boxes on the river boat to Portland worth a lot more money than the fish on the top layer."

In a 1998 issue of *The Sou'wester*, Helen Shagren Furlong wrote:

My cousin Tori, Ada and Ferd Nelson's daughter, tells about the times she used to go down to the garden to help [her uncle]

Bill weed. In just a little while, Bill would disappear for a long time. It was much later that she found out that the slough at the back of the garden was called Whiskey Slough because it was there that Bill ran the still. (No wonder Tori got stuck with most of the weeding.) The whiskey was distributed by leaving it in a prearranged spot by my father. Bill and my dad were out in public all the time and had ample opportunity for contacts.

Lou Stamp of Oysterville is too young to remember Prohibition but old enough to remember the stories that were told about the goings-on around Nahcotta, where he grew up. "You know that big tree at the end of Bay Avenue?" he said.

Charlie Nelson used to go and stand by that tree when the wind was just right and blow his horn. He had a big drum, too, and he'd pound on that and then blow on the horn some more. He'd build himself a bonfire and then wait for the Indians to come over from Bay Center and load up with bottles of hooch. There was a place called "Smugglers' Cove" right near Whiskey Slough, and that's where the hand-offs were made.

Escalating Arrest Rate

As the arrest rate escalated for liquor-related crimes, Hazeltine's *South Bend Journal* reports became increasingly detailed. The June 6, 1919 issue presents a story that would have done credit to the likes of Elliot Ness:

OFFICERS FIND "STILL" OPPOSITE SCHOOLHOUSE
ITALIAN AND 2 GREEKS HAVE CLEVERLY CONCEALED BOOZE PLANT
Soldato Gives Deputy Sheriff Stephens Five-Block Chase with Variations—Get Quantities of Liquor Which Was Concealed Under Trap Doors in Floor—Charges Filed
A "still" raid that brought results and that also brought some thrills, was staged by Deputy Sheriffs T.J. Stephens and Jack Yoes last Friday night.

The raid was on a building opposite the Broadway school occupied by Andrew Soldato, an Italian, and Gus Krigias and Nick Cavata [sic], *two*

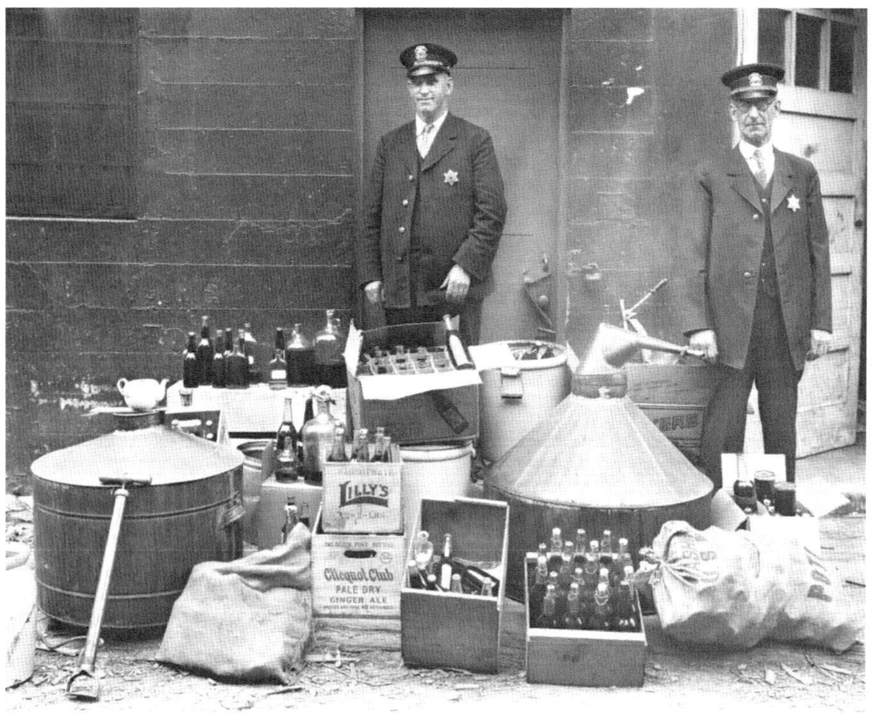

Typically, perhaps, this photograph from the days of raids by federal revenue agents is titled simply "Confiscated Booze," with no other identifying information. *PCHS.*

Greeks. These three were arrested and two charges have been filed against them, one charging the manufacture of liquor, and other charging being a jointist.

Soldato was not captured until he had given Deputy Sheriff Stephens a chase of five blocks, during which Soldato experienced the peculiar sensation of having an officer fire four shots at him.

Besides their capture of the men, the officers gathered in a complete still. Between 40 and 50 gallons of raisin mash, and about a dozen gallons of liquor. The liquor was bottled, and one five-gallon carboy was prepared for shipment.

The officers visited the place three times before they discovered the plant which was hidden in a completely walled-in room between the kitchen and the woodshed, and the only entrance to which was through a trap door in its ceiling, the door being reached by a ladder from the woodshed. To find the plant, the officers chopped out the rear wall of the kitchen when they noticed the apparent difference in the dimension of the kitchen inside and out. Soldato had built a partition across the kitchen five feet from the rear wall and had carefully papered the partition, leaving no opening.

In the still room the officers discovered as complete a plant as has been found in this section since dry law became effective. Water was piped into the room, a large oil stove furnished the necessary heat for the distilling process, there were vats for handling the mash and the liquor during the fermenting and distilling process, and every implement necessary to the production of liquor in considerable quantities.

When the officers went through the house the first time they were shown about by Soldato who was most polite and apparently anxious to show everything about the place. But when they returned for a second search and Stephens began to take up the matting on the hall floor Soldato made a break for the door. Stephens took up pursuit and after a chase of five blocks caught his man. Yoes remained at the house with Krigias and Cavata.

Under the matting was a trap door in the floor which, when lifted disclosed numerous bottles of whiskey. Beneath a bed was another trap door which covered a similar store.

County officials believe that these arrests will result in cutting off a large part of the liquor supply that has given the officers much work in recent weeks.

Increased Diligence

The reason for the increased diligence by the sheriff's deputies and the escalating numbers of arrests is perhaps explained by an article in the June 6, 1919 *Journal*—an article that clearly places blame on the juries for the inconsistent trial results. Reluctance to find friends and neighbors guilty of breaking the dry laws was a community problem that would continue throughout the years of Prohibition.

CARRY ACTIVE FIGHT TO ENFORCE DRY LAW
JUDGE HEWEN TELLS SHERIFF'S OFFICE THERE MUST BE NO LET-UP
Propose to Hunt Out Every Still and Prosecute Every Bootlegger and Booze Manufacturer Found—
Stream from California via Lumber Vessels Drying Up Somewhat
Acting under instructions of Superior Court Judge H.W.B. Hewen of the Pacific County Court, Sheriff A.B. McDonald and his deputies have

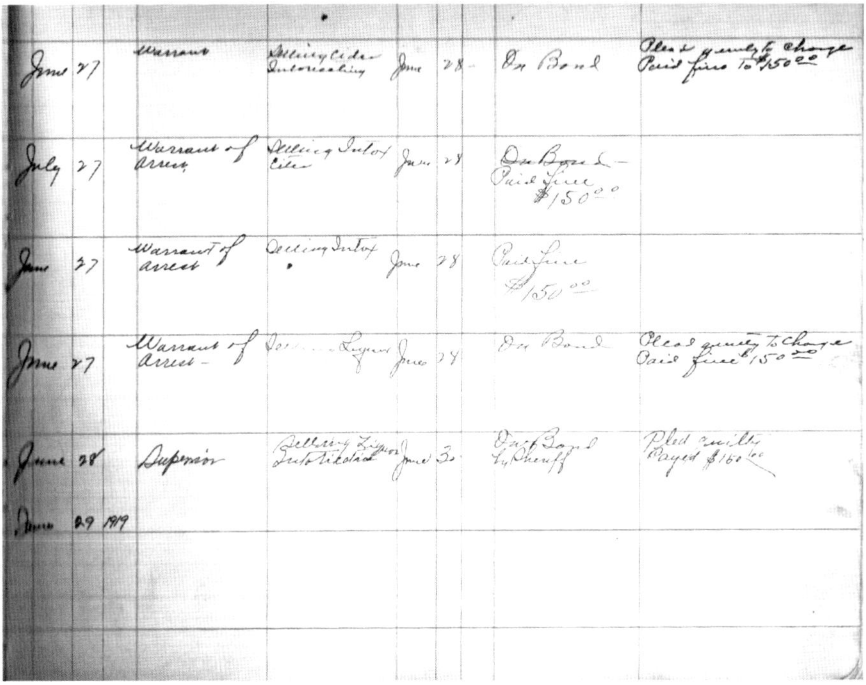

Though Washington had been "dry" for four years, alcohol-related arrests in Pacific County reached an all-time high with the ratification of the Eighteenth Amendment. *Sydney Stevens photo.*

redoubled their efforts to put an end to the liquor traffic in this county. The running down of the still operated by Andrew Soldato and associates in the east end of the city was but the first stop in a campaign that will be carried on until every such plant in the county has been sought out and put out of business, the sheriff declares.

Large quantities of liquor have come in at various times on lumber vessels from California. This traffic, however, has been curtailed to a large extent by the careful searches that the sheriff and his deputies make of every incoming vessel. The steamer Avalon, which was considered the worst offender because of the many arrests made aboard her and the quantities of liquor seized, has been completely "dry" the last two trips, the sheriff says.

The court's instructions were given because during the last jury term the majority of persons arrested on bootlegging charges were acquitted by the jury. Judge Hewen declares that there must be no let-up for any cause whatever and that prosecutions of persons mixed up in liquor transactions must continue until such transactions cease.

Though there are several more entries in the old jail book, the July 27 arrest of M.B. Arsiff is the last that concerned alcohol. The final entry is dated September 20, 1919, with no notation regarding the reason. Presumably, Pacific County clerks continued to keep a record of arrests in the months before and after the Eighteenth Amendment went into effect on January 20, 1920. And presumably, the arrests for liquor-related crimes continued at a high rate. However, the remaining pages of the volume called *Prison Record No. 1 Pacific County* were left blank.

BIBLIOGRAPHY

Archives and Websites

Department of Corrections, WA State. "A History of the Washington State Penitentiary." "McNeil Island Corrections Center History." http://www.doc.wa.gov.

Espy Family Archives. Oysterville, Washington and Washington State Historical Society Research Center, Tacoma, Washington.

Find a Grave Memorial #62785362, "Miles Standish Griswold." www.findagrave.com.

HistoryLink.org Essay 2640: "Native Americans Organize the Indian Shaker Church in 1892." www.historylink.org.

HistoryLink.org Essay 7850: "Shoalwater Bay Oysters Begin Feeding San Francisco in 1851." www.historylink.org.

HistoryLink.org Essay 8647: "Washington State Reform School Opens in Chehalis on June 10, 1891." www.historylink.org.

"Lumber Industry, Centralia Washington, 1910s." Reuther Library Collections, Wayne State University. http://reuther.wayne.edu.

Medora Espy Archive. Washington State Historical Society Research Center, Tacoma, WA

Books

Anderson, Nancy Bell. *The Columbia River's "Ellis Island": The Story of Knappton Cove*. Gearhart, OR: Heritage Folk Press, 2012.

Crossley, Rod. *Soldiers in the Woods: The U.S. Army's Spruce Production Division in World War One*. Portland, OR: TimberTimes, 2014.

Espy, Willard R. *Oysterville, Roads to Grandpa's Village*. New York: Clarkson N. Potter, Inc., 1977.

Feagans, Raymond. *The Railroad that Ran by the Tide*. Berkeley, CA: Howell North Books, 1972.

Hazeltine, Jean. *Willapa Bay, Its Historical and Regional Geography*. South Bend, WA: South Bend Journal, 1956.

Lloyd, Nancy. *Observing Our Peninsula's Past*. Vol. 1. Long Beach, WA: *Chinook Observer*, 2001.

Oesting, Marie. *Oysterville Cemetery Records*. Ocean Park, WA: Marie Oesting, 1988.

Stevens, Sydney. *Dear Medora, Child of Oysterville's Forgotten Years*. Pullman, WA: WSU Press, 2007.

Swan, James G. *The Northwest Coast, or Three Years' Residence in Washington Territory*. New York: Harper & Brothers Publishers, 1857.

Webster's New World Law Dictionary. Hoboken, NJ: Wiley Publishing, Inc., 2010.

Williams, John G. *Johnny Stories*. Seaview, WA: Rosemary Folklore, © Joan Frances Mann, 1987.

Magazines

The Sou'wester, Quarterly Magazine of the Pacific County Historical Society, 1966–2013: 2, no. 4 (1967); 10, nos. 2 and 4 (1975); 11, nos. 3 and 4 (1976); 12, nos. 1–4 (1977); 13, nos. 1, 4 (1978); 17, no. 3 (1982); 4 (1984); 19, nos. 1, 2, 4 (1985); nos. 1–4 (1989); 30, no. 4 (1995).

Newspapers

Chinook (WA) *Observer*, various issues 1900–2011.

Ilwaco (WA) *Tribune*, 1952–1958 issues.

(Portland, OR) *Oregonian*, 1890, 1892 issues.

Seattle Post Intelligencer, various issues, 1890–1891.

South Bend (WA) *Journal*, various issues 1890–1920.

(South Bend, WA) *Enterprise*, 1890.
(South Bend, WA) *Willapa Harbor Pilot*, various issues 1891–1968.

Official Records

Census, Washington Territory, Pacific County, 1887.
Oysterville Baptist Church Records, 1892–1980. Espy Family Archives, Oysterville and Tacoma.
Oysterville Cemetery Association. "Old Linen Map." 1855.
Territory of Washington, *Plaintiff v. Marcus* [*sic*] *Schuldrup, Defendant.* Justice Court for Oysterville Precinct, April 15, 1886.
U.S. Board on Geographic Names. Department of the Interior.
Washington Supreme Court Records #109 and #110, 1891.

INDEX

F

G

H

Y

About the Author

Sydney Stevens remembers playing law and order in the dilapidated old jailhouse in Oysterville when she was a little girl. "Somehow, I knew that my great-grandfather had been the county sheriff in 'the olden days,' so I always wanted to play his part. What I didn't know," she laughs, "is that he had resigned after only a few months in office. The county wouldn't pay for his badge, and he said that, in that case, he wouldn't serve. Things were a lot different back then!"

The great-grandfather of whom Sydney speaks was Robert Hamilton Espy, co-founder (with Isaac Alonzo Clark) of Oysterville in 1854. Espy family members have been living in the little village ever since, and it is through her interest in their stories that Sydney has become a primary keeper and disseminator of Oysterville and Pacific County history.

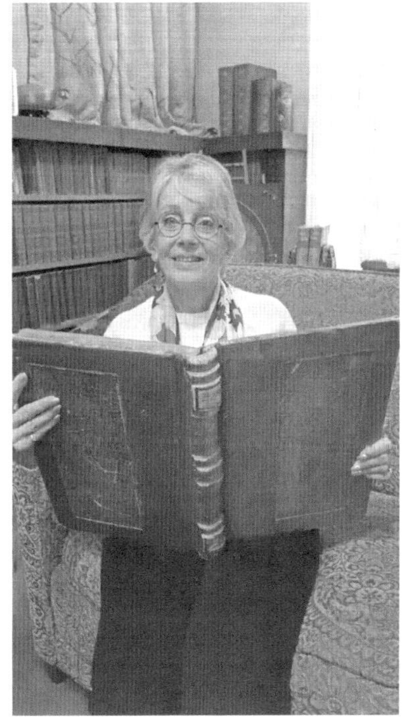

"Captivating!" says author Sydney Stevens about the bits of information revealed in this old log book—*Prison Record No. 1 Pacific County*. *Nyel Stevens photo.*

"When I first saw the huge volume with *Prison Record No. 1 Pacific County* embossed on its spine, I felt it might be a chance to see law and order from a somewhat different perspective. That turned out to be the case, but not in quite the way I had imagined. I found myself looking at our community from the inside out...literally! It wasn't always a reassuring view."